Amanda Jillings
Foxbury, Crabtree Lane,
Westhumble, Dorking
Surrey RH5 6BQ, UK
01306 880554 / 07767 657363
mandy@jillings.net

D1826082

Are We One?

Are We One?

Jewish Identity in the United States and Israel

Jerold S. Auerbach

Rutgers University Press

New Brunswick, New Jersey, and London

Library of Congress Cataloging-in-Publication Data

Auerbach, Jerold S.
 Are we one? : Jewish identity in the United States and Israel /
Jerold S. Auerbach.
  p. cm.
 Includes bibliographical references (p.) and index.
 ISBN 0-8135-2917-4 (alk. paper)
  1. Jews—United States—Identity. 2. Jews—United States—Attitudes
toward Israel. 3. Israel and the diaspora. 4. Jews—Cultural
assimilation—United States. 5. Jews—Cultural assimilation—
Israel. 6. Zionism and Judaism. I. Title.
 DS143 .A94 2001
 305.892'4073—dc21   00-045682

British Cataloging-in-Publication data for this book is available from
the British Library.

Manufactured in the United States of America

For Sus
with love

Contents

Are We One?

If you walk in my statutes, and keep my commandments, and do them . . . I will give peace in the land, and you shall lie down, and none shall make you afraid. . . . And I will walk among you, and will be your God, and you shall be my people. . . .

But if you will not hearken to me, and will not do all these commands . . . I will set my face against you, and you shall be slain before your enemies; they that hate you shall reign over you; and you shall flee when none pursues you.

Lev 26:3, 6, 12–15, 17–19

Introduction

The story is told that when Czar Nicholas I of Russia met with his cousin Emperor Franz Joseph of Austria to discuss affairs of state, their conversation quickly turned to their shared Jewish problem. The Czar, who instigated pogroms to keep Jews subservient, was puzzled by his cousin's leniency. In Russia, the Czar observed, we deny Jews civil and religious rights, and thwart them at every turn. But you, he said in evident puzzlement, intend to emancipate them, to make them the equal of Christians. Why would you wish to liberate such terrible parasites, he asked? The Emperor curtly replied: You are free to destroy the Jews in your own way. Please permit me to destroy them in mine.

On a steamy August night nearly three decades ago, when I arrived at Lod Airport (as it then was called) to begin a sabbatical year in Israel, I was a fully emancipated and comfortably assimilated Diaspora Jew. I did not even dimly comprehend that I was somehow implicated in the unfolding history of the Jewish people. Nor did I realize, as my taxi began its labored climb into the Jerusalem hills, that my own journey of Jewish discovery had finally begun.

Long before that sabbatical year ended, I was already filled with fantasies about living in the Jewish state. Indeed, I left Israel somewhat disconcerted by the fervor of my new attachment. Nearing forty, I felt like a love-smitten sixteen-year-old, drifting in and out of dreamy reverie, yearning for another glimpse, a smell, a touch—not of a beautiful girl, but of a country that unexpectedly had enabled me to feel more securely at home than I ever had during my entire adult life in the United States.

I had not felt such passion for the United States since my brief surge of boyhood patriotism during World War II. To help my country win its war against tyranny, I had avidly sold war bonds, collected tin foil, cultivated radishes and lettuce in our school "Victory Garden," and secretly exchanged coded notes with third-grade friends lest our loose lips sink American ships.

How could Jewish youngsters do otherwise? The grandchildren of Eastern European immigrants, we were expected by our parents to erase any lingering traces of family foreignness by demonstrating our abiding loyalty to the United States. Emulating the real Americans we aspired to be, we asked the Lord's blessings on Thanksgiving, dreamed of a white Christmas, dressed as Halloween goblins, hunted for Easter eggs, and enthusiastically cheered the marines for defending American freedom from the halls of Montezuma to the shores of Tripoli.

Not long after the war, however, my patriotic fervor subsided into cynical detachment. I belonged, as I subsequently learned, to the "Silent Generation," intimidated into fear and passivity by the wave of political repression known as McCarthyism. American Jews, I now realize, were especially vulnerable to Senator McCarthy's reckless allegations of disloyalty. Our foothold in the United States was still too precarious, and memories of Hitler were too recent and horrific, for many of us to assume the risks of self-identification as Jews. Although the fate of atomic spies Julius and Ethel Rosenberg was never discussed in my family, I have little doubt that their trial, conviction, and execution made Jews of my parents' generation—the Rosenbergs' generation—tremble with apprehension lest all American Jews be implicated in the Rosenbergs' betrayal.

By the time that I graduated from college, just a few years later, almost everything was possible for American Jews of my generation—as long as we shed any lingering vestiges of Jewish distinctiveness. That was not very difficult. Guided by the examples of my assimilated parents, relatives, and Jewish friends, I had already become the very model of a non-Jewish American Jew. With fantasies of becoming the next Clarence Darrow, arguing First Amendment cases before the Supreme Court, or Joseph Welch, confronting the next anti-Communist bully, I was also the prototypical Jewish liberal, eager to crusade for the rights of the oppressed and downtrodden—as long as, to be sure, they were not Jews.

When my dream was punctured by the reality of law school, I turned to history. Most of my fellow graduate students—especially in the social sciences and humanities—were Jews. This was hardly coincidental. At some level of subconscious intuition, we all knew that mastery of American history or literature could serve as our passport to American respectability. We may have sensed that once Jews finally were permitted to instruct Gentiles in the subtle nuances of American civilization—most academic precincts having been closed to all but a tiny handful of the most assimilated Jews until after World War II—we would truly be at home in America.

At the time, however, such thoughts were far from my mind. Ever since my own flight from Judaism began, no later than the day after my bar mitzvah, I imagined that I had made peace with my Jewish identity, such as it was. In fact, like almost everyone I knew, I had merely consigned Judaism to the nether realms of my consciousness. There it slumbered undisturbed, for nearly twenty-five years, in the company of other discarded childhood embarrassments. I was not even a three-day-a-year Jew; on Rosh Hashanah and Yom Kippur, as on all other days, I behaved like the real American I was.

But my Jerusalem sabbatical shook loose some quite confused feelings about myself as an American Jew. I began to wonder whether, like Irish Americans or Italian Americans, I belonged to a distinctive American ethnic group. Certainly I was not (nor had my grandparents ever been) Russian American or Romanian American. Was I, then, more like Catholics and Protestants, for whom religion alone identifies their distinctiveness? But I was not religiously identified or observant. Was I an *American* Jew, who belonged—as so many Israelis seemed inclined to assert—to the Jewish people? Or was I a *Jewish* American, a citizen of the United States who happened to be Jewish? In Israel, my tidy categories of self-identification had become sources of confusion, not clarification.

My bewilderment about these issues of modern Jewish identity was not, of course, unique or personal. Trained as a historian, I could more easily locate my own identity dilemma, as an American Jew coming of age in the United States after World War II, within the larger sweep of modern Jewish and American history. I was hardly the first Jew to be tormented and fascinated, in roughly equal measure, by the dilemmas of Jewish identity in the modern era. It did not take long to discover that Zionism itself—one answer to all those nagging questions about the place of Jews in modern society—had emerged from precisely this conundrum of secular Jewish identity in the modern era.

Long before I was fully aware of my own Jewish problem, I had witnessed—from a safe historical perspective, to be sure—the torments of American Jewish identity for someone else. While I was a graduate student at Columbia, I spent a year writing the biography of Joseph M. Proskauer, a retired New York lawyer, judge, and, at a crucial moment in American Jewish history, Jewish community leader. During the years preceding and following the birth of Israel, he was president of the American Jewish Committee, the most influential (anti-Zionist) Jewish organization of its time. I discovered, to my fascination, how vulnerable Proskauer had always been to the conflicting tugs of American and Jewish loyalties.

During my early months of research, I was frequently puzzled by the extreme sensitivity that Proskauer had long displayed toward even the slightest intimation of dual loyalty. Eager to absolve American Jews of "political schizophrenia," he worried incessantly lest the Zionist movement, to say nothing of its culmination in a Jewish state, divide the loyalty of American Jews and, in the eyes of other Americans, compromise their loyalty to the United States.

The critical episode in Proskauer's adult life had been his devoted service as a political adviser to Alfred E. Smith, the popular governor of New York in the 1920s who became the first Catholic to be nominated by a major party for the presidency. Smith's 1928 presidential campaign was marred by virulent expressions of anti-Catholic bigotry. Crosses were burned along his campaign trail, and even respectable magazines like the *Atlantic Monthly* questioned whether Smith owed his highest allegiance to the Constitution or to the Pope. Proskauer was greatly alarmed by these insinuations of divided loyalty, which, after all, might as readily be levied against Jews as against Catholics. Drafting Smith's public reply, Proskauer emphatically insisted that there could be no conflict between religious faith and patriotic loyalty.

During his rise to Jewish communal leadership in the 1930s, after Smith's political career ended, Proskauer insistently demanded unyielding Jewish support for American government policy. From public protest against the Nazi regime (when he counseled silence) to Jewish statehood (which, before 1948, he vehemently resisted), Proskauer remained staunchly opposed to any display of Jewish assertiveness. Jews had absolutely no "moral right," he claimed, to pursue exclusively Jewish interests. "For Jews in America, *qua* Jews, to demand any kind of political action," he warned, "is a negation of the fundamentals of American liberty and equality." In Proskauer's convoluted logic of loyalty, Jews must become second-class citizens, by stifling their political voices, in order to be recognized as genuine Americans.

Eventually, as Proskauer may have anticipated all along, Smith's loyalty problem became his own. Fearful that Jewish statehood would compromise the loyalty of Jews to the United States, Proskauer became a leader of the anti-Zionists, who were then numerous and influential in American Jewish affairs. "From every point of view of safety for Jews in America," he declared when he became president of the American Jewish Committee in 1943, "there has got to be an open, vocal Jewish dissent from nationalism and political Zionism." A Jewish state, he believed, would be "a Jewish catastrophe." American Jews did not suffer from "political schizophrenia. . . . We are bone of the bone and flesh of the flesh of America."

Yet in 1948, ironically, Proskauer's loyalty concerns finally compelled him to endorse Jewish statehood. Once President Truman recognized Israel, on the day the Jewish state was born, Proskauer had no choice but to become a Zionist. Anything less would have expressed precisely the opposition to American government policy, on a Jewish issue, that he was so resolutely determined to avoid.

Proskauer's loyalty dilemma, I realized, was the dilemma of American Jews writ small. It had penetrated deeply into the American Jewish historical experience, ever since the German-Jewish immigration of the mid-nineteenth century. How, American Jews had endlessly asked thereafter, can we remain Jews yet become good Americans? From the earliest Reform modifications of traditional ritual and liturgy, American Jews struggled, usually quite successfully, to make their Judaism conform to American specifications.

The Zionist movement, and then the existence of Israel, immensely complicated the lives of American Jews. Beneath the surface unity of "We Are One!"—the enthusiastic fund-raising slogan for Israel—and not very far beneath it at that, there has always been an undercurrent of apprehension lest Israel compromise the most important unity of all, the unity of American Jews with the United States. The key to understanding the intricacies of the historical relationship of American Jews to Israel, as fifty years of uneasy ambivalence toward the Jewish state demonstrate, is the nagging issue of divided loyalty.

From long before the Rosenbergs, to well beyond Jonathan Pollard, American Jews have remained determined to protect their American flank against allegations of disloyalty. For that reason, above all, the "Israel" with which American Jews identify must be a miniature America: a secular, liberal democracy and a Jewish state that is all but indistinguishable, in its political and cultural essentials, from the United States. Whenever Israel has significantly departed from American norms, whether in religion or politics, to pursue a distinctively Jewish agenda, American Jews have uncomfortably confronted the painful dissonance between their identity as Jews and as Americans.

It was in Israel, paradoxically, that I came to a clearer understanding of the abiding loyalty concerns of American Jews than I had ever achieved in the United States. I can still remember how often during my first months in the country that I met an Israeli with whom I had, usually within fifteen minutes, some variation on the following dialogue:

Israeli: "When will you move to Israel?"
Me: "I am American. Why should I?"
Israeli: "Because you are a Jew. Your home is here."
Me: "A Jew can be at home anywhere."

My answer, needless to say, was as incomprehensible to my Israeli interlocutors as their question was to me.

It did not take long, however, before I began to wonder about some familiar Diaspora certitudes. I had never imagined, for example, that in the United States I lived in anything remotely resembling Jewish exile. Was I, then, just another victim of the Diaspora myopia that had deluded Jews from ancient Babylon to modern Berlin into believing that they were at home wherever they lived? Had Israel, precisely according to the Zionist argument, transformed personal choice into Jewish obligation? Could a Jew truly be "at home" outside the Jewish homeland?

I was no longer oblivious to Zionist pleas for the ingathering of Jews, including American Jews, from exile. Nor, however, was I entirely persuaded by them. Modern Jews, after all, confront an unprecedented array of choices. Will life be lived in Zion, the old-new land of the Jewish people? Or in Torah, the portable homeland of Jews ever since their forced exile by the Romans? In the Diaspora, where vibrant

Jewish communities have survived, and often thrived, ever since the Babylonian exile? If there, will it be in synagogue and prayer, or in the enticing world of modernity, where Judaism no longer is an inherited destiny but a matter of purely personal "lifestyle" choices?

During that year in Israel, and many times since, I spent an inordinate amount of time meandering through the Old City of Jerusalem. Its complex maze of streets and intricate mosaic of ethnic and religious neighborhoods—with all those tantalizing Middle Eastern sights, sounds, and smells—were endlessly alluring. Somewhere along the way, however, I realized that these were not merely pleasant outdoor excursions but a serious, if convoluted, interior journey of self-discovery. Where, after all, was there a better place than Jerusalem, any archeologist's dream, to excavate the buried layers of my own Jewish self?

The newly restored Jewish Quarter often became my own *altneuland*, where antiquity and modernity were linked in ways that even Theodor Herzl's inflamed imagination could not have anticipated. Above ground are sparkling new buildings, built after nineteen years of destruction and abuse during the Jordanian occupation. Faced with Jerusalem stone, they change color from rosy pink to bleached white to golden orange to faded mauve as the sun rises and sets. I often sat at the edge of the central square, in the shade of a gnarled olive tree, absorbing the ebb and flow of Jewish neighborhood life as it had been lived for centuries in the shtetl culture of Eastern Europe, until modernity and the Nazis obliterated it.

When the summer heat or crowds of tourists became oppressive, I went below ground to explore recent archeological excavations of ancient Jerusalem. Literally beneath the plaza from which I had just descended are extraordinary remnants—charred walls, mosaic-tiled floors, stone tables, plates, and jugs—from the last moments of the Second Temple era, when the Romans sacked and torched Jerusalem and drove Jews into nineteen centuries of exile. Beneath the modern city, transported back through centuries of time, I could almost reach the bedrock of Jewish history.

On damp and chilly winter days, I often took refuge in the nearby stone-vaulted chambers of Wilson's Arch, adjacent to the Western Wall. The audible rhythms of Jewish prayer frequently lulled me into contemplation of the remarkable links between Jewish antiquity and modernity. For all those centuries, exiled Jews had dreamed in prayer of returning to this place—where it is possible to share a common language of ritual with Jews from anywhere in the world, and from almost any century in time. I had forgotten most of the words, but even to this wandering Diaspora Jew the melodies of Jewish prayer remained reassuringly familiar, indeed hauntingly evocative.

Yet my new attachment to Israel was also deeply unsettling. It made me wonder whether this was what had been missing in my relationship to the United States ever since I was a teenager. If so, had Israel, even as it made it easier for me to feel comfortable as a Jew, also managed to complicate, if not compromise, my identity as an American? When I returned home after that year in Israel, I wondered whether it was even home any longer. Suspended between two countries, between American and Jewish culture, I felt acutely uneasy. Those feelings of discomfort, more or less acute depending upon changing American and Israeli contingencies, remained with me until quite recently.

Now, the problem of national identification has become even more complex. Although Israel remains the pivot upon which so many Jewish identity questions still turn for Diaspora Jews, the Jewish state is experiencing its own acute identity crisis. As far back as 1948, following the Israeli proclamation of independence, the philosopher S. H. Bergmann asked: "What is a Jewish State?" Half a century later, the answer to his deceptively simple question still remains frustratingly elusive and, indeed, the source of bitter controversy in Israel. The complexities and contradictions of Jewish identity in the modern era, in Israel no less than in the Diaspora, seem ever more acute and insurmountable.

Most Israelis are quite content to live in a state of the Jews, where Hebrew is spoken and Jewish time is loosely marked (and easily disregarded) by the Hebrew calendar. They certainly do not want a *Jewish* state. Indeed, that prospect, which instantly conjures fearful images of fanatical Orthodox rabbis intruding into every corner of their private lives, alarms them far more than all the external dangers to their country from their avowed Arab enemies.

To these Israelis, a truly "Jewish" state portends a deformed Israel, even more of a pariah state culturally than it has been politically ever since its birth. As it did for Herzl a century ago, Jewish normality still seems to require a state that emulates Switzerland (Herzl's favorite example), or, a far more inspiring model these days, the United States. A state dominated by Judaism—the extraordinarily rich and complex religious and cultural inheritance of the Jewish people—would be truly abnormal. This is precisely what the relentless Zionist thrust toward normalization is determined to stifle.

During my last visit to Jerusalem, nearly a decade ago, I was invited by my friend Chava to explore a recently discovered Second Temple village at the southern edge of the city, near Bethlehem. Chava had always delighted in showing me the newest archeological excavation, or most recently discovered artifact, that strengthened the link of the Jewish people to their ancient homeland. No corner of Jerusalem, from Templar houses in the German Colony to subterranean cathedrals beneath the Jewish Quarter, escaped her interest.

On the way to our destination, she detoured to show me the newest pride and joy of Zionism. Not, this time, an ancient synagogue in the Jewish Quarter, or an inscription of the priestly blessing on an Iron Age juglet in the Israel Museum, or Herzl's perfectly restored Viennese study on Har Herzl. Rather, astride a recently leveled hilltop, we gazed at a splendid pleasure palace, a temple of consumerism, surely the grandest of its kind in the entire Middle East. It was the sparkling new Jerusalem shopping mall. Was this, I found myself wondering, the fulfillment, or betrayal, of the Zionist dream?

The amazingly rapid pace of Americanization, now so evident in Israel, leaves me more than a little uneasy about the Jewish future of the Jewish state. What is Jewish, after all, about the McDonald's, Pizza Huts, and Tower Records that now dot the Israeli landscape? Or the discos blasting pop music on Friday nights, even in Jerusalem? Or the fondness of Tel Avivians for Shabbat, and even Yom Kippur, at the beach? By the standards of American consumer culture, Israelis already seemed quite normal to me. But can this be good for the Jews? If Israel is determined to become, culturally, the fifty-first American state, why should Jews not prefer the North American original to its Middle Eastern replica?

To be sure, Israel hardly stands alone among the nations of the world for its eager absorption of the more tasteless excesses of American mass culture. But only Israel is a *Jewish* state, obligated by the innermost imperatives of Jewish history to resist the foreign enticements that must inevitably corrode its distinctiveness. That much I had learned from weeks, months, ultimately two years of living as a Jew in

Jerusalem, the restored capital of the first Jewish state in two thousand years.

The Americanization of Israel goes beyond the "Coca-colonization" of malls and McDonald's. It is also expressed in the insidious spread of post-Zionist values through Israeli intellectual, academic, media, and artistic circles. The relentless assault of Israeli secular elites, not only on Judaism but on Zionism itself, indeed on the very morality of the existence of a Jewish state, has reached pathological extremes. Israelis have absorbed the corrosive moral relativism that has infused American culture since the 1960s, and redirected it toward their own history, myths, and national institutions. The accompanying loss of Jewish meaning and purpose, as Israelis scramble to dismantle the uniqueness of Zion, has become Israel's distinctive attribute at the turn of the millennium. Israeli culture, writes Yoram Hazony in his exploration of the current struggle over Israel's Zionist soul, "has become a carnival of self-loathing, offering little from which one could construct the renewed Jewish civilization that was to have arisen in Israel."

That raises a troubling question: is assimilation in Israel any less problematic for Jews than its Diaspora variations? A Jew, after all, can live as easily in exile in Tel Aviv as in Los Angeles. Indeed, tens of thousands of Israelis have already taken the logical next step, preferring a home in California to one in the Jewish homeland. Might it be that now, at the beginning of the twenty-first century, "we are one" in ways quite different than the American Jewish cheerleaders for Jewish unity ever could have imagined?

Once, Israel forced me to confront the Jewish hollowness of my Diaspora existence. As a result, my Jewish identity, indeed my entire life, was transformed: I actually became a Jew. Now, however, I am stunned by the Jewish shallowness of contemporary Zionism. Like a sponge, it has soaked up culture from the West, especially from the United States, as the sources of Jewish vitality atrophy in Israel. It is not only astonishing, even miraculous, but also profoundly disturbing that Herzl's prophetic vision of Jewish normalization has already been so fully realized in contemporary Israel.

There still are, to be sure, pockets of Jewish passion in post-Zionist Israel. In recent years, I found the most vibrant Zionism among the religiously observant Zionists (American immigrants conspicuous among them) who, since the Six Day War, have chosen to live in Judea and Samaria. But these Israelis, pejoratively labeled "settlers" when they are not cursed as zealots, are widely castigated for having the temerity to dwell amid Arabs in the ancient homeland of the Jewish people. Their Zionism, with its taproots in Torah—the biblical record of God's promise of the Land of Israel to the Jewish people—is indifferent to Western consumer fashion. And their sharp critique of Zionist normalization challenges the convergence of mainstream Zionism with Western secularism. For that, they are roundly pilloried by secular Israelis for whom Zionism has come to mean a night at the disco, Shabbat at the mall, and exotic foreign vacations.

With which Israel—normal Israel or Jewish Israel—are American Jews "one"? Certainly not with the Israel of settlers, Orthodox rabbis, and their unabashedly Jewish followers. For their passionate fusion of Zionism and Judaism, these Zionists are despised and calumnied as demented fundamentalists by Diaspora Jews and secular Israelis alike. American Jews strongly prefer a secular liberal Zionist state, one that defines Judaism by American standards. This is also what most Israelis now seem to wish for themselves.

If we—American Jews and Israelis—are indeed one, what now defines our unity? The attachment may have originated in our ancestral heritage or sacred texts, but these sources have lost their vitality to Jewish identity in the modern era. Toward such traditional sources of Jewish inspiration and renewal, increasing numbers of Jews in both countries are abysmally ignorant, willfully indifferent, or overtly hostile. Rather, most American Jews and Israelis—except for the Orthodox minorities in both countries—seem to share a determination to dilute Judaism with an American infusion of free-choice individualism.

In their own distinctive ways, Jewish communities in Israel and the United States seem driven by the powerful acculturation imperative that was released by emancipation two centuries ago. Beginning in France, and spreading throughout Western Europe, Jews were cautiously invited to become "normal" citizens with equal rights in the modern nation-state. Everywhere, however, their acceptance was made conditional upon their divestment of the most distinctive attributes—whether religious or national—of Jewish peoplehood. Jews eagerly accepted the bargain wherever it was tendered, gratefully adopting the manners and mores of their host nation.

Zionism was offered as a Jewish solution to the emancipation problem. But the normalization of Zionism, like the assimilation of Diaspora Jews that it so closely resembles, is the logical and historical culmination of the emancipation impulse. For Israelis now, as for cultured European Jews two centuries ago, and for the uprooted immigrants whose children became American Jews, the road from the ghetto seems to lead, inexorably, to assimilation. Only in return for relinquishing their Jewish distinctiveness can Israelis hope to live normal lives and gain acceptance among the family of nations, whose approval they so desperately seek.

Just as American Jews have always fervently believed

in the compatibility of Judaism with Americanism, so Israelis now imagine that the more normal their country becomes the closer it approaches Zionist fulfillment. Sadly, if ironically, they are correct. After nearly a century of isolation and conflict, their yearning for integration and acceptance is understandable. But the question remains: how much longer will it take before Herzl's dream of an old-new Jewish homeland becomes a Jewish nightmare?

It may seem strange, just half a century after the horrific atrocities of the Nazi era, to dwell on the perils of freedom for Jews. But two centuries of freedom may have more insidiously undermined Judaism, if not actually imperiled Jews, than the murderous deeds of any tyrannical despot except, perhaps, Hitler. There can be no argument, at least, that emancipation created, sustained, and continues to intensify the fundamental tension inherent in modern Jewish life, whether it is lived in the United States or Israel: how do Jews, as free citizens in modernity, define and preserve their coherence as a people? Can Jews, the modern legatees of an ancient culture that traces its history for nearly six thousand years, find ways to live both as equal citizens and as Jews?

Not very long after the Czar and the Emperor had their memorable conversation, the plight of Eastern European Jews became all but intolerable. Trapped between discrimination and persecution, with no discernible prospects for improvement, Jews began to abandon the Pale of Settlement where they had lived, and where Jewish culture had thrived, for centuries. The overwhelming majority of Jews who left Eastern Europe behind, beginning in the 1880s, came to the United States. Their story is familiar, and justly celebrated: downtrodden and impoverished, but inspired by the promise of individual opportunity and civic equality, they clung desperately to their precarious foothold in the United States, their newly proclaimed *goldene medina*. Within two generations, their faith in their adopted homeland had been so abundantly rewarded that their children and grandchildren, indisputably free and equal citizens of a benevolent democratic nation, were accepted and rewarded beyond the wildest dreams of their immigrant ancestors.

A tiny handful of European Jews, no less determined to escape persecution for freedom, chose a different destination. Inspired by dreams of Jewish national rebirth, which had been nurtured ever since their expulsion from the land of Israel in the first century of the Common Era, they journeyed east, not west. Turning their backs on the brash new land where streets were paved with gold, they set out for the biblical homeland of the Jewish people. As long and as fervently as Jews had prayed for their return to Zion, this was an astonishingly bold step. No other people, before or since, has come close to replicating their remarkable achievement: to restore a people to national sovereignty, in its ancient land, after an interruption of two thousand years.

Two fragments of one people, making completely different choices about the meaning of Jewish freedom. Where else but the United States could an individual Jew hope to enjoy freedom from want and fear amid such boundless opportunities for personal fulfillment? Where else but Zion could Jews, collectively, become a free people, empowered by the irrepressible hope to determine their fate and define their Jewish future in their own homeland?

For all its trauma and horror, the twentieth century marked an era of freedom for Jews unprecedented in their history. In the American Diaspora, as in the Jewish national home, Jews are now freer than they have ever been to decide what kind of Jews they will be. And therein lies the Jewish problem, embedded in post-emancipation Jewish modernity. How were Jews in the United States to become

Americans, yet remain Jews? How were Zionists in Israel to become a normal people in a Jewish state? And, no less urgent, how were these two Jewish communities, which in tandem all but define the parameters of Jewish existence in our time, to settle the terms of their co-existence?

The dialogue between Jews who insist that they are at home wherever they live and Jews who assert that Jews can only truly be at home in the land of Israel goes back to the time of the Babylonian exile. Since the sixth century before the Common Era, Jews have intermittently, and at times quite passionately, argued with each other about the meaning of "home." With the beginning of the Zionist era, just over a century ago, and especially since the creation of the State of Israel in 1948, this argument has involved American Jews, whose fate has been implicated by decisions made in Basle, Kishinev, London, Tel Aviv, and Jerusalem. As fervently as American Jews have asserted "We Are One!" to demonstrate their unyielding identification with Israel, their uneasiness about the relationship has characterized the American Jewish experience.

Israelis have had their doubts, and for good reason, about the fidelity of American Jews to Zionism. Fewer than one American Jew in three has even visited the Jewish state, no less actually contemplated living there. Most American Jews, most of the time, live in blithe detachment from the concerns of Zionist or Jewish consequence that can agitate Israelis on an hourly basis. Convinced that their Diaspora home defines the best of all possible worlds for modern Jews, American Jews have tenaciously resisted, never more than now, the Zionist appeal for the ingathering of Jews from exile. How, they wonder, can anyone imagine American Jews to be in exile when they are so evidently at home in the United States?

Yet from its inception Zionism compounded the manifold problems of acculturation that are inherent in American Jewish life. Jews, after all, have always comprised a tiny fragment of the American population, with all the real and imagined vulnerabilities that accompany their minority status. Zionism, the ideology of Jewish nationalism, and Israel, the Jewish state, necessarily implicate American Jews in the issues and actions of a foreign nation. It is not surprising, therefore, that American Jews have often defined themselves, and their differences with each other, first by their responses to Zionism and, more recently, to what the government of Israel may say or do. Zionists may have finally wearied of imploring American Jews to make aliya, by now surely recognized as a hopeless cause. But Israel continues to complicate the terms of existence for Jews in the United States.

By now, each Jewish community looks to the other for a measure of self-definition and self-validation. They both grapple with what it means to be—or not to be—a modern Jew. When David Ben-Gurion called upon American Jewish parents to send their youngsters to Israel, when Israelis debate "Who is a Jew?" or when Israeli soldiers fire rubber bullets and tear gas at marauding Palestinians, American Jews are deeply implicated. Similarly, when an American president withholds loan guarantees from Israel, or snubs an Israeli prime minister, or American Jewish women wish to conduct prayer services at the Western Wall, Israelis take notice. Each Jewish community is affected by the other.

But neither Jewish community, in the United States or Israel, has ever been unified behind a common understanding of Judaism, either in religious or cultural terms. That, too, is a legacy of emancipation. For quite different reasons, rooted in their own sectarian identities, Zionism aroused the ire of Reform and Orthodox Jews in the United States, and it took many decades before the divisions healed. The

Reform movement, historically attentive to the Christian
mainstream, warily kept its distance from Zionism until
the eve of World War II. Orthodoxy, fiercely hostile to human efforts to supplant divine power, did likewise. (Ironically, its impassioned support for Zionism ever since the
Six Day War has made American Orthodoxy anathema to
secular Israelis, who treat all forms of Jewish religious enthusiasm, even for Zionism, with undisguised hostility.)
Conservative Judaism, guided early in the twentieth century by Rabbi Solomon Schechter, embraced Zionism within
its creative synthesis of Jewish law and nationalism with
American patriotism. But the Conservative movement did
not attract a plurality of affiliated American Jews for another half century. For many Eastern European immigrants,
too European for Reform and too American for Orthodoxy,
yiddishkeit remained a religion and culture of its own.

In Israel, too, there are sharply polarized disagreements
over the terms of Jewish existence in the modern era. Secular Ashkenazi Jews, entrenched virtually since the founding of the state in the arts, media, and universities no less
than in government circles, comprise the governing class.
It has never been reticent about asserting its cultural superiority, its secular imperatives, and its identification with
Western liberal norms. By now, its adherents denigrate religious Judaism, as well as any notion of Israel as a mani-
festly Jewish state, with all the fervor that their ancient
forebears once displayed in worshipping the Golden Calf.
The Orthodox communities, excluded from the ruling consensus unless their votes are needed to form a governing
coalition, are reciprocally hostile to secular Zionism. The
ultra-religious *haredim* display unbridled contempt toward
any vestige of modern secular authority, whether it is made
in America or an expression of godless Zionism. Sephardic

Jews, whose grandparents emigrated from Middle Eastern and North African Arab countries, display their own blend of tolerant Orthodoxy and Israeli secularism.

Although Israel and the United States have their own distinctive national trajectories, both nations share some illuminating historical affinities. Each has defined itself, Americans metaphorically and Zionists literally, as a reincarnation of the biblical promised land. The Puritans, the earliest American settlers from England, articulated their mission in explicitly biblical terms. Before they left for America, they were reminded of God's promise to "appoint a place for my people Israel." They identified their journey with the exodus from Egypt; if they followed the admonitions of the Hebrew prophets, John Winthrop reassured them, they would surely be blessed in their new home and "finde that the God of Israell is among us."

When Puritans reached the shores of Massachusetts, they knew that they had left "Babylon" behind for "God's new Israel." The linkage was explicit: "*Jerusalem* was, *New England* is, they were, you are God's own, God's covenant people." As Cotton Mather told them, "You may see an Israel in America." So closely identified were the two Israels in Mather's mind that he was certain that his congregants "know not, whether I am giving an Account of *Old Israel*, or of *New England*: So surprising has been the Parallel!"

Nor was preoccupation with the promised land an exclusively Puritan conceit. By the time of the Constitutional centennial in 1887, Oscar S. Straus, the most prominent and respected American Jew of his generation, found the resemblance between ancient Israel and modern America "remarkable." The history of Israel, he realized, had been "a glorious example and inspiring incentive to the American people." Straus concluded that "the bright sun of Canaan" was still shining upon the United States, where Washington, Franklin, and Adams were the spiritual descendants of Moses, Joshua, and Samuel.

Promised land imagery, of course, fills the Hebrew Bible, punctuates Jewish prayer, inspired the Zionist dream, and explicitly defined the purpose of Jewish statehood. "The land of Israel," proclaims the Israeli declaration of independence, "was the birthplace of the Jewish people." Exiled from their land, Jews "kept faith with it throughout their dispersion, never ceasing to pray and hope for their return to it." Inspired by their "historic and traditional attachment" to their divinely promised land, Jews were determined to realize "the age-old dream, the redemption of Israel."

Jews now inhabit two promised lands, one Zionist and the other American. Each community of Jews has linked itself to Jewish antiquity to affirm its own legitimacy. For Jews in the American Canaan, promised-land imagery demonstrated the required convergence of their American and Jewish identities. For Zionists in the Land of Israel, even the most resolutely secular among them, Zionism made sense only when it drew upon the very biblical sources whose authority they rejected.

Both the new world American Zion and the Zion that became Israel are nations of immigrants, proudly defining themselves by the sanctuary they offer to beleaguered, freedom-seeking refugees. Around the turn of the last century, as Jews from Russia, Romania, and Poland fled to the United States, they encountered a settled, prosperous community of German Jews who worked diligently to scrub these "Oriental" newcomers clean of their distasteful Jewish attributes. Similarly, the Sephardic Jews who fled to Zion after 1948, like the Holocaust survivors who arrived around the same time, were absorbed by Israelis with a sense of urgency about the necessity of conforming to Labor Zionist ideals—and prejudices.

In any nation of immigrants, identity and loyalty are endlessly contingent and frequently contested. In the United States, loyalty to their adopted nation has been repeatedly proclaimed by Jews who were understandably anxious lest their Jewishness, however it might be defined, set them apart from other Americans. American Jewish history can hardly be recounted independently of the concerted efforts, for nearly two centuries now, to interweave two disparate traditions, one Jewish and the other identifiably Christian, into a single, coherent American Jewish culture.

While American Jews struggle to reconcile their American and Jewish identities, Israelis confront the widening disjunction between Zionism and Judaism. Does Zionism require Israel to be a Jewish state, a state of the Jews, or a state of all its citizens, Jews and non-Jews alike? How are the historic and religious claims of covenantal Judaism, which originate in the biblical text, to be reconciled with the imperatives of Zionist normalization in the modern era?

In the end, American and Israeli Jews (excepting the Orthodox, whose Jewish identity, by definition, is less malleable) have adopted strategies of accommodation that attempt to reconcile, if often uneasily, their competing identity commitments. To be a modern Jew is to be pulled between tradition and modernity, between religious and secular imperatives, between insularity and universality. Jews must delicately, and endlessly, renegotiate their own identity to accommodate to the majority cultures that surround them. Sooner or later, American Jews and Israeli Zionists will need to confront their own nagging identity contradictions, lest they disappear altogether as identifiable Jewish communities.

The extraordinary peculiarities of the long and tangled

history of the Jewish people are deeply embedded in the structured cycle of Jewish memory. They are woven into the repetition of days and holy days, seasons and festivals, occasions for celebration and lamentation. Jewish time hardly encourages normalization. Yet Jews, who are now free to disregard the Jewish calendar and its imperatives, are more vulnerable than ever to the endlessly alluring enticements of the global village.

Contemporary Jewish historiography, for the most part, is accepting of these modern acculturation trends. Most American Jewish historians, like most American Jews, have secular liberal commitments that resonate in their work. Imitating nineteenth-century Reform rabbis, they see no incompatibility between the American and Jewish traditions. Following Louis D. Brandeis, the revered leader of the American Zionist movement in its formative era, they recognize no contradiction between Zionist and American values, or, since 1948, between American and Israeli national imperatives. Instead, they spin a seamless web of unity and harmony in which underlying conflicts, which precisely identify where American Jewish history becomes fascinating, are all but eradicated.

In Israel, the era of Zionist historiography has now given way to virulent post-Zionist revisionism. For decades after the worst catastrophe in Jewish (or, indeed, world) history, the Jewish state was exalted for saving the remnant of the Jewish people who survived the Holocaust. Its remarkable state-building and nation-preserving achievements were the source of Zionist pride. In recent years, however, Israel has been incessantly tarnished by post-Zionist historians, who not only accuse their nation of the "original sin" of dispossessing Palestinians, but castigate it for the subsequent sins of invasion, domination, exploitation, and religious fanaticism.

Regardless of their substantial disagreements, both Zionist historiographical currents draw upon the secular leftist politics of their practitioners. The unrelenting, even oppressive, secularism of Labor Zionism is taken as a given, along with its occasional ruthlessness toward its political enemies on the right. Israel, not Israel's unyielding enemies, is usually made to bear virtually the entire burden for peace or war. There has been little, if any, sympathetic understanding of the post-1967 religious Zionists who overcame immense obstacles to return Jews to Judea and Samaria, the biblical homeland of the Jewish people. Rabbis, religious parties, and religiously observant communities of Jews are routinely treated as irrelevant at best, or, at worst, malevolent. Religious nationalism, an ancient Jewish synthesis, has become a modern curse. Indeed, anything tinged with Judaism in the Jewish state is suspect. Both the Zionist and post-Zionist narratives have all but abandoned Jewish culture as a source of something worth saving in Israel.

Instead, Israeli historians, like so many Israelis (and Jews everywhere), pursue the goal of harmonious integration into the wider world. Their secular universalistic imperatives drive their irrepressible hostility toward Judaism and even Zionism, both of which seem hopelessly contaminated by Jewish parochialism. Their trendy moral relativism, in conjunction with their repudiation of the authority of Jewish history, Zionist achievement, and Israeli national purpose, plays well to an international audience that enthusiastically applauds the defamation of the Jews.

My own reading of modern Jewish history, and within it the contemporary plight of American Jews and Zionists alike, locates me far outside the contemporary historiographical mainstream. Rejecting liberal universalistic premises, which invariably submerge Jews and Judaism, I try to remain attentive to the overriding theme of modern

Jewish history: how foreign cultures have relentlessly impinged upon Jewish identity and autonomy, even in the Jewish state.

During two millennia of exile, until the beginning of the nineteenth century, Jews had no difficulty retaining their identity as Jews. Now, after two centuries of freedom, Jewish identity is more problematic than ever and, Zionism notwithstanding, no less so for Israelis than for American Jews. The fragmentation and polarization in both countries reflects the sharp rupture in Jewish life once the foundations of communal stability, based upon *halakha* (Jewish law) and rabbinical legal authority, were fatally compromised by emancipation. Even Zionism, the national liberation movement of the Jewish people, has been powerless to resist this accelerating process of disintegration. Indeed, Zionism now hastens it along.

In the end, it now seems clear, only the continued dilution of Judaism can assure harmonious reconciliation with the liberal pro-choice values that so many American Jews and Israelis fervently embrace. Adrift on a sea of relativism and revisionism, their Jewish compass badly battered by the enticements of modernity, Jews follow the siren song of assimilation and normalization wherever the gusts of changing fashion may take them. If Jews are ever again to find their way home, it will require a long and difficult—perhaps impossible—journey back to the sources of Jewish historical distinctiveness. At the very least, however, Jews can attempt to understand how we lost our way.

1

In Exile

at Home

The Emancipation Dilemma

The American people have demonstrated an extraordinary ability to escape the past, create the present, imagine the future, and realize its promise. Confident, brash, and innovative, Americans have long asserted their uniqueness among all the peoples of the world. American Jews have enthusiastically embraced these expectations and fully realized them. Yet try as Jews may to emphasize how American they are, they also fall within the long shadow of Jewish Diaspora history, which still asserts its claims, often in unexpected ways. If any ancient prophecy has been fulfilled in our time, it is that of Jeremiah, the prophet of Diaspora survival.

After the Babylonian conquest in 597 B.C.E., Jeremiah provided a remarkably prescient prescription for the renewal of Jewish life in the Diaspora. In a letter that still occasionally resonates for American Jews, the prophet conveyed his understanding of God's instructions to the exiled community:

> Build houses, and dwell in them; and plant gardens, and eat the fruit of them; Take wives, and beget sons and daughters . . . that you may be increased there, and not diminished. And seek the peace of the city into which I have caused you to be carried away captives, and pray to the Lord for it: for in its peace shall you have peace. (Jer. 29:5-8)

Rejecting any form of active resistance to conquest and dispersion, Jeremiah urged his people, abruptly wrenched from their homeland, to accept the normality of exile. Demanding accommodation to Babylon, he advised them to pray for the welfare of their foreign rulers. Jeremiah's advice was, and remains, entirely sensible. How else, after all, were Jews to survive in exile? But it should also be noted that his plea for docile accommodation to heathen rule, however pragmatic, marked a sharp departure from the biblical norm, which certainly did not counsel placid accommodation to foreign domination.

Nor was that all. In one of his memorable parables, Jeremiah actually praised the exiled Babylonian captives as "good figs" for remaining loyal to God. But he castigated the remnant that remained behind in Jerusalem as "bad figs," evil-doers whose transgressions were "a horror." Those Judeans who still lived in the promised land, he warned, would intermingle and intermarry with their idolatrous neighbors. Geography alone, Jeremiah implied, offered no assurance of Jewish integrity or continuity.

Was Jeremiah, as some Israelis have claimed, a despicable traitor, who placidly accepted defeat and exile? His counsel of capitulation to pagan rulers may, after all, have subverted the resolve of his people to resist foreign domination. Was there any religious obligation, the renowned biblical scholar Yehezkel Kaufmann inquired caustically, to surrender Jerusalem and the Temple "to a heathen king"? Jeremiah may have paid dearly for his prophecy of doom—he was despised, denounced, and cast into a slimy pit by his own people. But that hardly compensated, Kaufmann noted, for "the gravity of his offenses," which all but constituted treason.

Or was Jeremiah, as Diaspora Jews have long insisted, the prophet of Jewish survival? Certainly, Jeremiah accepted exile as a necessary, if temporary, condition of Jewish life. He shrewdly calculated the risk, at one extreme, of misguided zeal for national restoration and, at the other, of craven assimilation. His letter carefully balanced the competing claims on their allegiance that Jews confronted. Ingeniously, he transformed loyal citizenship in a foreign state into Jewish religious obligation. Indeed, so persuasive was his counsel that the rabbis subsequently reworked his legacy of accommodation into a model for post-exilic Jewish survival outside the Land of Israel.

Jeremiah's vision of exile may have been more complex than either his Israeli detractors or Diaspora admirers—each with their own ideological axe to grind—have recognized. His letter addressed an urgent theological and existential problem for the new Diaspora community in Babylon. Had God accompanied Jews into exile, they surely wondered, or were they abandoned to their fate? Recording their uncertainty, the Babylonian psalmist poignantly wondered, "How shall we sing the Lord's song in a foreign land?" Indeed, could it be sung there at all?

Jeremiah's letter was reassuring on precisely that point: even in a foreign land, the "Lord's song"—prayer—could still be heard. The homeland might be lost, but God had not abandoned the children of Israel. Sooner or later, the prophet promised, the exiles would return to their promised home. Indeed, Jeremiah tangibly displayed his faith in national redemption. During the bleakest moments of the Babylonian siege of Jerusalem, he had purchased a field in his nearby birthplace of Anatoth, delivering the deed with the ringing declaration that "houses and fields and vineyards shall be bought again in this land."

The devastating shock of foreign conquest initiated a debate over the meaning of exile and home that has persisted, unresolved, throughout Jewish history. Then and ever since, Jews have disagreed among themselves over their geographical and spiritual destiny as a people. The Babylonian Talmud, compiled many centuries after the exile, asserted that "whoever lives in the land of Israel is as one who has a God . . . and whoever does not live in the land has no God." And, according to the Mishnah, the Land of Israel is "holier than any other land" (a sentiment that would please even the most resolute atheist among modern secular Zionists).

But Jeremiah, for one, might have disagreed with such a Zion-centered reading. So did other sages, whose dissents the Talmud recorded. Rabbi Judah affirmed the primacy of Babylon, declaring: "Whoever lives in Babylonia is as if he lives in the Land of Israel." Indeed, anyone who left Babylon to return to Israel transgressed a positive commandment, for the rabbis instructed their communities that God alone, not human effort, could terminate the exilic punishment of the Jewish people. This very principle would be asserted many centuries later when the Zionist movement elicited stiff rabbinical opposition to its call for national restoration by dint of human effort.

With the Babylonian exile, Jewish life in dispersion began. Even when given the opportunity to return some seventy years later, relatively few members of the exiled community abandoned the comforts and pleasures of Babylon for Jerusalem. Diaspora communities also flourished in Egypt, in both Alexandria and Elephantine, where Jews adapted to the land of their ancient bondage. There was "a unique and rewarding polarity" in Jewish antiquity, historian Elias Bickerman has suggested, with Jerusalem and the Diaspora communities co-existing in creative tension. Then as now, Diaspora Jews adapted to their host cultures even as they faced Jerusalem in prayer and implored God to return them to their holy land.

About one thing, at least, Jeremiah surely was prescient: Jews in the Land of Israel were not immune to the enticements of foreign cultures. When Ezra led the exiled community from Babylon back to Jerusalem, he discovered a shockingly "unclean" land. The transgressions of the Israelites were evident: they "have not separated themselves from the peoples of the lands, doing according to their abominations." The homeland was no assurance of fidelity; Israelites had intermarried with strangers and worshipped foreign idols.

The problem of cultural assimilation, even among those who remained "at home," persisted. Centuries later, as the celebrated story of the Maccabees reminds us, Mattathias and his sons stood virtually alone in their rejection of King Antiochus's command for idolatrous worship. Modern renditions of the Hanukkah story, both in Israel and the United States, tend to evade the troubling fact that the first target of Maccabean wrath was not a foreign occupier but an assimilated Jew. In their national homeland, as in their Diaspora homes, Jews found the enticements of Hellenistic civilization—the civilization of foreigners—quite irresistible.

After the first-century Jewish uprising against Roman rule was suppressed, Jews were once again exiled from their homeland. With only a tiny remnant remaining behind in the Land of Israel, Jewish history began to unfold in the Diaspora. Yet the longing for Zion was preserved, even as any efforts to satisfy that longing by human endeavor were vigorously suppressed by rabbinical authorities.

The creation of a religious culture that could survive the loss of the homeland was, by any measure, a stunning achievement. By spiritualizing the land, and encasing it in memory and yearning, the rabbis managed to contain the impulse to return to Zion within the bounds of prayer, ritual, and hope. Sovereignty was lost and the people were scattered, but Jews everywhere remained bound by Jewish law and sacred time. Zion was desolate, but the Jewish people dwelled securely within the portable homeland of Torah.

Throughout the Diaspora, for nearly two millennia, Jews remained clearly recognizable, to themselves and to Gentiles, as Jews. Living together in enclosed communities, their lives, religiously and culturally, were distinct and separate. Jews might borrow extensively from their neighbors (as the architecture of synagogues and the design of ritual objects so vividly demonstrates), but integration, to say nothing of assimilation, was impossible. With few exceptions, Jews could hardly imagine it and, regardless, Gentiles would not permit it. Over time, Jews internalized Jeremiah's admonition to adjust their lives and prayers to Diaspora reality.

It would be foolhardy to suggest that every Diaspora Jew, during more than two thousand years, practiced what Jeremiah preached. But his admonition was embedded in a fundamental and enduring principle of Jewish law—*dina d'malkhuta dina* (the law of the state is the law)—that reconciled civic and Jewish obligation. To this day, Jeremiah's letter is still cited favorably by American Jews as a recipe for Jewish survival.

The internal coherence of Jewish life, and the communal insulation that sustained it, survived until the beginning of emancipation at the end of the eighteenth century. First in France, and then throughout Western Europe, Jews were encouraged to abandon their ghettos to exercise the rights and enjoy the opportunities of citizenship. Eagerly responding to this enticing invitation, they reformed Judaism into a diminished religious affiliation that would be unlikely to offend their Christian neighbors. The fateful emancipation bargain—national citizenship in return for Jewish assimilation—was the transforming event of modern Jewish history.

The emancipation process, so elaborately choreographed in France, is fascinating to reconstruct. It began in 1791, when the French National Assembly recognized Jews, identified as "individuals of the Jewish persuasion," as citizens of France. But civic equality in France implicitly mandated Jewish renunciation—or, at the very least, a radical redefinition of Judaism that would all but obliterate the distinctive national identity and sense of Jewish peoplehood that was historically embedded in the core of Jewish life. Once Jews were invited to become French citizens, the foundation of Jewish communal autonomy crumbled. Personal choice, the measure of civic freedom in the modern West, replaced the rule of Jewish law as the final arbiter of Judaism.

To newly emancipated French Jews, the benefits of the exchange vastly outweighed any discernible cost. As Berr Isaac Berr, a merchant from Nancy, exulted: "We are now, thanks to the Supreme Being, and to the sovereignty of the nation, not only Men and Citizens, but we are Frenchmen!" In gratitude, Berr implored his fellow Jews to relinquish any "narrow spirit, of Corporation and Congregation" that might still set them apart. To deserve the esteem and friendship of fellow citizens, for which every emancipated Jew yearned,

"We must absolutely appear simply as individuals, as Frenchmen, guided only by a true patriotism."

Yet doubts lingered about the Jews. Were they truly prepared, after so many centuries of isolation, to divest themselves of their irritating peculiarities? In 1806, a Jewish Assembly of Notables, whose gestures of Jewish renunciation were carefully arranged by Napoleon, was convened to respond to lingering questions about the ultimate loyalty of Jews to the state. Its answers would determine whether French Jews could indeed become "faithful subjects" of an enlightened modern state.

The questions varied: were polygamy, intermarriage, divorce, and usury still governed by Jewish law? Would rabbis continue to exercise legal authority, judicial power, and police jurisdiction? Did Jews consider other Frenchmen "brethren or . . . strangers"? What conduct did Jewish law mandate toward Gentiles? And, at the heart of Napoleon's concern: "Do the Jews born in France, and treated by the law as French citizens, consider France as their country? . . . Are they bound to obey the laws, and to follow the directions of the civil code?" Their answers to these questions would determine their civic worthiness.

The Jewish Notables dutifully responded. Comprising "enlightened men of the Jewish persuasion," the assembly (rather abjectly, it must be said) subjected itself to "the paternal goodness of His Majesty." Eager to assure Napoleon, their benevolent "Christian Prince," that rabbinical functions were limited "to preaching morality in the temples, blessing marriages, and pronouncing divorces," the deputies hastened to repudiate all vestiges of rabbinical legal authority, which for so long had preserved Jewish communal autonomy. "France is our country," the Notables affirmed; therefore, "all Frenchmen are our brethren." They recognized that Jews "must, above all, acknowledge and obey the laws of the prince," for "in every thing relating to civil or political interests, the law of the state is the supreme law."

Even this unequivocal affirmation of loyalty did not fully satisfy Napoleon. In a master stroke, replete with historical irony, he convened a Sanhedrin in Paris to ratify the surrender of the Notables. In ancient Palestine, the Great Sanhedrin of the Jews had exercised supreme judicial authority. Now, in modern France, a Christian ruler convened the Sanhedrin to repudiate all vestiges of Jewish legal authority.

The French Sanhedrin, lavishing fulsome praise on Napoleon as the instrument of divine will, readily complied. Eager for Jews "to be one with the great family of the State," it insisted that Judaism was fully compatible with the civil laws that governed society. "We are in no wise separated from the society of men," the Sanhedrin declared. Dividing Jewish law into "political" and "religious" categories, it dismissed the former as inapplicable "since Israel no longer forms a nation." Jewish sacred laws, it noted approvingly, "religiously enjoin on all obedience to the State in all matters civil and political."

Napoleon had every reason to be satisfied. The "moral regeneration" of the Jews, implicit in emancipation, was complete. Jews were now free, as the Sanhedrin recognized, "to build, to sow, to reap, to cultivate all human knowledge." The process of emancipation would take more than a century to run its course, but the essential principles were already in place by 1807 when the French Sanhedrin, its work of Jewish renunciation accomplished, vanished into oblivion.

With emancipation, Judaism was converted from an encompassing way of life, framed by legal obligation, into a spiritualized (and increasingly marginalized) "religion." Duly reformed, it bore more than a slight resemblance to

Christianity. With the dismantling of Jewish legal obligation, rabbis, traditionally the legal arbiters of Judaism, were
now expected to do little more than preach morality in their
temples and minister to their congregants, whose civic loyalty was channeled exclusively and passionately to the state.

The nineteenth-century era of personal freedom, which
proved sufficiently expansive to include the freedom from
Judaism, had dawned for Western Jews. Yet as avidly as
French citizens of the Mosaic persuasion pursued their journey from emancipation to assimilation, they still remained
Jews—potentially disloyal aliens who, in the eyes of others,
were forever suspect. As Captain Alfred Dreyfus discovered
toward the end of the century, even passionate patriotic
devotion might not suffice. With cries of Dreyfus's "treason" resounding through Paris in 1894, a thoroughly assimilated Viennese Jew such as Theodor Herzl could still feel
vulnerable. Shocked by the anti-Semitic frenzy over Dreyfus,
Herzl prepared his bold and desperate call for Jewish
statehood.

But why a Jewish state, and why then? After all, as
Shlomo Avineri has noted, Jewish history was "a chronicle
of discrimination at the hands of Christians and Moslems
alike." What made Jews react to nineteenth-century persecution "by turning toward Zion"? To be sure, Jews had always remembered Jerusalem and prayed for their return.
Yet only toward the end of the nineteenth century was this
longing finally translated into political activism and resur-
gent nationalism. Why did an abiding religious yearning
suddenly become such "a potent force for action" in the
realm of politics?

Why? Because Zionism alone offered to bridge the widening abyss between traditional Judaism and modern national identity. Rejecting Diaspora Judaism for its rigorous
religious traditionalism, Zionism nonetheless rested its

claim to a Jewish national homeland on biblical promises. Yet it also afforded Jews an opportunity to remain Jewish by defining themselves in national, not religious, terms.

As deeply embedded in Jewish religious consciousness as the dream of returning to Zion surely was, political Zionism floated on the modern currents of secularism, liberalism, and nationalism. Zionism was a thoroughly secular yet undeniably Jewish answer to the Jewish Question—the identity and destiny of Jews in modern society. It was hardly coincidental that the boldest Zionist theoreticians—from Hess and Pinsker through Herzl and beyond—all plundered Western ideology for their assorted nationalist programs. Jewish identity, after emancipation, had become malleable, contingent, a matter of personal choice and political preference. Once Jews entered European society as civic equals, there were abundant possibilities. Why *not* Zionism?

Consider Leo Pinsker, the assimilated doctor from Odessa. Like Herzl, whose Zionist argument he anticipated, Pinsker was a disillusioned emancipated Jew. Stunned by ferocious anti-Semitic pogroms after the assassination of the Czar in 1881 (as Herzl would be shocked fifteen years later by the Dreyfus case), Pinsker felt compelled (as Herzl did not) to reappraise the benevolent promise of emancipation. In an impassioned plea to Russian Jews, he insisted that "the eternal problem presented by the Jewish question . . . remains unresolved."

After nearly a century of emancipation, Pinsker wrote bitterly, the Jew remains "everywhere a guest, and nowhere *at home.*" So adaptable were Jews to foreign, even hostile, cultures, that they had all but divested themselves of their own distinctiveness as a people. The price of their new freedom, he concluded sadly, was Jewish self-renunciation.

Pinsker described the alluring promise of civic equality as merely "a rich gift, splendid alms," extended by Christians.

(And, as European Jews would ultimately discover to their horror, it was a gift all too easily rescinded.) But whether Jews were "persecuted, tolerated, protected, [or] emancipated" mattered less than the "degrading dependence of the eternally alien Jew upon the non-Jew." Pinsker despaired of efforts to integrate Jews into society—even in a society based upon liberty and equality. Only as "a nation among nations" would the Jewish people finally rehabilitate itself, "in our own eyes and in the eyes of the world." Modern Jews "wish to live like other men," Pinsker wrote, "and be a nation like the others."

"We must first of all *desire to help ourselves*," Pinsker insisted. Auto-emancipation—"the creation of a Jewish nationality"—was the answer. The self-respect of Jews required a home of their own (whose geographical location mattered as little to Pinsker as it would to Herzl). "Help yourselves," he implored Jews, "and God will help you!" Yet precisely here, even at his most daring, Pinsker remained bound by emancipation premises. Jews could only free themselves, this radical Jewish thinker insisted, by emulating everyone else.

It remained for Herzl to devise the most compelling Zionist blend of national self-assertion and Jewish assimilation. Zionism did not come easily to this cultured Viennese journalist, who only recently had felt trapped as a Jew, "condemned to an identity he could neither assume nor reject." For his son's sake, he had confessed just after Christmas in 1892, he would "rather convert today than tomorrow. . . . But I cannot do it." (Herzl, for a time, even nurtured the bizarre fantasy of the mass conversion of the Jews.) Yet just a few years later, Herzl became the Zionist messiah, the savior of the Jewish people. His unequivocal answer to the vexing Jewish Question was Jewish nationalism. But nationalism, Herzl insisted, was only to hasten Jewish normalization. About Jewish distinctiveness, after all, Herzl was abysmally ignorant.

Herzl's response, like Pinsker's, suggests that from the moment of its articulation, Zionism itself was trapped in the emancipation dilemma: Jewish "freedom" meant assimilation. For all the power of his assertion that Jews were one people, needing a state of their own, Herzl's Zionist ideas were far more deeply rooted in Western than in Jewish sources. He fantasized an "aristocratic republic," modeled upon Switzerland, which would become an "outpost of civilization as opposed to barbarism" in the Middle East. He wanted nothing less than Vienna-on-the-Mediterranean, where emancipated Jews could finally live normal lives like everyone else.

The virulence of French anti-Semitism had convinced Herzl that the Jewish problem could only be solved by Jewish statehood. His central, compelling insight about Jews was that "we are a people—*one* people." His diagnosis was unerring: "We have sincerely tried everywhere to merge with the national communities in which we live, seeking only to preserve the faith of our fathers. It is not permitted us." His stunning achievement was to propel Zionism to the center of the debate over Jewish identity in the modern era, and even beyond that, into the arena of international politics—where it has remained ever since.

Modern anti-Semitism, Herzl concluded, "is an outgrowth of the emancipation of the Jews." It would not abate; any expectation of human perfectibility, he warned, was "sentimental drivel." Yet assimilation was impossible: "The surrounding peoples . . . will not let us be. After brief periods of toleration, their hostility erupts again and again." Therefore, Herzl's "quite simple," yet audacious, plan: "Let sovereignty be granted us over a portion of the globe adequate to meet our rightful national requirements; we will attend to the rest." Only in their own state, paradoxically, would Jews enjoy the freedom to assimilate.

Herzl's Zionist dream, explicated in *The Jewish State* and, several years later, in *Altneuland*, was conspicuous for its Jewish barrenness. Herzl cited Jewish history as a burden from which emancipated Jews must finally escape; his occasional Jewish allusions invariably were dismissive. "We do not mean to found a theocracy, but a tolerant modern civil state," he wrote. Therefore, "our clergy" will not have "even the slightest chance to assert their whims. We shall confine them to their temples," precisely as Napoleon had demanded.

In Herzl's multilingual Jewish state, "every man can preserve the language in which his thoughts are at home." ("Who among us," Herzl wondered, "knows enough Hebrew to ask for a train ticket?") But Yiddish, the "stunted and twisted jargon" of Eastern European Jews, should be eradicated. It symbolized the ghetto from which Jews must escape to a cosmopolitan homeland of their own. Its location hardly mattered. As between Argentina and Palestine, Herzl was indifferent, prepared to take "what is given us and what is selected by Jewish public opinion."

Herzl's expanded vision of the Zionist future, described in *Altneuland*, was a utopian commonwealth where emancipated Jews, all but indistinguishable from Western European Christians, lived harmoniously with grateful Arabs who appreciated their civilizing virtues. Quite evidently, his source of inspiration for Jewish nationalism was not Jewish history but the enlightened West, with its "ideas which are the common stock of the whole civilized world." If modern anti-Semitism was an outgrowth of emancipation, as Herzl insisted, then so too was Herzl's Zionist response.

Herzl's genius was to devise a way to secularize Jewish yearning for national restoration. Even as Zionism absorbed

Jewish symbols and myths, he asserted, it must remain recognizably European. The virtues of Jewish statehood, for
Herzl, were expressed in the modern secular language of
the Enlightenment: "justice, truth, liberty, progress, humanity, and beauty."

Herzl's personal visage exemplified the duality of Zionism, in which the ancient yearning of Jews was expressed
in modern Western terms. His dark beard evoked images of
a traditional Jew, even as his elegant sartorial style, with
top hat and white gloves, identified him as a respectable
Viennese gentleman. Recasting religious yearning in secular form, Herzl appealed to godless Jews in Eastern Europe
who were desperately searching for an escape route to Western freedom.

Because Zionism has been ratified by history, at least
until recently when so many Israelis have wearied of its
burdens, it is seldom recalled how furiously Herzl's plan
was denounced by anti-Zionists and Zionists alike. Responding to the call for a Zionist Congress, the German
"Protestrabbiner" (Herzl's derisive term for his rabbinical
opponents) issued a sharp disclaimer. In a most incongruous alliance, seldom repeated, Reform and Orthodox rabbis
converged in their hostility to secular nationalism. "Religion and Patriotism," the protest rabbis declared, obligated
"all who have the welfare of Judaism at heart" to resist the
siren song of Zionism.

Reformers reasoned from emancipation premises to the
inevitable conclusion that "Judaism obliges its followers to
serve the country to which they belong with the utmost
devotion." Jewish nationalism, according to the prominent
American Reform rabbi Isaac Mayer Wise, was nothing but
"a momentary inebriation of morbid minds." Jews already
stood on "freedom's holy soil" in the United States, another
Reform leader claimed. Judaism must remain a religion only,

devoid of national content. To Reformers, Zionism was a dangerous repudiation of the assimilationist promises of emancipation, upon which their decorous edifice of enlightened Judaism had been constructed.

Orthodox hostility was fierce. Zionism contradicted their faith in "the messianic promises of Judaism," their belief that only God could decide when it was appropriate for Jews to return to the Land of Israel. A Grodno rabbi, writing in 1900, asked dismissively: "How can I bear that something be called 'the State of Israel' without the Torah and the commandments (heaven forbid)?" The separation of Jewish nationalism from religion, warned Rabbi Abraham Isaac Kook, about to leave Europe for Palestine (where he would become Chief Rabbi during the Mandatory era and the foremost theoretician of religious Zionism), was an "abomination."

Herzl's critics were not all rabbis. No sooner had the First Zionist Congress in Basle concluded its work than Asher Ginsberg, to become known by the pseudonym Ahad Ha'Am (one of the people), penned his vigorous dissent from Herzl's preoccupation with nationalist trappings and diplomatic negotiations. Ginsberg, a brilliant yeshiva student in his youth, became a formidable Zionist theoretician who was galvanized by Herzl into a life-long quarrel with Zionism.

Ahad Ha'Am's first published essay, *Lo ze ha-derekh* (This Is Not the Way), secured his reputation as an astringent Zionist critic. Too agnostic for the Orthodox, too spiritual for Herzl's secular Zionist followers, he questioned Zionism to its very core. With his challenge, Zionism moved from a simple prescription for a state to a complex (and still unresolved) debate over the meaning of Jewish statehood.

Ahad Ha'Am, like Pinsker, denigrated emancipation and its consequences. In a scathing attack on the notion that the "rights of man" were the "new Ten Commandments," he denounced the condition of emancipated Jews as "spiritual slavery under the veil of outward freedom." He detected a cruel historical irony: emancipation, both morally and intellectually, had enslaved Jews. To be sure, many emancipated Western Jews had successfully integrated themselves into their host societies—as army officers, civil servants, and professors. But Ahad Ha'Am was not impressed. "Do I envy these fellow-Jews of mine their emancipation?" he asked. "No! a thousand times No! The privileges are not worth the price! I may not be emancipated; but at least I have not sold my soul for emancipation."

Ahad Ha'Am's soul was no less troubled by Zionism than by emancipation. For if the Jewish national revival should fail to liberate Jews "from the *inner* slavery, from the degradation of the spirit caused by assimilation," then the Jewish Question would remain tragically unresolved. Politics and diplomacy were fine preoccupations for normal nations, he conceded, but Jews did not constitute a normal nation. Zionism, therefore, must mean more than practical politics. Ahad Ha'Am—who would never attend another Zionist Congress—confessed that in Basle he felt "like a mourner among the wedding guests."

Ahad Ha'Am did not precisely define "the living inner spiritual force of Judaism" that political Zionism, in his judgment, had failed to absorb. For Orthodox Jews, of course, this force was precisely the Torah-based *halakhic* Judaism that Asher Ginsberg had rejected as a young man. For the adult Ahad Ha'Am, however (as for so many modern Jews who wished to escape the yoke of Jewish religious tradition), it was the teachings of the ancient Hebrew prophets, who had implored Israel "to respect only the power of the spirit and not to worship material power." He insisted that "the Jewish state can only find peace when universal justice will ascend to the throne and rule the lives of the peoples and the states."

An important clue to Ahad Ha'Am's conception of spiritual Zionism was located in first-century Yavneh. During the Jewish war against Rome, while the Zealots in Jerusalem were slaughtered by Titus's legions, Rabbi Yohanan ben Zakkai had escaped to open his academy for Torah study and prayer. For Ahad Ha'Am, who remembered his yeshiva lessons well, Yavneh was a familiar inspirational story. It marked the emergence of rabbinic Judaism from the ashes of national destruction. Despite exile, and without national sovereignty, Judaism—spiritual Judaism—could survive.

For political Zionists, however, Yavneh was a deeply flawed source of inspiration. While valiant Jews fought to their death on the walls of Jerusalem to preserve national independence, Yohanan ben Zakkai had himself smuggled in a coffin to safety. For permission to open his academy, he humbled himself before Vespasian, the Roman commander, whose imperial rule he recognized. Was he, then, a Jewish hero or a Jewish quisling? And was not the political passivity of rabbis ever since Yavneh precisely what Zionism must repudiate for the Jewish people to be restored, in pride and dignity, to their ancient homeland?

Regardless, Ahad Ha'Am remained contemptuous of Herzl's Western arrogance and Jewish ignorance. In a scathing review of *Altneuland*, he mocked Herzl's foreign imports (the restored Temple in Jerusalem, for example, where "on Friday nights they sing 'Lecho Dodi' to organ music, just as they do in the Vienna synagogue"). An infuriated Herzl, unwilling to confront Ahad Ha'Am directly, asked Max Nordau to respond. In one of his kinder asides, Nordau referred to Ahad Ha'Am as "a crippled, round-backed victim of intolerance" who had the temerity to chastise Herzl's fondness for "academies, opera houses, and white gloves."

But Ahad Ha'Am's roots, unlike Herzl's, extended deep into Eastern European Judaism. They were richly nourished by indigenous religious, historical, and cultural sources. His Odessa, to say nothing of the Eastern European shtetl and *shteibel*, had nurtured Jewish continuity, vitality, and diversity for centuries. In Vienna and Paris, by contrast, emancipated Jews like Herzl so keenly felt their exclusion from Gentile society that they redoubled their efforts to emulate its manners and mores.

Ahad Ha'Am scorned "the great men of the West," those European Zionists (like Herzl) who could not even speak Hebrew, for turning to Jewish statehood to alleviate their own sense of cultural inferiority. As he noted, "Almost all our great men—those, that is, whose education and social position have prepared them to be at the head of a Jewish State—are spiritually far removed from Judaism." (Surely he was thinking of Herzl, but more than a few modern Israeli political leaders come readily to mind.)

Herzl's Zionism promised a state like every other state, where a Jew "could find at home all that he now sees outside, dangled before his eyes but out of reach." But Ahad Ha'Am despised mere statehood, which would sanctify "material power and political domination," while severing "the thread that unites us with the past." Statehood, an idea borrowed from the West, was likely to do little more than impose foreign standards on Jewish culture.

Ahad Ha'Am cited a disturbing historical precedent. The Second Jewish Commonwealth in Palestine under Herod was, at least in name, a Jewish state. But, Ahad Ha'Am continued, "the ruling house did everything in its power to implant Roman culture in the country and frittered away the resources of the nation in the building of heathen temples, amphitheaters, and so forth. Such a Jewish State will spell death and utter degradation for our people. Such a

State . . . would be estranged from the living inner spiritual force of Judaism." He demanded "not merely a State of Jews but a really Jewish State."

Despite Ahad Ha'Am's reservations, and Zionist limitations, it must be acknowledged that Herzlian Zionism radically transformed modern Jewish life. By converting the Diaspora from a requirement to a choice, Zionism shifted the entrenched Jewish religious preoccupation with sacred time to the novel political question of Jewish space. With Zionism, the question became—and, a century later, still remains—where can a Jew best live a fulfilling Jewish life, and is Jewish political sovereignty its prerequisite?

After Herzl, for better or worse, Jewish identity no longer was exclusively religious. Zionism irrevocably redefined it in territorial, and therefore explicitly political, terms. The consequences for Diaspora Jews have been profound and unsettling. The very idea of a Jewish state, to say nothing of its eventual reality, stripped the Diaspora of its monopoly on Jewish life. For the first time in nearly two thousand years, the Jewish Diaspora existed in relation to a nascent Jewish polity, aspiring to national sovereignty and asserting its own competing claim for Jewish allegiance. Since 1948, every Diaspora community has been compelled to define itself in relationship to Israel, whether in unbounded affection or uneasy apprehension.

Indisputably, emancipation and Zionism have been the defining Jewish liberation movements of the modern era. Emancipation confronted Jews with their fateful rendezvous with Western (Christian) civilization. Zionism promised to return Jews to the Land of Israel, the historic source of Jewish civilization, for the ambiguous purpose of Jewish normalization. But it is less clear than it once was whether these historical processes offered competing or complementary visions of the Jewish future.

Now, two centuries after emancipation and over one hundred years since the First Zionist Congress, Jews everywhere are indelibly defined by their dual inheritance. Even the most ultra-Orthodox rabbi in Brooklyn or Jerusalem, who repudiates emancipation and Zionism as modern blasphemies, defines his own Judaism in opposition to them. ("Orthodoxy," after all, is itself a post-emancipation badge of Jewish religious identification.) Similarly, the most assimilated non-Jewish Jew, whose freedom is rooted in emancipation, remains vulnerable to judgments against Israel, and by implication all Jews, in the court of world opinion.

How does it all look now, soon after the celebration of fifty years of Jewish statehood (precisely when Herzl had predicted)? "You were right," a secular Israeli might say to Herzl. Build the state first, a state like any other state, and ultimately the rest will take care of itself. Zionism may indeed have been formed from the theory and practice of modern nationalism; but today, from synagogue to shopping mall, in the *shuk* or in Knesset debate, in its language and calendar, Israel remains recognizably Jewish.

"*You* were right," an unrepentant Diaspora Jew might say to Ahad Ha'Am. Only if the spirit of Judaism radiates from a truly *Jewish* state, not merely a state of the Jews, will Zionism elude the quicksand of assimilation. Otherwise, as abundant evidence already confirms, Israel will be powerless to resist the steady erosion of Jewish content from Zionism; worse yet, it will eagerly absorb foreign culture and call it "Jewish." Zionists, as the Hasidic rabbi of Lublin instructed Ahad Ha'Am and Herzl at the turn of the century, may "appear to be zealous on behalf of Judaism," but instead they are "digging a mine beneath our faith."

Jews from the far-flung Diaspora, dreamers and dispossessed alike, were driven by zealous commitment or horrific necessity to rebuild the Jewish national homeland in Zion.

Ever since, the State of Israel has become a seething cauldron of contentious dispute over the meaning of Zionism and the terms of its relationship to Judaism.

Diaspora Jewry, by and large, has remained indifferent to this internal Zionist debate (except when its own self-interest has been directly affected). Any devoted Zionist must be puzzled, even angered, by the unwillingness of Diaspora Jewry—American Jews especially—to finally dissolve itself by emigrating to the Jewish state. Meanwhile, large numbers of Israelis have been drawn to the competing vision of Jewish freedom and opportunity afforded by the American dream. It may be sad, but it is nonetheless true, that there are now many more Israelis living in the United States than American Jews living in Israel. Where, finally, is the promised land of the Jews?

Between our respective communities, we virtually define the possibilities of Jewish existence in the modern era. Zionists have built their state, while American Jews have remained faithful to Jeremiah's counsel. As loyal Americans, Jews have built houses and planted gardens; Jews have married (and, of late, just as eagerly intermarried), raised families, and faithfully sworn allegiance to this country.

To be sure, a serpent of temptation lurks in our American Eden. Ours may be the freest Jewish community in history. Yet precisely because of that freedom, we American Jews may not, for very much longer, be able to raise new generations of Jewish children. We are already deeply divided among ourselves over "Who is a Jew? " (and infuriated by the efforts of the Orthodox rabbinate in Israel to answer the question decisively, in ways that nullify our proclivity to intermarry). In fifty years, if our intermarriage rate continues to accelerate, the American Diaspora may well be reduced to its Orthodox core, comprising the only Jews who did not permit the enticements of emancipation to obliterate the obligations of Judaism.

But is the problem of intermarriage and assimilation, whose seriousness is beyond dispute, unique to the Diaspora? Jeremiah's "bad figs," after all, lived in Jerusalem. Ezra, upon his return from Babylon, was appalled by Israelite transgressions. Perhaps American and Israeli Jews alike are fatally attracted to the assimilationist enticements of emancipation, which even Zionism is powerless to resist. What if both Jewish communities, the Jerusalem and Babylon of modernity, are bound by little more than a shared affinity for a vapid Jewish variant of secular liberalism, rampant consumerism, and freedom of choice?

If so, what does that portend for the continued distinctiveness of the Jewish people, without which our extraordinary history will become ever more incomprehensible to the generations that come after us? If we are all emancipated Jews, responding to the modern siren song of freedom, does it really matter where we live? We know, as a matter of historical fact from two millennia of Diaspora history, that Judaism has never required a national foundation to endure. And we also know, from the bitter lessons of the First and Second Commonwealths, that Jewish nationalism alone has never assured the survival of Jews or Judaism.

Perhaps we are edging toward yet another momentous turning point for the Jewish people. The Zionist revolution succeeded, beyond the wildest expectations of even its most zealous advocates. Yet the current post-Zionist reaction, with its eviscerating cynicism about Israeli national history and Zionist purpose, gathers intellectual and cultural momentum. Israelis are weary of incessant conflict, eager for world acceptance, and responsive to the American dream.

This does not bode well for Zionism. Israelis are coming ever closer to resembling those newly emancipated Jews in the nineteenth century whose desperate eagerness to embrace Western culture prompted them to jettison Judaism with hardly a look backward.

Among American Jews, to be sure, the picture is no brighter. For one hundred years now, in the first Zionist century of modern Jewish history, the Diaspora identity of American Jews has reflected their passionate embrace of the United States. Despite all the protestations of unity, there has been a palpable distance between American Jews and Israel, a stubborn resistance to the Zionist idea. Briefly closed in 1948 following Israeli independence, and again in 1967 with the Six Day War, the latent conflict between these Jewish communities endured, widened, and grew especially deep between 1977 and 1992, and again between 1996 and 1999.

At this moment in Jewish history, any convergence between Israel and the Diaspora seems highly unlikely to deepen Jewish consciousness or commitment. With Jews from both countries equally at home chatting on cell phones and surfing the Web, our two communities of non-Jewish Jews grow ever more disturbingly similar. Emancipated Jews that we are, we seem to be far more comfortably at home in the global village than in Jerusalem.

2

Zionism as

Americanism

Despite enthusiastic, even passionate proclamations of unity between American Jews and Israel, a century of Zionism, including more than fifty years of Jewish statehood, has vastly complicated the lives of American Jews. Israel, some would argue, has saved American Jewry from disappearing into the oblivion of assimilation. Without the existence of a Jewish state, American Jews might have chased the American dream with virtually no Jewish content to their lives. (Even with the existence of Israel, this remains the preference of a significant majority.) There is no doubt that by embracing Israel, American Jews found a rather easy way to remain Jewish. But scratch the surface of this Zion-centeredness and one uncovers persistent anxiety, lest too strong an identification with the Jewish state be taken as compromising their loyalty to the United States.

American Jews have always, and understandably, worried about their status as Americans. Until quite recently just a generation or two removed from Eastern European shtetl culture, their passionate affirmation of the United States as their promised land was the natural response of

Jews who were highly sensitive to loyalty issues. Once Jewish statehood explicitly threatened the comfortable terms of American Jewish acculturation, Zionism was recast as Americanism, and Israel, in turn, became a miniature replica of the United States.

Long before Herzl, the United States had already become the promised land for Diaspora Jews. The keynote of American Jewish yearning was sounded at least as early as 1841, when Gustavus Poznanski, blessing a new Reform temple in South Carolina, located Jerusalem in Charleston and Palestine in the United States. The rapid Americanization of Judaism in the nineteenth century expressed the determination of a generation of German-Jewish immigrants to reform their religion, and themselves, until they became all but indistinguishable from the Protestant majority.

The German Jews who arrived in the United States before the Civil War fervently pledged their allegiance to their adopted homeland. The United States was their Israel, their truly promised land. Rabbi Kaufmann Kohler, the intellectual leader of nineteenth-century American Reform, which decorously blended Judaism with the prevailing form of Protestant worship, proclaimed the United States to be "the land where milk and honey flow for all."

Toward the end of the century, the arrival of hundreds of thousands of Jewish immigrants from Eastern Europe challenged the prevailing terms of American Jewish accommodation. The assimilated, "reformed" German Jewish community was discomforted by the evident foreignness of the newcomers. Immigrant Orthodoxy, in their eyes, marked a regression from their own decorous modern Judaism to primitive "Orientalism." The Eastern European Jews were conspicuously Jewish, and foreign. Were they not, therefore, dangerously un-American?

The convergence of mass immigration with the first

stirrings of Zionism was deeply unsettling. Zionism might only be the wistful fantasy of handfuls of Russian Jews, but it immediately provoked insinuations about the loyalty of all Diaspora Jews. In the founding statement of American Zionism, Richard Gottheil, president of the nascent Federation of American Zionists, asked the fundamental question that has agitated American Jewry ever since: "What is to be our relation to the new Jewish polity?" Gottheil conceded that Jews comprised more than a religious entity (which was the constricted emancipation definition), perhaps even "a nation." But if Jews everywhere constituted a single nation (as Zionists boldly proclaimed), then the implications for the undivided loyalty of American Jews to the United States were ominous.

A Jewish national refuge, Gottheil insisted, hardly meant that every Jew must return to Palestine. The Zionist ingathering was reserved for Jews from "places in which it has become impossible for them to live." The United States, by clear implication, was excluded. To Gottheil, the American problem was not too few Jews, but too many. The influx of "Jews who are not Americans," warned Gottheil, would surely pose "a continual menace" to American Jews.

Zionism offered Gottheil a solution to continued Jewish immigration to the United States. "It is more than an open secret," he conceded, "that we cannot cope with the 400,000 Jews in [New York]; Boston, Baltimore, Philadelphia, and Chicago will give you the same answer." What, then, would become of hundreds of thousands of Jews who were desperately seeking to leave Russia, Poland, and Romania for a secure haven elsewhere? Their Jewish safety valve must be Palestine—not the United States. Zionism deserved the support of American Jews because it promised to divert Jews from the United States.

Zionism confronted American Jews with a novel, and

unsettling, challenge: how to reconcile their allegiance to
two promised lands. Divided loyalty was rarely mentioned
in public, at least not explicitly. But it is not difficult to
discern the preoccupation of American Jews with it. Jacob
Schiff, the prominent turn-of-the-century banker and Jewish communal benefactor, declined even to meet with Herzl
lest he be contaminated by contact with a real Zionist.

During the formative era of American Zionism, between
the world wars, the most revered American Zionists were
Louis D. Brandeis, Judah L. Magnes, and Henrietta Szold.
Their leadership in the American Zionist movement derived
from their ability to reconcile the competing national claims
that Zionism provoked. Indeed, by World War II, the compatibility of Jewish nationalism with loyal Americanism had
become the mantra of American Zionism. In the famous
Brandeisian *non sequitur*: "To be good Americans, we must
be better Jews, and to be better Jews, we must become
Zionists."

Brandeis first achieved renown as a lawyer, then as a
Progressive reformer, and finally as a jurist, the first Jew to
be appointed to the Supreme Court. But his unrivaled esteem as the "American Isaiah," who forged an unbreakable
link between Zionism and Americanism, may have been
his most stunning achievement. Intuiting the loyalty dilemma that tormented American Jews, because at some level
it also may have tormented him, he found the language with
which to conceal the tension between Zionism and American patriotism.

Although Brandeis's identification with Zionism was
both belated and circumscribed, it has been enclosed in the
myth of a compelling conversion story: the wandering Jew
who finally returned to his people to endorse their yearning
for national liberation. But his rather tortured reconciliation of Zionism and Americanism became a self-evident

truth only because it told American Jews what they most wanted to hear. If a Zionist could become an associate justice of the Supreme Court, then—precisely as Brandeis insisted—surely there was no conflict between an identification with Zionism and loyalty to the United States.

Brandeis easily discovered so much in common between Zionism and Americanism because he knew so little about Judaism. He grew up in a family whose primary ethnic identification was German. Although his revered uncle Louis Dembitz was a knowledgeable and observant Jew, Brandeis did not emulate his Jewish observance or scholarship. Indeed, there was little in his early years, or even in adulthood, to identify him as a Jew. From his boyhood in Louisville to his days as a Harvard Law School student, his tastes reflected a yearning for the cultivated refinement, and approval, of Brahmin Boston. (He succeeded admirably; one prominent Boston dowager had no idea, despite his prominence in the Boston bar, that he was a Jew.) Brandeis candidly conceded: "I have been to a great extent separated from Jews. I am very ignorant in things Jewish."

Like so many of his German-Jewish contemporaries, however, Brandeis worried that new Jewish immigrants from Eastern Europe would endanger the comfort of assimilated Jews, like himself, in American society. There was no place in the United States, he warned bluntly, for "hyphenated Americans." In his first address to a Jewish audience, in 1905 when he was nearly fifty years old, he sternly demanded loyalty to "American institutions and ideals." His tepid Jewish identification was well known to the assimilated German Jews who organized the American Jewish Committee in 1906 to combat anti-Semitism. They shunned Brandeis for a leadership position, noting that "he has not identified himself with Jewish Affairs and is rather inclined to side with the Ethical Culturists," a group of disaffected New York

Jews led by Felix Adler who had broken with Judaism some decades earlier.

Not until 1913, at a dinner honoring the European Zionist Nahum Sokolow, did Brandeis find anything positive in Zionism. After hearing Sokolow speak, Brandeis told him with evident feeling: "You have brought me back to my people." Not long afterward, Brandeis met Aaron Aaronsohn, a Palestinian agronomist who came to the United States to raise funds for his agricultural field station near Haifa. Brandeis was inspired by Aaronsohn's reference to "the little communities" of law-abiding Zionists that flourished in Palestine (in contrast, Brandeis noted critically, to the Lower East Side of New York, where Jews had earned unwelcome notoriety for criminal activities). That touched a responsive chord in Brandeis. To the Brahmin Jew of Boston, Palestine suddenly came to life—as the modern reincarnation of seventeenth-century New England!

Brandeis's Zionist frame of reference was—and remained—colonial Massachusetts. It was the source, real or imagined, of all that he cherished in American civilization. "My approach to Zionism," he readily acknowledged, "was through Americanism." The Jewish national revival in Palestine, for Brandeis, reenacted "the birth of New England." Zionism, he claimed, was "the Pilgrim inspiration and impulse all over again." The Zionist *halutzim*, tilling the soil on their Palestinian frontier, exemplified the rugged virtues that Brandeis associated with hardy Puritan pioneers. He imagined that "the values of the Massachusetts founders were being carried on in far-off Palestine."

New England historical analogies, no matter how contrived, served an important function for Brandeis. They enabled him to transform American Zionists into patriotic citizens whose "loyalty to America can never be questioned." If, as he claimed, "the Jewish spirit . . . is essentially modern and essentially American," then it followed that "there is no inconsistency between loyalty to America and loyalty to Jewry." Truly, "the Zionist ideal, the highest Jewish ideals, are essentially the American ideals." No American, he insisted, should imagine "that Zionism is inconsistent with Patriotism."

Despite his leadership of the American Zionist movement through the World War I era, Brandeis remained staunchly opposed to the political fulfillment of Herzl's Zionist dream. "I am but expressing the views of . . . all Zionists with whom I have personal relations," he wrote on November 2, 1917, the day the Balfour Declaration was issued, "when I state that they and I neither advise nor desire an independent state." A Jewish state, for Brandeis, was "a most serious menace."

To whom? Surely to American Jews, whose loyalty to the United States Brandeis was determined to secure. His supreme achievement as an American Zionist leader was to devise the terms of reconciliation between Zionism and Americanism. His reiteration of the congruity between them told American Jews what they most wanted to hear. A thoroughly Americanized Zionism, stripped of Jewish content, would not endanger American Jews. Brandeis led by example: Zionism could hardly pose a problem of loyalty once a Zionist served on the Supreme Court of the United States.

Brandeis never imagined that an American Zionist was obligated to live in Zion. Few American Zionists did. But two prominent American Jews, after years of dedicated Zionist activity in the United States, actually moved to Palestine. Like Brandeis, their American ideals of democracy and social justice, activated by the liberal reform movements of the Progressive era, framed their Zionist commitment—and led them, ultimately, to oppose Jewish statehood. Yet their decision to live in Palestine, inspired as it was by Zionism, ultimately depended on their equation of Zionism with American values. For Judah Magnes and Henrietta Szold, American Zionism was a Progressive reform with a slight Jewish accent.

Magnes, born in California in 1877, blended western independence with his own distinctive style of Jewish non-conformity. As a student at the Hebrew Union College in Cincinnati, the bastion of rabbinical anti-Zionism, Magnes boldly challenged the conventional Reform wisdom. The land of Israel, he asserted, was the only alternative to the inevitable withering of Judaism in the Diaspora. Despite the insistent claims of Reform Jews, Magnes seriously doubted that the United States was "Palestine."

Studying in Berlin, Magnes experienced a Jewish trans-formation. Encountering Eastern European Jews for the first time, he discovered (as Brandeis had) "complete" Jews, sus-tained by "Talmud Judaism," who displayed a "tremendous spiritual power" that American Jews lacked. ("God help them," Magnes warned, "if . . . our cracked-up ideas of 'progress,' etc. ever reach them.") Newly inspired by these encounters to grapple with "the questions concerning the Jewish people," Magnes suddenly became a Zionist and pro-claimed his determination "to live more like a Jew." Zion-ism, he informed his parents, "is more to me than anything else in the world."

Magnes embraced Zionism as the alternative to Diaspora assimilation. In the United States, he concluded, "we can-not produce Jewish forms of life," for "Americanization means . . . dejudaization." Only in "the old historical land" of the Bible could there be "Jewish standards for everything." Zionism served another purpose for Magnes (as it also did for Gottheil and Brandeis). "The Jewish immigration to America is already a danger to the Jews of America," he warned. Therefore, "we must endeavor to turn the stream of immigration towards the Orient." Not only could Eastern European Jews "develop themselves in the land of our fathers," but their diversion to Palestine would enhance the security of American Jews.

After nearly two decades of exhausting public activity—as rabbi of Temple Emanu-El, secretary of the Federation of American Zionists, founding leader of the New York *kehilla*, and pacifist dissenter during World War I—Magnes yearned for a respite. In May 1922, he sailed with his family to Palestine for an extended rest. Two years later, still uncertain whether he belonged there or in the United States, he was named chancellor of the new Hebrew University in Jerusalem. The appointment changed his life. A maverick Jew in the United States, he became an American individualist in the Jewish homeland, a "dissenter in Zion."

Magnes, like so many other modern Jews with a frayed attachment to the Judaism of commandment and obligation, drew inspiration from the ancient Hebrew prophets. As a rabbinical student, he had absorbed the Reform reading of prophecy as a spiritualized alternative to Jewish law and, therefore, the nourishing source of an ethical, liberal Judaism that was suitable for the modern age. He yearned (borrowing from Ahad Ha'Am) for "a Jewish spiritual center" in Palestine, "a country where nationalism is but the basis of internationalism, where the population is pacifistic and disarmed—in short, the Holy Land." Would Jews in Palestine, Magnes brooded, become "devotees of brute force and militarism as were some of the later Hasmoneans"? Or, as he fervently hoped, "will the Jews of Eretz Israel be true to the teachings of the Prophets of Israel," redeeming their nation "through righteousness and peace"?

The ultimate question, Magnes asked Zionist leader Chaim Weizmann, is "do we want to conquer Palestine now as Joshua did in his day—with fire and sword? Or do we want to take cognizance of Jewish religious development since Joshua . . . and repeat the words: 'Not by might, and not by violence, but by my spirit, saith the Lord'?" Jews must do nothing, Magnes insisted, "that cannot be justified before the conscience of the world."

Defining himself as "a radical liberal," Magnes remained a genteel Progressive reformer, a stanch American individualist, and an ambivalent Jew in the Middle East. As a "moral gadfly," however, his jeremiads from the university heights on Mount Scopus—so effective in an American setting that valued the moral preaching of dissenting ministers— rendered him increasingly marginal, if not actually obstructive, to the Zionist cause. During the interwar decades, when Jews were ravaged by Arab violence in Palestine and Nazi barbarism in Europe, Magnes was reduced to pitiful pleading with his own people to be peaceful, righteous, and merciful.

Renouncing the Zionist goal of national independence, Magnes persistently advocated a bi-national Arab-Jewish state. This left him with no following among Jews in Palestine, beyond the handful of like-minded German intellectuals who orbited around Martin Buber in his tiny B'rit Shalom (Covenant of Peace) circle in Jerusalem. Even in the United States, by the outbreak of World War II, his most appreciative audience comprised militant anti-Zionists in the American Council for Judaism and Arabists in the State Department, who applauded his presumably unintended service to their cause.

Magnes, as his biographer notes, "stood out as the authentic product of a liberal America." His rhetoric drew upon the prophetic writings so dear to American Jewish liberals. Amos and Isaiah, filtered through Reform or Progressive lenses, enabled American Jews to pledge their allegiance to Jewish tradition even as they rejected it for modern liberal politics. But as Shmaryahu Levin, the Eastern European Zionist, once told Magnes, it was precisely his moral sermonizing that demonstrated that "you are really an assimilated Jew." Magnes may have left the United States for Palestine, but he always carried his American baggage with him. From Zion, ironically, his characteristically liberal distortion of ancient Hebrew prophecy encouraged the most resolute American opponents of Jewish statehood.

Among Magnes's devoted admirers was Henrietta Szold. A rabbi's daughter, Szold was born in Baltimore on the eve of the Civil War. Her childhood on the Mason-Dixon line sensitized her to the plight of oppressed minorities. (In her later years, she would insist upon concluding Passover seders with Negro spirituals.) As a young girl she yearned to become "a Quaker lady," hidden demurely beneath a bonnet of personal modesty while passionately serving humanity.

A sharp influx of Russian Jews to Baltimore, fleeing the pogroms that followed the assassination of the Czar in 1881, aroused her empathy. "My heart bleeds for them," she wrote. "I have no greater wish than to be able to give my whole strength, time, and ability to them." Responding to their needs (and, not incidentally, to her own), she established one of the earliest night schools for new immigrants, where she taught English, sewing, carpentry, and other attributes of good citizenship.

Szold's German-Jewish upbringing, which instilled a strong sense of *noblesse oblige*, framed her response to the new immigrants. Blending sensitivity and pity, she condemned "the pride of the rich Jew, the parvenu," whose arrogance toward Russian Jews was "inexcusable." But she despaired of the "shocking grammar" and "despicable smartness of the street and factory" displayed by immigrant children. With the fastidiousness so typical of German Jews, she referred to native-born American Jews as her "coreligionists," carefully distinguishing them from the "race-Jews" of Eastern Europe.

As a generation of post-Victorian American women moved from domesticity into public life around the turn of the century, Szold, nearing fifty, finally ventured beyond the comfortable but confining world of Jewish books. Like Jane Addams at Hull House, she blazed new trails, carrying Victorian "women's work"—teaching, nurturing, and healing—into the public arena. For Addams, a visit to the London slums was the stimulus for Hull House; for Szold, the road to Hadassah began in Jaffa.

Accompanied by her mother, Henrietta Szold visited Palestine for the first time in 1909. Both women were repelled by the misery and disease that plagued its inhabitants. In Tiberias, they encountered emaciated children with bony sticks for legs. In Jaffa, Henrietta wrote, "we saw a most horrible sight: children with a wreath of flies around their eyes." Her equally "horrified" mother admonished her: "You should do practical work in Palestine."

Szold's Palestine experience surely deepened her Zionist commitment, but its transformative impact, like Brandeis's conversion, is easily exaggerated. To be sure, she plunged ever more deeply into Zionist activities. But in her new position as secretary of the Federation of American Zionists, she found herself engaged in the dreary task of reorganizing "a hopeless muddle" of paperwork. "I cannot flatter myself that I am doing Zionist work," she conceded; "cleaning up other people's Augean stables is too far removed from Jewish ideal hopes to be a solace." Inspired to do noble work, she dutifully filed correspondence for the Federation of American Zionists, while in her spare time proofreading and indexing for the Jewish Publication Society.

Five years after her visit to Palestine, a private donor enabled Szold to reorganize her literary group, the Hadassah

Circle, into a medical unit. She bestowed upon it a prophetic, and self-revealing, motto (from Jeremiah): "The healing of the daughter of my people." Just before the outbreak of war in Europe, Hadassah sent its first visiting American nurses to Jerusalem. Szold, sounding exactly like a Progressive reformer encountering an urban slum, insisted that a "sane, healthy life" in Palestine depended upon "the problems of the cities" being solved "in a modern, systematic, organized way," with "modern, American-style" techniques.

No one would benefit more from the healing work of Hadassah than Szold herself. In 1920, nearing sixty and with a diagnosed heart problem, she arrived in Palestine on a two-year assignment to administer the enlarged Hadassah medical unit. "Whether I ought to be here" perplexed her; and her first months were exceedingly difficult. "The life here does not make me happy," she confessed; "Palestine is for the young." In less than a year, however, a rejuvenated Szold realized that she had finally embarked "on the great adventure of my life."

For Szold, accustomed to "homekeeping like a cat," Palestine was dislocating, yet inspiring. She felt "a strenuous stirring"—both in her people and in herself. Like Magnes, she imagined Palestine as "a center from which Jewish culture and inspiration will flow . . . dominated wholly by Jewish traditions and the Jewish ideals of universal peace and universal brotherhood." But she had no illusions about Zionists, whom she primly described as "inefficient, spiritually poverty-stricken, uncouth, and unmannerly."

Hadassah was a distinctively Progressive export to Zion. Szold detected the local resentment of its pervasive "Americanism." It could hardly be otherwise, for her passion for efficiency and organization was not a conspicuous Zionist attribute. "I love order. Disorder nauseates me," she admitted. But the new immigrants to Palestine (like Russian Jews in Baltimore forty years earlier) were "systemless. They hate efficiency." Indeed, in one of her sharper observations, she referred to "the flotsam and jetsam of East European Jewry which is washed up on these Palestinian shores." Szold realized that to the Zionists she was merely "a dear little old lady—so devoted! so idealistic!" But she insisted, with unusual asperity: "I am not a saint, I *am* an American."

Szold's Hadassah appealed to American Jewish women who, like their model heroine in Palestine, were prepared to venture, if cautiously, beyond home and family. Caring for the weak, the ill, and the disadvantaged offered a personally rewarding, and socially acceptable, escape from the trap of domesticity, while simultaneously expressing domestic virtues. For Szold, Hadassah was the ideal combination of Judaism and liberalism, Zionism and Progressivism. Committed to practical, nonpartisan tasks of health, hygiene, and sanitation, Hadassah retained its moral purity amid the nasty swirl of Zionist politics. Under Szold's guidance, Hadassah deftly eluded the hazards of dual loyalty that always lurked at the edge of American Zionist activity. She made it possible, indeed easy, for American Jewish women to transform their compassion into Zionist dedication.

Szold, like Magnes (a friend since her years at the Jewish Theological Seminary), viewed the Middle East through American liberal lenses. Indeed, she admired the "sweet reasonableness" of his proposal for a bi-national state at a time when Zionists were far likelier to denounce it as bordering on treason. Her (limited) comprehension of the Arab-Jewish conflict was permanently framed by her girlhood perceptions of American race relations. Arabs and Jews, she thought, like blacks and whites, were locked into "race-tight compartments" that fed "race hatred." Szold could not understand how an infusion of American-style tolerance and good will could fail to resolve even so bloody a struggle for national survival as engaged the Zionists in Palestine. Jews must not, however, prevail "by the power of brute force, but by the spirit of divine law and love."

"A gentle woman," one historian has written, Henrietta Szold "devoted her life to securing justice for her people." True enough. But Szold deserves better than the reverential canonization that admirers have bestowed upon her. She would be the first to defend her own complexities against such simplistic praise. Like her Zionist mentor Brandeis (who paid Szold his highest compliment when he referred to her, quite aptly, as a Jewish Jane Addams), and her dear friend Magnes, she struggled to balance American and Jewish loyalties that were more acutely conflicted than they could ever comfortably acknowledge.

Brandeis, Magnes, and Szold all were jolted by their encounters with Eastern European Jews—whether in Europe, the United States, or Palestine. Suddenly, the shallowness of their own Americanized Judaism was starkly exposed. In their first encounters with what they perceived as Jewish authenticity, they felt a connection to their people and to the national yearnings that stirred among them. But they could only embrace Zionism by infusing it with American content, legitimating Jewish nationalism by submerging it in American history or Progressive liberalism. Even the most devoted Zionist, as Brandeis insisted and Magnes and Szold demonstrated, could remain reassuringly American. Indeed, their creative achievement was the transformation of Zionism into a most unlikely affirmation of American values.

From its inception, American Zionism absorbed the tenets of American liberalism—and the apprehensions of American Jews. American Zionists could never completely elude the fundamental premise of their opponents: that

Zionism compromised the loyalty of American Jews to the United States. To combat this insinuation, indeed to suppress it, American Zionists molded their Jewish nationalism to fit the requirements of American patriotism. To Zionists in Palestine, such adulterated Jewish nationalism might be pallid and all but unrecognizable. Americanized Zionism, however, was entirely compatible with the main currents of liberalism that transformed American political culture in the twentieth century. American Jews could become Zionists, yet remain assured of their place in the American liberal mainstream.

To this day, the historical icons of American Zionism remain Brandeis, the Boston Brahmin, Magnes, the California maverick, and Szold, the Quaker lady from Baltimore. They all framed Zion with American imagery. "The Israel of American Jews," as historian Jonathan Sarna has tellingly observed, "the Zion that they imagined in their minds, dreamed about, and wrote about—was . . . a Zion that reveals more about American Jewish ideals than about the realities of Eretz Israel." To Brandeis, Magnes, and Szold, Zionism meant the American dream transported to Palestine.

The gathering support of American Jews for Zionism in the 1930s and 1940s, amid the annihilation of European Jewry, was no less inhibited by American patriotic constraints. The most passionately committed Zionist youth movements often presented Zionism as a variant of Americanism. Even the unquestionable devotion of American Zionist idealists who actually made aliya to Palestine was constrained by American inhibitions.

American Zionist teachers located the kibbutz, the most distinctive Zionist innovation, securely within the American historical experience. When *halutz* (pioneering) values were taught to American youngsters, their sources in European socialist theory were conveniently overlooked. Instead, the kibbutz became the embryonic expression of (American) democracy, justice, and equality. In Zionist literature, the *shomer* (guard) was compared to American "minutemen," standing valiantly at Lexington and Concord to defend their new nation. The kibbutznik, riding and shooting like a "western cowboy," became a Zionist sheriff defending law and order on the Middle Eastern frontier. Arguably the most authentic Zionist of the *yishuv*, the Jewish community in Palestine, the kibbutznik was recast as "the ultimate American."

For a summer camp project during the 1930s, a Zionist manual instructed counselors to "compare [the kibbutz] to the American stockade." (As the manual noted helpfully, "A model of a tractor can be bought at Woolworth's.") Among the topics for discussion was "The Ideal of the Pilgrims and the Chalutzim," a Brandeisian concoction in which Zionists were depicted as Pilgrims and Arabs as Indians. The real Pilgrims, however, were described as resolute individualists who seized land from the Indians, while Zionist *halutzim* were lauded as communal pioneers "who did not want to take land away from the Arabs." Campers were taught that Pilgrims and Zionists shared a common struggle against "primitive conditions" on their respective frontiers.

Mizrachi (religious) Zionist youth chapters received instruction in the "striking similarity between the ideals and aspirations of the Jewish people and those of Abraham Lincoln." In a program about "Abraham Lincoln and the Jewish Spirit," these young Zionists learned that Jewish religious principles expressed Lincolnian virtues: honesty, sincerity, righteousness, peace, and freedom. "Judaism and liberty," Mizrachi noted proudly, "are equivalent."

When Lincoln did not inspire young American Zionists, Jefferson might. In a public relations pamphlet published

by the Zionist Organization of America, the Zionist commitment to rebuilding the ancient Jewish homeland was
located among the wish of "every people [for] the inalienable right to life, liberty and the pursuit of happiness."
Zionism, therefore, fulfilled the core principle of the Declaration of Independence. The Intercollegiate Zionist Federation, addressing a more sophisticated audience, tried to rally
its followers to Zionist activity with a rousing quotation
from Ralph Waldo Emerson!

The conspicuous fondness for citing American sources
reassured even the most committed young Zionists that they
were, after all, genuine Americans. Young Judeans, between
the ages of ten and seventeen, professed their devotion to
the Jewish people while affirming: "I promise to be loyal to
America." Did Zionism, worried the American Student Zionist Federation, imply that "we all must go to Palestine"?
Was it merely a nationalistic political movement, "where
Jews can rule and perhaps control Arab lands nearby"? Or
was it, preferably, a "liberal-progressive" American ideal?
American Zionists always needed reassurance that even in
Palestine they were genuine liberals pursuing the Ameri-
can dream.

Despite these efforts, movement elders remained con-
cerned lest Zionism be interpreted as undermining "Americanism and patriotism." The American Zionist Youth
Commission adopted explicit Brandeisian language: "There
is no conflict with Americanism, and there can be none,
in the effort of Jews to regain self-confidence and self-
respect. . . . Zionists are advancing the loftiest ideals of
Americanism." The writer Marion Magid, a Habonim summer camper at the age of fourteen, fondly recalled her summer Zionist idyll (and other blossoming loves) "in the hill
country of Vermont—Ethan Allen and the Green Mountain
boys. There was no contradiction."

No sooner was Israeli statehood declared in 1948 than the education committee of the American Zionist movement rushed back into print Brandeis's seminal 1915 speech, "The Jewish Problem and How to Solve It." Brandeis had then insisted that "multiple loyalties are objectionable only if they are inconsistent." But, he concluded, "the Zionist ideal, the highest Jewish ideals, are essentially the American ideals." A new generation of Zionist youth would be nurtured on his patriotic premises.

Even Habonim, the movement of young Labor Zionists that was most avidly committed to settling in the Jewish national home, stumbled over the loyalty issue. Habonim precepts might be resolutely Zionist ("personal realization of Zionism through aliya"), while remaining passionately socialist (Israel as "a democratic socialist state"). But these Zionist "builders and dreamers," as they proudly identified themselves, still struggled to reconcile their own commitment to *"am echad,"* one Jewish people, with their identity as Americans.

Habonim always elevated the American ideal of "personal freedom and the democratic process" above socialist collectivism. Aliya might be a Zionist imperative, and a movement preference, but these youngsters, as American individualists, must remain free to decide the question for themselves. Pluralistic in its tolerance of personal choice, Habonim never succumbed to the doctrinaire Zionist ideologies that were molded in Eastern Europe.

But the question of aliya certainly exacerbated the latent conflict between American and Zionist values. In kibbutz Gesher Haziv, where an American Habonim *garin* (founding group) settled near the Lebanese border, the opportunity "to build something new and exciting . . . a state on our own principles," generated impassioned Zionist commitment. But "American pluralism and pragmatism" constantly intruded, justifying everything from assertive individualism to religious indifference. As one young American settler wrote, "We came here for positive reasons. . . . It wasn't because we dislike the States. . . . On the contrary, there's a hell of a lot to the American way of life, beginning with ice cream and ending with John Dewey."

But not even Dewey, the American philosopher of pragmatism, could resolve the irrepressible tension between Zionism and Americanism. At the very least, Zionism required a wrenching choice between national homes. Long after handfuls of Habonim recruits actually moved to Israel, they still agonized endlessly over competing American, Zionist, Jewish, and liberal claims. Was there too much socialism in their kibbutz? Too little democracy? Were Arabs treated fairly? Or "are we bastards"? Was there a place for religious Judaism in the Jewish state? A Passover seder on a kibbutz? An *oneg Shabbat*, welcoming the Jewish sabbath—or American "boogie-woogie" music? The choices and conflicts between Zionist and American values were endless, and they tugged at the consciences of young *olim*.

In Israel, the Habonim pioneers remained recognizably American. They boasted of the origins of their movement "in a free, 'Anglo-Saxon' culture." Zionism could not compel them to relinquish their commitment to civil liberties— or their fondness for softball. Their inclination to define Jewish "culture and heritage" (minus religion) as "basic moral and ethical precepts" was characteristically American in its Jewish shallowness.

Like nineteenth-century Reform rabbis and Progressive-era Zionists, Habonim Americanized Jewish "tradition" by recasting it as liberalism. Habonim members were determined to build an American liberal enclave in the Jewish state. There they could have it all: ice cream and falafel; Dewey and A. D. Gordon; in sum, a Zionist New Deal. But

"I never believed," one Habonim kibbutznik wrote sadly, "that Habonim kids could be so ignorant of what [Jewish] tradition really means."

Habonim envisioned itself as a Zionist beacon to American Jews. But the overwhelming majority of American Jewish youngsters, like their parents, were conspicuously indifferent to the Zionist cause. "With a background estranged from Jewish environment, culture, and tradition," a Zionist publication lamented, they remained committed to "an individualistic life within a small family circle." Youngsters who went to Palestine, according to one report, were likely to "drift about helplessly and remain the same Americans they were before." Nowhere, observed an American Zionist who made aliya, "have the disintegrating influences of Galut life been so visible as among us." Young American Jewry, he lamented, "wanders in a maze."

Even the tiny minority of committed youngsters who actually joined Zionist youth groups, their teachers complained, were the undernourished children of an "anaemic" Jewish culture. American Zionism itself was scathingly characterized within the Zionist Youth Organization as "a short-sighted combination of sentimentality and philanthropy," which promised a haven for European refugees but "never promised anything" to American Jews. In the United States, observed the chairman of a Zionist youth education committee, Jewishness had become "an accident of birth rather than . . . a conscious and proud sense of belonging." Young American Jews, he concluded shrewdly, were "obsessed by the fear of what the American gentile world around them would think. . . . This fear is for their status as Americans."

By the end of World War II, Zionists were convinced that Nazi Germany had brutally and finally demonstrated "the humiliating tragedy of Jewish assimilation." Surely Zionism, as the expression of "a liberated Jewish self," would be recognized as the only alternative. But "the bridge between Israel and American Jewry is yet to be built," declared a Habonim editorial a year after the birth of Israel. American Jewish youngsters, a Zionist official noted, "are not with us." The overwhelming majority "were completely indifferent to the dramatic events in Israel." Without "a deep Jewish consciousness," worried one Habonim leader, "what have we to say to Jewish youth?"

So little, apparently, that a tiny group of applicants who wished to enlist in Americans for Haganah, formed in 1947 to help the Jews of Palestine in their struggle for independence, included few Jewish respondents. The letters from volunteers were revealing. A nineteen-year-old Irish American from the Bronx could hardly wait to join the Jewish army in its "fight for the new land." A navy veteran from Kentucky identified the cause of Jewish statehood as the cause of "true freedom-loving men everywhere." An Italian-American Catholic from New Jersey pleaded: "I believe in your cause and I am willing to die if necessary to defend it." Few Jews applied. One, a young man from Massachusetts, was "willing to do my part," but only in "civilian work" that would "help my people in their quest for a peaceful new country." And he insisted that he be permitted to return home by mid-September to begin the new school year.

In fact, American citizens were prohibited by law from volunteering for military service in Palestine. Yet hundreds of young men found ways to elude that restriction. One of them was Bill Bernstein, who had served in the merchant marine during the war. Bernstein became a Zionist hero, but in the end, his story reveals the Jewish apathy and Zionist indifference of even the bravest American Jews who served the Zionist cause.

The journey of the *Exodus* in 1947, as every American

Jew learned from Leon Uris's popular novel, was a heart-breaking symbol of Jewish yearning, Zionist tenacity, and British perfidy. The rickety ship seemed a most unlikely choice for a heroic, or historic, journey. Built in 1928, and designed for inland water traffic, it had served for years as a Chesapeake Bay honeymoon cruise ship. Purchased and re-fitted for the Haganah, the primary Jewish fighting force in Palestine, it had barely left port in Baltimore when a hurri-cane battered it back to dry dock for major repairs. Months later, it finally resumed its mission to transport nearly five thousand Jewish refugees from the charnel-house of Europe to Eretz Israel.

The *Exodus* crew was an incongruous mix of Yiddish-speaking seamen and adventurous novices. Until the ship reached Europe, where it picked up the Haganah crew mem-bers who would sail the final leg of the journey to Palestine, there hardly was a knowledgeable Jew, or committed Zion-ist, among them. First mate Bernstein, a recently discharged twenty-three-year-old sailor, was a typical restless Ameri-can war veteran. He still needed to be on the move, search-ing for action and excitement. "If I tried to settle down," he patiently explained to his mother back in Brooklyn, "I would only get into trouble and bring misery to you and God knows what to myself." He was not yet ready for the "normal married, clean living life" that she, like any good Jewish mother, envisioned for him.

Bernstein, raised from his teens by his older brother Morris in San Francisco, had no Jewish education or affilia-tion. Shipboard photographs reveal a ruddy, curly-haired, carefree young man, clowning with his mates, clearly en-joying himself. His commitment, by all accounts including his own, was to adventure, not to Zionism. Palestine was a geographic destination, not a spiritual one. "There was no fanaticism in our makeup," recalled Eli Kalm, another crew member; "we were too typically American to worship the Martyr clause in the Haganah Contract."

Yet somewhere along the way, Bernstein was transformed. "He got it," Kalm acknowledged, "this crazy bug Eretz." In several shipboard letters to his brother Moe, Bill Bernstein described, with evident wonderment, his own interior journey. The *Exodus*, he wrote quizzically at the outset, was "a ship like none I've seen before." To his astonishment, almost everyone on board was Jewish. Nautical knowledge, the young sailor inferred, mattered less than Yiddish fluency. The chief mate was "a Palestinian" named Yitzhak. "I still jump when I hear someone shout his name," Bernstein confessed. "To hear the bosun give an order in Yiddish, and have everyone comply"—to the young merchant-marine veteran that was "the god-damndest thing!!!!!!"

"In all the time I've spent at sea," Bernstein marveled, "I have never yet heard the kind of talk I've heard here." The usual seabound subject, he conceded, was "women and the various means of enjoying them." On board the *Exodus*, however, "if you don't know integral calculus, at least one-third of the conversation at the dinner table is lost to you. If you don't know what Aristotle told his mother on his sixth birthday, another slice of the conversation is lost. And if, God forbid, you shouldn't know . . . how many calluses Yosha Heifitz has on the index finger of his left hand, you are completely ignored." Talk about sex, Bernstein quickly learned, was talking "like a Gentile"—a "*goy*."

After a refueling stop in the Azores, the ship finally reached Marseilles. Bernstein anticipated a two-month layover to prepare for the final run to Haifa. Then he expected to spend a few relaxing weeks touring in Palestine, followed by a pleasure jaunt to Europe, before he returned to the United States. But in Marseilles, where Haganah agents stripped the ship bare to its hull to maximize space for its awaiting passengers, a sense of Zionist purpose was suddenly awakened in Bernstein.

"Our people," he wrote excitedly, "have only one burning desire here,—Aliyah Beth! The second deliverance to Eretz Israel. The first migration was supposedly the handiwork of God, the second one we fight for. If we can fuck some goyem up in the process, all the better." Bill Bernstein, for the first time, identified with the Zionist cause.

What had happened, within a single week in Marseilles, to convert this young sailor, a bemused American observer of his Jewish shipmates, into an impassioned Zionist? As he explained to his brother Moe:

> Three days ago the Jews here in Marseille and aboard my ship celebrated the fourth anniversary of the Warsaw Ghetto. Every one of 60,000 Jews were massacred there defending a street with small arms against the German army. We held it for five days. Only five days of resistance in 4,000 years of persecution. Something we should be ashamed of.

The Warsaw Ghetto commemoration had been held in a refugee camp on the outskirts of the French port city. Although, in his Jewish ignorance, Bernstein got some of the details wrong, he was evidently seared by his encounter with the refugees. "They all speak Jewish [Yiddish], some speak Hebrew and all will eventually be in Eretz. . . . A good many of those kids have numbers tattooed on there arms as proof of the life they have lead for four years." Suddenly, Bernstein's sea-born lark was infused with Jewish meaning.

In his next letter, early in July on the eve of departure, Bernstein wrote ecstatically: "This is it! After working, hiding and chasing all over Europe for months, we've finally cleared the way for a seven day voyage." His pride was evident: the *Exodus*, he told Moe, was carrying "the greatest number of people ever transported in one ship" to Palestine. "The important thing," he knew, "is that these people are out of Europe and will definitely end up amongst their own people in their own country."

Bill Bernstein began his journey as an American Jewish innocent who could not comprehend the Jewish passion and Zionist fervor that swirled around him. During a brief port stop in Italy, to elude British spies who were tracking the *Exodus*, he found time to buy a rosary as a souvenir for his Catholic girlfriend. But after his encounter with Holocaust survivors, young Jews like himself, Bernstein identified passionately with the Jewish people. Suddenly, he became a zealot for Zionism. His metamorphosis was complete.

Early in the morning of July 18, nine days after his departure letter to Moe, the *Exodus*, trailed by British destroyers, neared the coast of Palestine. Bernstein, starting his watch, had just made his log entries. Ike Aronowitz, the young Haganah ship captain, joined him in the wheelhouse. The clock struck five bells. It was 2:30 A.M.

Suddenly the night sky brightened to mid-day as the searchlights from British ships illuminated the *Exodus* from bow to stern. Bernstein seized the ship whistle, its piercing wail reminding another sailor of "the shriek of an animal caught by beasts of prey." British destroyers rammed the fragile ship; then armed sailors and marines swarmed on board. As they raced for the bridge and wheelhouse to seize control of the *Exodus*, they sparked a frenzied battle. Desperate refugees hurled tin cans and potatoes, their only weapons, at the British invaders. After several hours of struggle, the Haganah finally conceded that further resistance was futile and the captain surrendered.

The battered *Exodus*, "its deck black with people," according to the *Palestine Post*, was escorted into Haifa harbor just before the sabbath. It took twelve hours, in the sweltering Mediterranean heat of summer, to remove all the passengers. That evening, three British prison ships, packed with nearly five thousand Jewish refugees from the *Exodus*, sailed back to Europe.

Not everyone on board the *Exodus* made the return trip. Two passengers, young Holocaust survivors, had been killed by British bullets. Scores of wounded remained behind, hospitalized in Haifa. Bill Bernstein, forcibly ejected from the wheelhouse, had grabbed a fire extinguisher to spray as he fought his way back. A British marine clubbed him on the head with a steel-tipped truncheon. Bernstein, his skull fractured, lay unconscious in the captain's cabin until the *Exodus* docked thirteen hours later.

A letter came to Moe Bernstein from the Haganah. It informed him that "Naval Officer William Bernstein was killed on the high seas in a brutal manner by sailors of the British Navy." The Haganah, it continued, "stands at attention at his fresh grave and pays a last tribute of respect to this young American Jew who made the supreme sacrifice while helping to bring the remnants of our people to our homeland. . . . American Jewry has lost one of its heroic soldiers."

Bill Bernstein, the fun-loving adventurer, was wrapped in an American flag and buried in the Martyr's Row of Haifa cemetery. His vision of Israel, compressed into the final weeks of his life, radiated with Zionist fervor. Until then, however, he had hardly been aware of himself as a Jew. Like so many other young men of his generation, he had fought in a war for democracy against fascism. There is no evidence that he knew about, or was particularly affected by, the extermination of European Jewry. The war ended; he was restless. A journey to Palestine offered ship-board adventure. He seized the opportunity.

It is impossible to know, more than half a century later, what to make of Bill Bernstein. A typical restless war veteran, he was a normal American Jew—and a most unlikely Zionist martyr. Is the meaning of his life to be found in his years of Jewish apathy and ignorance? In his purchase of rosary beads for his American girlfriend? Or in his conversion to Zionism? Surely it is to be found in the braiding of all these experiences within the single life that ended far more suddenly, heroically, and tragically than anyone had reason to expect.

Who might Bill Bernstein have become had he lived? Probably he would have realized his wish to tour Palestine and travel in Europe. Then he would have returned to the United States, to recount his odyssey to his beloved brother Moe while his wanderlust wound down. Sooner or later, he might have fulfilled his mother's dream: to settle down, get married (to a nice Catholic girl?), and raise a family. Perhaps he could even have reconciled who he was as an American with who he had become as a Jew and a Zionist.

The restoration of Jewish national sovereignty after two thousand years indisputably marked a momentous turning point in Jewish history. American Zionists greeted the birth of the Jewish state with unrestrained joy. In a typical tribute, Israelis were acclaimed as "taut-muscled young men and women" inspired by "the frontier spirit" who were being "molded in the sunlight of the Holy Land into a tough, athletic nation."

A new Jew, directly descended from the Maccabees and Bar Kochba, was emerging in the ancient biblical homeland. Gone forever was the "dank Ghetto" that had deformed the "sickly, undersized bodies" of Eastern European Jews. But despite this initial burst of euphoria, the impact of Jewish statehood on American Jewry was remarkably slight. Bill

Bernstein's conversion experience was the conspicuous exception, not the norm.

For most American Jews, the children of Eastern European immigrants who had emigrated to the American *goldene medina* before World War I, Franklin D. Roosevelt's New Deal had finally begun to unlock the gates to American opportunity. Until the 1930s, access to elite educational institutions, and to positions of economic and political wealth, power, and influence, had largely been reserved for Christians, and for a handful of German Jews like Oscar Straus, Jacob Schiff, Louis Marshall, and, of course, Brandeis.

After 1933, there were dramatic changes. The Roosevelt political revolution eroded the bastions of privilege that had been occupied, almost exclusively, by white Protestants. Talented Jews were welcome in the proliferating New Deal alphabet agencies. Ordinary Jews were eligible for welfare payments, public works jobs, and social security. For the first time, Jews belonged to the ruling political majority in the United States. For this miracle, which bound them heart and soul to the United States, their adoration of FDR would never diminish.

The Second World War accelerated the Americanization process for American Jews. For no group of Americans was the fight against fascism a more urgent priority. "The experience of the war years," as Lucy Dawidowicz wrote, "had a transforming effect on American Jews and on their ideas of themselves as Jews." By joining the American military forces that were waging war against Hitler, they proved their patriotism. Their Jewish identity had become all but indistinguishable from who they were as Americans.

After the war, American Jews made their great leap to educational achievement, economic opportunity, and social acceptance. By an accident of timing, Jewish national inde-

pendence coincided with this era of unprecedented possibilities for American Jews. Whatever was happening in the
Middle East, they would not be distracted from their yearning for a secure job, a suburban home, a two-child family,
and a two-car garage.

As universities eased their restrictive admissions quo-
tas (it no longer being fashionable, after Hitler, to discrimi-
nate against Jews), the horizon of social mobility seemed
limitless. Before too long, Jews would leave their mark everywhere from Hollywood cinema to Ivy League scholarship. In the movies they produced as in the books they wrote,
they converted their own success into an idealized version
of American democratic benevolence, whose blessings they
passionately affirmed.

The faith of Jews in the American dream indelibly
stamped them as Americans. During their own golden age,
amid postwar American affluence, their Zion was relocated
from the inner cities to the suburbs. They transformed Judaism into an occasional leisure activity, molded like everything else by American abundance. Yet no matter how
carefully American Jews insulated themselves from Israel
in their American Zion, the Jewish state was bound to ac-
centuate, and complicate, their dual identity. By becoming
Zionists, Brandeis had insisted, American Jews would demonstrate that they were good Jews and good Americans.
Whether his conflation of Zionism with Americanism resolved the problem or concealed it remained an open question.

3

The Crisis

of Diaspora

Loyalty

From Herzl to the Holocaust, American Jews may indeed have been ambivalent about the idea of Jewish statehood. They may also have tried to mold Zion in their own American image. But surely the birth of Israel—experienced by Jews everywhere as a miraculous moment of redemption—changed all that. Since 1948, according to the conventional wisdom, the identification of American Jews with Israel has been impassioned, unequivocal, and sustained.

"We Are One!"—for many years a compelling fundraising slogan for American Jews—nonetheless obscures an extremely unstable relationship between the American Diaspora and the Jewish homeland. Historical reality is more complex than the comforting myth of unity suggests. American Jews, to be sure, have taken Israel to their hearts. But not always, or unconditionally. Beloved though it has been, Israel has also deepened the loyalty anxieties of Jews who have never stopped worrying lest their identity as Jews, and their identification with the Jewish state, compromise their security as Americans.

The birth of Israel recast American Jewry as a Diaspora community. Not only did 1948 mark the renewal of Jewish statehood; it simultaneously re-created the symbiotic relationship between homeland and Diaspora that had been absent during nearly two thousand years of Jewish history. After 1948, for the first time, American Jews confronted a Jewish state claiming the authority, at least implicitly, to define Jewish authenticity, and even legitimacy, in national and religious terms.

During the "golden decade" of rising opportunity and prosperity following the end of World War II, American Jews seemed comfortably reconciled to the new state of Israel. "We American Zionists know that Zionism is good Americanism," declared *New Palestine* editors after independence. The new Jewish state, they predicted, would promote "the American ideals of freedom, peace and prosperity"—a curious purpose, indeed, for a Jewish state. But as long as it did so, American Jews were content.

Early on, however, there were signs of uneasiness. In 1949, when Prime Minister David Ben-Gurion appealed to American Jewish parents to send their children to Israel, there was an immediate eruption of shocked dismay. The leaders of the American Jewish Committee, which still represented the assimilated German-Jewish elite of American Jewry, were aghast at the prospect of a pied piper in Tel Aviv luring American youngsters away to the melodic strands of "Hatikva."

Jacob Blaustein, the committee president, made a hurried visit to Israel to demand Ben-Gurion's recognition of Diaspora legitimacy. American Jews, Blaustein reminded the prime minister, "vigorously repudiate any suggestion or implication that they are in exile. . . . To American Jews,

America is home." Ben-Gurion, stung by the sharp criticism from Israel's wealthiest American contributors, conceded that a Jew living outside the Jewish state "owes no political or legal allegiance to Israel."

After protracted discussion at a carefully orchestrated reconciliation luncheon at the King David Hotel in Jerusalem, the prime minister publicly acknowledged that American Jews "have only one political attachment and that is to the United States of America." The decision to immigrate to Israel was, therefore, an American choice and not a Zionist obligation. The prime minister's concession, Blaustein noted, was necessary if American Jews "in the minds of other Americans" were to be free from "the serious charge of dual-nationality."

The controversy subsided, but the loyalty issue continued to simmer beneath the surface of Israeli-Diaspora relations. Several years later, Ben-Gurion warned that Jews in the West faced "the kiss of death, a slow and imperceptible decline into assimilation" for which Israel provided the only alternative. Once again, the American Jewish Committee vigorously protested. Ben-Gurion, by his own admission, still failed to grasp the depths of American Jewish discomfort about divided loyalty. "I lack a full comprehension of the feelings of an American Jew," he conceded to Blaustein. Needing American financial and political support for his fledgling state, Ben-Gurion accepted the fundamental American precept of individual choice, which no conception of Zionist obligation would be permitted to contradict.

The American Jewish Committee, with its long history of anti-Zionism, was not alone in its discomfort with Israel. Even American Zionists remained wary of the implications of Jewish statehood for American Jews. In 1949, the Zionist Organization of America published what may have been the first American travel guide to the new State of

Israel. In this "concise and handy guide for the American tourist," the ZOA effusively encouraged American Jews to realize their "dream of a lifetime" by visiting the new Jewish state. But it prudently warned visitors not to impose an American framework upon this "valiant little country"—even as its description of Israel reinforced their inclination to do precisely that.

Prospective American visitors were instructed that Zionists had transformed a "neglected wilderness" into "a healthy, prosperous land," whose political institutions rested "on the ideals of social justice." But "woe" to any visitor who "compares everything with America, to the constant advantage of the latter." Israelis could be "helpful and friendly" to American visitors. But if their stunning achievements were measured by American standards, they were inclined to turn "cold, argumentative, and narrow." If American travelers did not find "a bed of roses" in the land of milk and honey, that was not attributable to Zionist deficiencies but to British indifference to the "progress or prosperity" of the pre-state *yishuv*.

The ZOA found its own prescription for cultural tolerance difficult to follow. Israeli delicatessens, the guidebook noted, were likely to be "a great disappointment" to American tourists, while Israeli ice cream "does not approach American standards." Americans were forewarned that religious observance might also be problematic. Tourists were unlikely to find any familiar Conservative synagogues in Israel. Indeed, American Jewish sensibilities were "apt to be disturbed by the rather free and easy attitude of the [Orthodox] congregants," which contrasted sharply with American conceptions of synagogue decorum. And, the guide noted with discernible regret, in Israeli synagogues there are "no sermons."

Israeli cities received mixed reviews. Tel Aviv, the burgeoning Zionist metropolis, was built by "indomitable will," but it must not be measured by sophisticated American urban standards. Jaffa was a "panorama of dress, language, and modes of life," but it had little to offer of Jewish interest. Jerusalem was "most interesting," with its "memorable landmarks," "beautiful residential sections," and "some touches of medieval Europe." But it sounded more like a provincial French town than the holy city of the Jews.

No trip to Israel in the early years was complete without a visit to a kibbutz, the shining symbol of Zionist pioneering achievement. Kibbutz "settlers" (in those days, an honorable designation among Israelis) were lauded as genuine pioneers who deserved the highest respect of Americans. But tourists were warned, yet again, not to measure the struggling kibbutz "settlements"—some of which "have not yet eliminated flies"—by the hygienic standards of American farms.

The ZOA tourist guide was soon followed into print by two popular guides to the young state, written by journalist Ruth Gruber. She urged American Jews to "Go now" to Israel, where they could witness the rebirth of "a once broken people and a once broken land." In Israel, she wrote excitedly, the Diaspora Jew is "transformed . . . into a new type of man: a tiller of the soil in peace, a fighter in war." Here was a people "released from fear," a country "built out of death for life."

Gruber's Israel closely resembled a mythologized America of bygone frontier days. In the Jewish state, American tourists were invited to glimpse "the growing pains of young Americans freeing themselves from British law." Not only did Israel resemble colonial America on the eve of independence; it would also remind Americans of their own "Wild West of the 1880s." (The Negev outpost of Beer Sheva resembled "Lost Gulch or Deadman's Creek.") Israel is "like

America," Gruber wrote reassuringly, where "you can find almost everything you look for"—even "the comforts and pleasures" of Florida.

After barely a decade of national life, Gruber proudly reported, Israel conspicuously displayed "its Yankee ways." American cars abounded. Frosted milk shakes and self-service laundries (with American washing machines) were available to satisfy tourist needs. In a Habonim kibbutz, Gruber was delighted to discover American-style toilets. Israeli children, she noted, learned the facts of life from Hollywood movies. Jerusalem, she wrote reassuringly, was "the Washington, D.C. of the Jewish State." Israel might be "a small frontier land making brave new experiments," but Gruber reminded Jewish women to bring their hats "for tea parties and afternoon receptions."

Early travel guides invariably depicted Israel as a newer, smaller, only vaguely Jewish version of the United States. The Zionist revolution might be creating bold, brave Jews, "suntanned, and determined, strong and beautiful," as one enraptured American wrote; and American visitors were encouraged to observe them in their native kibbutz habitat (variously described by visiting journalist Judd Teller as a "boy scout utopia," "a summer camp," and "a coal mine"). But there were constant reassurances that the new Jewish state fit snugly into American preconceptions and expectations.

The tour-guide profile of Israel in its early years of statehood conspicuously omitted anything of Jewish content or consequence. The dominant frame of reference was the American historical experience, not biblical sources or Jewish history. A young American-born instructor at the Hebrew University complained that American Jews who declined to make aliya lacked "the true, pioneering American spirit"—not Zionist will. There were "few better places in the world to study essential 'American history,'" he wrote, than Israel during its nation-building years.

The Americanized rendition of Israel was a reflex of self-affirmation by American Jews. A Zionist, it seemed, was a hardy American pioneer reborn in the Middle East. "Of all the countries that one may visit in Europe or Asia," wrote an American visitor, "Israel is the only one which gives a similar feeling of tempo and spirit to that felt in the United States." Israel, after all, must affirm the compatibility of Zionism with Americanism, the staple of American Jewish life ever since Jews in the Brandeis era first confronted the Zionist challenge.

The initial spasm of American Zionist enthusiasm for Israel should not be exaggerated. To the overwhelming majority of American Jews, Israel was geographically and spiritually remote. They paid little attention to it. In his classic survey of American Judaism, Nathan Glazer observed in 1957: "The two greatest events in modern Jewish history, the murder of six million Jews by Hitler and the creation of the Jewish State in Palestine, have had remarkably slight effects on the inner life of American Jewry."

The soothing rhetoric of compatibility between Israel and the United States belied the lurking potential for conflict. As a small, democratic nation (and a Cold War ally) struggling to preserve its independence, Israel quickly won American diplomatic support—up to a point. But during the Sinai campaign of 1956–57, when Israel, allied with England and France, went to war against Egypt to free its borders of cross-border terrorist raids, the blunt opposition of the Eisenhower administration, accompanied by sharp language from Secretary of State John Foster Dulles, suddenly brought American Jewry up short.

If an "open dispute" erupted between the two nations, the diplomatic gadfly Nahum Goldmann warned Ben-Gurion, "it will be impossible to mobilize an American-Jewish front" to support Israel. No matter what claims a Jewish state might have upon them, he predicted, American Jews would always demonstrate that they were Americans first.

This, after all, was the 1950s, when Americans experienced an acute crisis over national loyalty. The trial, conviction, and execution of the Rosenbergs for Soviet espionage left American Jews extremely vulnerable to allegations of disloyalty. The conspicuous presence of Jews in labor, academic, and entertainment organizations branded as subversive was worrisome. The anti-Communist crusade led by Senator Joseph R. McCarthy, FBI director J. Edgar Hoover, and the House Un-American Activities Committee made American Jews exceedingly wary of identifying with foreign countries or ideologies. In a political climate overheated by anti-radical zeal, an affinity for Jewish socialism in a foreign country had its risks.

A revealing barometer of American Jewish aspirations and anxieties during the fifties was the best-seller list for fiction. American Jews, like other Americans, avidly read and thoroughly enjoyed *Marjorie Morningstar* and *Exodus*, the blockbusters of American Jewish fiction in that decade. Herman Wouk's *Marjorie Morningstar* popularized and affirmed the American Jewish struggle for social mobility, while *Exodus* offered reassurance to its readers that the struggle for Jewish statehood was entirely compatible with American values.

Starry-eyed Marjorie Morgenstern was the American Jewish Everygirl, chasing Hollywood romantic fantasies but ultimately finding fulfillment in the American Jewish dream: marriage, affluence, and suburban respectability. Her aspiring immigrant parents had left their Bronx ghetto neighborhood for the affluent Upper West Side of Manhattan. In their luxurious Eldorado apartment on Central Park West, "where the good families live," they carefully groomed their daughter for a life of affluent domesticity.

Seventeen-year-old Marjorie preferred American fantasy to Jewish destiny. Judaism, after all, was merely a Stone Age vestige of "superstitious foolishness." Jewish observance, symbolized by her brother's bar mitzvah, was little more than carefully choreographed vulgarity, with all the garish excesses that family striving dictated. Marjorie, to be sure, attended synagogue, but only for dances. Her priorities were horseback riding, Columbia boys, and the forbidden fruits of sexual awakening provided by her bohemian friends. And why not? As Marjorie's mother conceded, "This is America."

Marjorie's ultimate temptation was Noel Airman (born Saul Ehrmann), an assimilated American rendition of the classic Jewish *luftmensch*. A suave and shallow songwriter, Airman had perfected his talents as a "connoisseur of Shirley," his generic label for the upwardly mobile Jewish princesses, like Marjorie, who were enraptured by his pseudo-sophistication. Stoking their fantasies of rebellion against diamond engagement rings and "domestic dullness," he lured them into his ritualized performance of sexual deflowering. Marjorie, his most "Raphaelesque" Shirley, fell easily into his romantic trap. After eating shellfish, she had nothing Jewish left to lose but her virginity.

Like any respectable American Jewish girl of her generation, Marjorie was plunged into guilt and mortification. Her true destiny, she finally realized, was not as Marjorie Morningstar in Hollywood. Instead, she became Mrs. Milton Schwartz, suburban wife and mother, devoted to her family, active in her synagogue, and, somewhat incongruously, keeper of a kosher kitchen. "The only remarkable thing about Mrs. Schwartz," an old friend muses at the end, "is that . . . she ever dreamed of being Marjorie Morningstar."

Wouk plucked at the heartstrings of his American Jewish audience. Marjorie, the "good little Jewish beauty," validated their yearning to reconcile Jewish continuity, as they defined it, with American freedom. She might crave romantic adventure, but she was dutifully apprehensive about going too far, too fast. Her bohemian friend Marsha struggled valiantly to reassure her: *"There's no hell.* You won't burn." But Marjorie never could relinquish her middle-class Jewish conscience. Her rebellion was too innocent to alarm anyone but her beloved Dr. Schwartz, who was shocked to discover that his prospective bride was not a virgin. Ultimately, Wouk reassured his readers, a Jewish daughter can be counted upon to fulfill her mother's dream of domesticity, not her own flight to freedom.

Families like the Morgensterns and Schwartzes were far too preoccupied with their own American strivings to concern themselves with Zionism. The Jewish state remained remote from the consciousness of American Jews until 1958, when *Exodus*, a runaway best-seller and then a record-breaking Hollywood movie, punctured a decade of American Jewish apathy toward the Jewish state.

Leon Uris unabashedly proclaimed the story of Israel "an epic in the history of man." His melodramatic tale of Zionist struggle, throbbing with adventure (invariably heroic) and love (invariably chaste), meandered from the Bible to the shtetl, from the Middle West to the Middle East. The Jewish state, Uris wrote emphatically, was the place "where God wants His people to be" and "a lighthouse for all mankind."

Lest American Jewish readers feel uncomfortably implicated in his rendering of the divine plan, Uris portrayed Zionism in reassuringly American terms. Setting his narrative in the pre-state months of 1947–48, he offered a modern Jewish retelling of the American revolution. In the

Middle East, as in the American colonies, the British Empire had perfidiously obstructed a freedom-loving people. Zionists, like the American revolutionaries they resembled, were struggling for independence from the yoke of British imperial rule.

American readers of *Exodus* encountered Zionism through the provincial sensibilities of Kitty Fremont, the "all-American girl" from "the all-American Midwest of Indiana." The proverbial "girl next door," every bit as American as "Mom's apple pie, hot dogs, and the Brooklyn Dodgers," Kitty stumbled inadvertently upon Jews in British internment camps in Cyprus. It was not easy, at first, for her to empathize with Jews or comprehend their Zionist yearnings. "A very beautiful American girl who is completely puzzled by these strange people called Jews," she just did not "feel right" in their presence. Jews, she observed, were "arrogant and aggressive," and possessed by the "strange obsession" of creating their own country.

Kitty's mission to Palestine was driven by her determination to rescue Karen, a teenage European refugee, from Zionist clutches. Karen actually had the temerity to believe that Zion was the homeland for all Jews, but Kitty wanted her to fulfill her Jewish destiny in "saddle shoes and pleated skirts" back in Indiana. American Jews, she explained to Karen, "love their country." In the United States, "we have many important Jews . . . and they are very happy and very much American."

Kitty's wholesome patriotism was echoed by Bill Fry, the American Jewish ship captain (loosely modeled upon Bill Bernstein) who was fated to die at British hands while steering a boatload of illegal immigrants to Palestine. "I love America," he insisted. "I wouldn't trade what I've got there for fifty Palestines." But he admired the Zionists because they are "fighting my battle for respect."

Kitty's Zionist protagonist, Haganah fighter Ari ben Canaan, aptly described her as "just a nice woman who looks at Jews as though she were looking into a cage at a zoo." But even Ari, the exemplar of Zionism (who proudly asserts "I'm a Jew. This is my country"), is recognizably American. As an Israeli film critic noted, Ari (as played by Paul Newman) epitomized "the very ideal of true blue American manhood." A rugged pioneer, he was as Jewish as Daniel Boone, whose frontier exploits he emulated. When Kitty finally embraced him, it symbolized Gentile approval of the Zionist cause—surely because it was so comfortably American.

Once Uris equated Zionism with the struggle for American independence, violence against the British—even from Menachem Begin's militant Irgun—seemed justified. The minutemen at Lexington and Concord, after all, had done no less. With the British finally driven from Palestine, Uris's narrative trickled into anti-climax; the desperate struggle for statehood, against invading armies from five Arab states, was hardly mentioned. With the departure of the British, the (American) cause of liberty and democracy had triumphed. After that, in the real Middle East at least, everything got much more complicated.

Kitty, speaking for the American heartland, had the final word. "There are many things I have learned to love here," she conceded, "but this is not my country and these are not my people." Prepared to return to Indiana, she reiterated the goodness of the United States—especially for Jews. "I do not believe the day will ever come," she proclaimed, "that American Jews must come to Israel because of fear or persecution." The United States, after all, was home.

The popularity of *Exodus* has often been taken as a benchmark of American Jewish identification with Israel. Thereafter, Israel was presumably woven into the self-consciousness of American Jews as their "redemptive homeland." Identifying with the Jewish state, they could finally "come to terms with their Jewishness." Their surge of Jewish pride crested, just a few years later, with the Six Day War.

Yet *Exodus* remains, at best, an ambiguous symbol of American Jewish self-consciousness and Zionist pride. With his Americanized rendition of the Zionist struggle, Uris (who only recently had scripted *The Gunfight at the O.K. Corral*) squeezed the Middle East into an engagingly familiar Hollywood Western format. His novel so Americanized the *yishuv* that Palestine could barely be distinguished from Kansas. That, of course, was precisely what American Jews most wanted to hear.

If *Exodus* encouraged American Jews to embrace Israel, their warm feelings ultimately depended upon the facile equation of Zionism with Americanism. In the end, *Exodus* vigorously affirmed the goodness of the American way. Nearly every major American character in the novel—Jewish and Christian alike—proclaimed that American Jews were finally and truly at home in the United States. For that reason Zionism, which finally earned the grudging respect of Gentiles like Kitty Fremont, was an altogether permissible identification.

Kitty's vapid universalism—"People are the same no matter what they're called"—expressed the conventional liberal wisdom of the postwar era (similarly exploited in the Broadway rendition of *The Diary of Anne Frank*, which muted Holocaust horrors with Anne's innocent proclamation of faith in human goodness). Ari's response may have seemed shockingly bold: "People are different. They have a right to be different." But Uris assured American Jews that they could be Jewish and identify with Zionism without being so different as to put their American patriotism at risk. Despite its ostensible Zionist triumphalism, *Exodus* affirmed the goodness of the American way.

Exodus and *Marjorie Morningstar* offered complementary visions of the postwar drama of American Jewish acculturation. Wouk and Uris, in effect, collaborated to affirm the validity for Jews of the American dream. Marjorie ratified middle-class affluence as the culmination of American beneficence. *Exodus*, while resounding with Zionist heroism, achieved popularity precisely because it converted Israel into a safe attachment for American Jews. By 1961, when El Al promoted its own *Exodus*-based tour of Israel with clips from the movie, even Israelis were willing to permit Zionist reality to be defined by Hollywood.

Nor is this surprising. We know that a bevy of American Jews in Hollywood—men like Louis B. Mayer and the Warner brothers—had long since made the film industry a projection screen for their own highly romanticized vision of the American dream. As frightened and insecure immigrants, they were driven by what Neil Gabler calls their "ferocious, even pathological, embrace of America." Determined to erase a Jewish past rooted in the shtetl culture of Eastern Europe, they "embarked on an assimilation so ruthless and complete" that from their new empire in Hollywood they created the cinematic America of their deepest yearnings.

Exodus, for all its superficially muscular Zionism, exemplifies Gabler's point. Produced and directed by Otto Preminger, an Austrian Jew who had immigrated to the United States in 1935, the screen version of Uris's novel presented a Zionism that sanctified the American way. *Exodus* (like *Marjorie Morningstar*) demonstrated that Hollywood could produce films with explicitly Jewish themes without offending Gentile audiences. The Preminger formula affirmed that Jews, wherever they lived, were indistinguishable from Gentile Americans. With Paul Newman as a Zionist freedom fighter (and Natalie Wood as Marjorie), Jews were quite evidently like everyone else, only more so.

That was precisely what American Jews in the postwar era wanted to hear. Their eagerness to Americanize was, for the first time, matched by their opportunity. The Lower East Side may have been their ancestral foothold in America, but after World War II Jews abandoned crowded tenements and claustrophobic *yiddishkeit* for new American frontiers. Glittering beyond Scarsdale and East Coast suburbia was California, the most alluring destination of all. In an updated version of the Gold Rush, tens of thousands of Jews migrated west (and, in lesser numbers, south to Florida) to their new paradise in the American Zion.

The great lure of the sunbelt frontier was the opportunity it afforded to escape a Judaism that even in the United States still seemed much too encumbered by tradition, religious prescription, and ritual. In Los Angeles and Miami, by contrast, Jews could be reborn as Americans, with their Judaism redefined as freedom of choice and personal pleasure. There, they could become "whatever types of Jews they wanted to be." Liberated from the constraints of religion and ethnicity, the sunbelt migrants found great pleasure but little Jewish content—the perfect combination—in what one historian (without irony) has called the "continuous sabbath" of their new leisure Judaism.

Sunbelt Judaism offered a new and appealing form of "spiritual recreation." So enthusiastically did the new Jews of California and Florida blend sybaritic pleasure with "spiritual sanctity" that within a single generation their Judaism of personal gratification all but defined mainstream American Judaism. The postwar migration patterns of Jews to California and Florida accelerated the dilution of Judaism into leisure-time Americanism.

Lest these American Jews be judged too unkindly by Zionist standards, it is worth remembering that before too long, in a cruel twist of Zionist irony, Israelis themselves were enticed by Hollywood definitions of the American dream. By the tens of thousands, Zionists flocked to their new Zion in Los Angeles. The allure of non-Jewish Judaism has not been confined to the American Diaspora.

It is nonetheless indisputable that the prolonged indifference of American Jewry to Israel was finally, and abruptly, shattered in the 1960s. The trial of Adolf Eichmann at the beginning of the decade riveted world attention on Israel. It was a pivotal experience for Israelis. They not only confronted the Holocaust, and were compelled to reconsider their own discomfort with survivors; but they became the first Jews since the destruction of the Second Temple to sit in judgment on crimes against their own people. Elsewhere, however, Jews had their doubts about Israeli jurisdiction over crimes that antedated Jewish statehood. Their legalistic argument expressed some of the concern that Diaspora Jews may have experienced when, against their will, events in Israel implicated them.

In 1967, Jews worldwide were terrified by the evident intention of Arab states to annihilate the Jewish state. While Arab armies massed at Israel's borders, and the United Nations and the United States looked on indifferently, Jews confronted with horror the prospect of another Holocaust.

But the stunning Israeli victory in the Six Day War was a transforming moment. For Jews, anguish gave way to wonder; "*terror* and *dread*," Rabbi Abraham J. Heschel wrote, became "exultation." After that momentous week in June, American Jews basked in the glow of their new identification with a daring, courageous, triumphant Israel. The Jewish state, until then a remote presence, suddenly became a tangible symbol of Jewish pride and power. For American Jews who had all but left Judaism behind, Israel was their new religion.

Yet what seems remarkable in retrospect was the brevity of this passion. The stunning Israeli victory notwith-standing, sociologist Charles S. Liebman still detected "the ambivalent American Jew," torn between "acceptance into American society" and "Jewish group survival." Liebman, almost alone, understood that a victorious and powerful Is-rael was bound to intensify, rather than moderate, the loy-alty dilemma of American Jews. For the moment, Israel had won their ecstatic acclaim. But the political and religious ramifications of victory all but assured their eventual dis-comfort with the Jewish state.

For Israel, suddenly and euphorically, was reunited with the biblical homeland of the Jewish people, from Shechem to Hebron, from Jericho to Jerusalem. The unexpected re-turn of Jews to their holy places in Judea and Samaria re-leased a wave of religious enthusiasm. Even soldiers from kibbutzim, the ideological stronghold of secular Israel, imag-ined that "we were inscribing a new chapter in the Bible, a chapter of miracles, wonders and greatness. . . . The whole of the Promised Land is ours." General Moshe Dayan's ring-ing proclamation from the Old City of Jerusalem emphati-cally asserted: "We have returned to all that is holy in our land. We have returned never to be parted from it again."

Israelis, suddenly liberated from what diplomat Abba Eban called their "Auschwitz borders," were thrilled with the opportunity to roam at will across the biblical landscape. By the tens of thousands, they flocked to Rachel's Tomb outside Bethlehem, to Machpelah in Hebron where the pa-triarchs and matriarchs of the Jewish people are buried, to ancient Jericho and biblical Shechem, and to the hill coun-try of Judea and Samaria where the Maccabees had fought and died for Jewish freedom. After a long separation, Zionism and Judaism had finally converged.

To the enemies of the Jews, however, Zionism suddenly became a cruel ideology of conquest, domination, and ultimately—and most preposterously—"racism." The stunned numbness of Arab defeat was converted, before too long, into raging and indiscriminate terrorism against Israeli civilians. As Palestinians wrapped themselves in the mantle of victimization, they became heroes among revolutionaries and radicals from the Arab souks to Harvard Square, for whom Jews, once again, were to blame for the suffering of others.

All this resonated deeply for American Jews. In the 1960s, as the struggle for racial equality and civil rights was diverted into the quest for Black Power, the assertion of racial, ethnic, religious, and gender "identity" became an American passion. Jews, like African Americans, Italian Americans, Native Americans, women, and gays, "came out," boldly asserting their own distinctive identity and brusquely repudiating the melting pot values of assimilation. For a decade after 1967, Israel made American Jews unabashedly proud to be Jews.

But identity consciousness quickly proved to be double-edged. With Israel found guilty in the court of world opinion for oppressing Palestinians, American Jews were implicated in the transgressions of the Jewish state. To Black Power advocates in the United States, Israel was just another wealthy Jewish landlord, callously exploiting its downtrodden tenants. As the alliance between blacks and Jews disintegrated, American Jews confronted a disturbing conflict between their commitment, as liberals, to the civil rights of disadvantaged minorities and their identification, as Jews, with Israel. For Jewish radicals, who were disproportionately represented in New Left politics, the choice was easy: Israel, after South Africa their favorite pariah state, was dispensable. For mainstream Jews, who disproportionately flocked to liberal causes, the discomfort was acute. What if they must choose between liberalism and Judaism?

That choice was not long in coming. In 1977, with the

stunning election of Menachem Begin as prime minister, Israeli voters, for the first time in thirty years, rejected the Labor party. Begin, leader of the Irgun before and during the struggle for independence, retained his militant Revisionist vision of a Jewish state within the expansive boundaries of biblical Eretz Israel.

This was not a pleasing prospect to many Americans. Even before Begin took office, the American media depicted him as a symbol of reckless terrorism, unyielding fanaticism, and dangerous demagoguery. The *New York Times* described him as "a former guerrilla" with "a fiery past." That august newspaper, whose unrelenting anti-Zionism had guided its editorial policy for decades before 1948, drew solace only from the prospect that the new government "may not last long." *Time*, much less restrained, labeled Begin a "terrorist," "superhawk," and "strong-willed little Polish immigrant," whose name, it crassly noted, "rhymes with Fagin."

American Jewish leaders dutifully pledged their "support and commitment" to the new government, affirming "the indissoluble ties" that bound American Jews to Israel. But their uneasiness with Begin was palpable. The most they could bring themselves to say about the stunning Israeli political transformation was that it had occurred "freely and peacefully," thereby demonstrating "the democratic process at work."

Begin contradicted romantic visions of Israel as the land of muscular kibbutzniks who resembled Paul Newman. He was the first prime minister of Israel to conspicuously identify himself as a Jew, rather than as an Israeli. He actually wore a *kipa* in public and prayed at the Western Wall. His post-election visit to that symbolic home address of the Jewish people graphically expressed his claim to be not only prime minister of Israel but leader of world Jewry.

Yet Begin, paradoxically, was a shtetl Jew from Poland, whose ill-fitting suits, Yiddish-accented English, and frequent Holocaust analogies touched deep, often discomforting, feelings among American Jews. He had a disconcerting way of reminding them of their Old World relatives, whom they preferred to forget. His lost world of Eastern European Jewry was the Old Country that they had twice abandoned, first when their parents emigrated and again when Hitler annihilated those who remained behind.

Begin was "a different kind of Prime Minister," an Israeli journalist wrote, "a more 'Jewish' leader." One of his first acts as prime minister was to visit a new Jewish settlement near Nablus, biblical Shechem. There he claimed Judea and Samaria as part of Israel, insisting that the land be identified by its biblical names. Like a vision from Ezekiel's valley of dry bones suddenly restored to life, Begin pointedly reminded modern Jews of their historical attachment to their ancient homeland. As he grafted explicitly Jewish symbols to Israeli public life, the state of the Jews actually began to resemble a Jewish state.

Inevitably, Begin antagonized the president of the United States. Jimmy Carter's political sympathies were well known. Urging Israeli withdrawal from nearly all the territory acquired in 1967, he had called for a Palestinian homeland and asked for reparations for displaced Arab refugees—which even Arab leaders had not yet demanded. Begin, at first, discounted the president's hostility. "Carter knows the Bible," the prime minister confidently declared, "and that will make it easier for him to know whose land this is."

But as Begin prepared for his first Washington visit, American Jewish leaders were evidently uneasy. Their effectiveness, after all, depended upon the absence of friction between Israel and the United States. They were accustomed to prime ministers who did not make excessive demands on them as Jews. Then, as now, American Jews preferred Israeli politicians who capitulated graciously to American definitions of Israel's best interests. Yet Begin, to their dismay, identified himself as a proud Jew who would bend his knee only to God.

The Israeli political revolution of 1977 had momentous consequences, which still reverberate for American Jews. Begin's right-wing politics undermined the unity that American Jews had always insisted was a permanent attribute of their relationship to Israel. But "unity," as Begin's election quickly demonstrated, was politically contingent. It rested upon some fundamental, if unspoken, assumptions about the politics of Zionism and its compatibility with American Jewish liberalism.

The overriding commitment of the American Jewish community had always been to demonstrate its undivided allegiance to the United States. The danger of Zionism was evident from the moment that Jewish statehood emerged as an issue in international politics. As Henry Morgenthau, American ambassador to Turkey, warned after the Balfour Declaration was issued in 1917, Zionism "would cost the Jews of America most of what they had gained in liberty, equality, and fraternity."

Although Brandeis and his Zionist followers had vigorously rejected any incompatibility between Zionism and Americanism, the persistence of their denials, down to 1948 and beyond, suggests how irrepressible their loyalty concerns really were. A Jewish state posed an implicit choice between American home and Jewish homeland. It could not help but activate the deepest anxieties of American Jews. Above all, American Jews did not want to be trapped between two nations, both of which made claims on their political allegiance.

American Jews were extremely uncomfortable with

anything, especially anything distinctively Jewish (like religious nationalism), that challenged their own political and religious liberalism—or the strict separation between them. Long before 1977, they had persuaded themselves that Judaism and liberalism were indistinguishable and that liberalism was good for the Jews. The identification of liberalism with religious freedom (and indifference), social-welfare legislation, church-state separation, and Democratic party platforms had coaxed Jews from the ghetto and guided them into the American mainstream. By voting for Democratic candidates, Jews convinced themselves that they were fulfilling the "social justice" mandate of the ancient Hebrew prophets. Their liberal course had been set ever since FDR, their American Moses, led them to their promised land of economic opportunity, social mobility, and religious equality.

Begin's assertion of transcendent Jewish unity, irrespective of national identity and citizenship, upset the fragile consensus that had enabled American Jews to identify safely with the Jewish state. Nobody, Begin insisted, "will frighten the great and free [Jewish] community in the United States. They will stand by us; this is the land of their forefathers. They have the right and duty to support [Israel]." Like Ben-Gurion, however, Begin failed to understand American Jews. When he invited them to respond to Israel as Jews, rather than as Americans, they quickly backed off. Like children trapped between quarreling parents, they became palpably anxious.

Until Begin's election, criticism of Israel from American Jews had been marginal and ineffectual, outside the liberal consensus. It was largely confined to the American Council for Judaism, a militantly anti-Zionist alliance of Reform rabbis and Sears Roebuck chairman Lessing Rosenwald, who had fought in vain against Jewish statehood. But the politics of the 1960s created new possibilities for hostility to Israel. On the seam between political radicalism and Black Power, anti-Zionism had converged ominously with anti-Semitism. Third World radical posturing, which appealed to many New Left activists, routinely denounced Israel for its "racist" and "imperialist" venality.

With Begin's election, a sharp critique of Israel emerged on the American political left where, predictably, Jews were conspicuous. Journalist I. F. Stone, who had traveled to Palestine with illegal Jewish immigrants back in 1946, complained that the "moral gravity" of Zionism had shifted toward Begin's "cold-blooded nationalistic calculation." How, Stone asked, "can we talk of human rights and ignore them for the Palestinian Arabs?" To retain his liberal and Zionist credentials, Stone pledged allegiance to "the other Zionism," a Zionism of "the deepest ethical motives" that he located in "that spirit of fraternity and justice and conciliation that the Prophets preached."

Rabbi Arthur Hertzberg, long an activist in Zionist causes, responded to Begin's tongue-lashing of the American ambassador to Israel by wondering how American Jews could support "a different country from the one its founders had intended," a country that no longer was based on "a moral passion for a better Jewish people." The commitment of American Jewry, Hertzberg insisted, was to "the liberal dreams" of Israel's founders. Israel must remain "a moral cause, consonant with America's highest ideals." For Israel to deserve the support of American Jews, suggested Stone, Hertzberg, and others, it must demonstrate undiminished fidelity to American liberal values.

With Yitzhak Shamir's accession to power after Begin's resignation in 1983, the Israel dilemma of American Jews intensified. Shamir was, if anything, even more intransigent than Begin. His pre-state command of the militant Stern Gang offended American Jews, while his obdurate resistance

to American-sponsored negotiations with the Palestine Liberation Organization exasperated them. The chill of the
Begin-Carter years seemed mild by comparison to the frosty
relations between Shamir and President Bush. As American Jews found themselves trapped between nations actively
competing for their allegiance, the crisis of Diaspora loyalty to Israel deepened.

Once the *intifada* erupted, and stone-throwing Palestinians became the newest insurrectionary heroes of the
American media, Israel was routinely pilloried—especially
by Jewish liberals—for betraying liberal ideals. In a remarkable confession in the *New York Times*, Reform spokesman
Albert Vorspan offered a revealing explanation for their
wrath. American Jews, he wrote, were "traumatized" by
events in Israel. Suffering "shame and stress," they wanted
"to crawl into a hole," where they might escape guilt by
association with "the political and moral bankruptcy"
of Israeli policy. American Jews, Vorspan insisted, were
"implicated" by the actions of the Jewish state. "It's about
us."

It was, indeed, about "us." Implicated by Israel in the
court of public opinion, liberal American Jews turned bitterly against the Jewish state. A refrain of liberal disaffec-
tion, shading into an indictment of Israel for high crimes of
political immorality, became the new conventional liberal
wisdom. On the *Times* Op-Ed page, Anthony Lewis relentlessly hectored Israel for its infidelity to the liberalism of
Brandeis and (Lewis imagined) the prophet Isaiah. The maga-
zine *Tikkun* was founded by Michael Lerner, a veteran
sixties radical, to save liberalism from neo-conservative
defenders of Israel like *Commentary* editor Norman
Podhoretz. A stream of books offered variations on the theme
of fallen Israel, fatally compromised by its abandonment
of liberal values. The moral decline and fall of the Jewish

state became the reflexive allegation of disaffected Jewish liberals.

The motif of this Jewish melodrama, whose reiteration was designed to enhance the moral virtue of its proponents, was "the tragedy of Zionism." The story of Zionist decline, from liberal democratic homeland to Revisionist holy land, bitterly proclaimed the ascendance of an "utterly nationalist, self-absorbed" Zionism, menacingly identified with "power, Bible, defiance, [and] settlement." Journalist Milton Viorst recounted how Israel, after 1967, had wandered into "a moral desert." Ruled by a coalition of Sephardic Jews accustomed to "mob politics," and Orthodox Jews who gave theological legitimacy to Begin's "'muscular Zionism,'" a once "humane" Israel had descended into the moral abyss of militarism and imperialism.

The liberal Jewish diatribe against Israel achieved national prominence with Thomas Friedman's *From Beirut to Jerusalem*, published in 1989. Friedman recounted his experiences as a *New York Times* reporter in the Middle East during the turbulent eighties, which began with the Lebanese civil war and ended with the *intifada*. The intrusive subtext of the book, however, was Friedman's personal odyssey to disillusionment with Israel—justified, of course, by its moral collapse during the Begin-Shamir years.

Friedman was the Everyboomer of postwar American Jewry. Growing up in a middle-class Minnesota family as a "three-day-a-year Jew," he was suddenly awakened to his Jewish identity during the Six Day War. Thereafter, he claimed (somewhat disingenuously), he wore Israel as a "badge of pride"—until 1982 when the Israeli army turned its back while Lebanese Christians slaughtered Palestinians at the Sabra and Shatila refugee camps outside Beirut. Suddenly, Friedman was overwhelmed by Jewish guilt, shame, and outrage. "The Israel I met on the outskirts of Beirut," he wrote bitterly, "was not the heroic Israel I had been taught to identify with." In his *Times* articles, he conceded, he "buried . . . every illusion I ever held about the Jewish state."

Propelling his book up the best-seller list, Friedman reiterated the newly fashionable theme of the Israeli betrayal of liberalism. Projecting the self-image of a morally anguished innocent who suffered a "personal crisis" as the once "heroic" Israel stripped away his illusions, he concluded that "something had gone terribly wrong" in the Jewish state. Like so many American Jews, Friedman filtered the Jewish state through American lenses. With astonishing journalistic agility, he converted Palestinians who threw stones and Molotov cocktails into sixties-style civil-rights activists practicing "non-lethal civil disobedience." Their stones, Friedman insisted, were merely political symbols of frustration and victimization (although more than a few Israelis were maimed, or even killed, by such "symbolic" assaults).

Friedman's tortured rationalizations may have subverted his journalistic objectivity, but they certainly protected him from the implacable enemies of the Jews whom he encountered in the Middle East. Friedman noted that when Arabs, scanning his "Mediterranean features," inquired about his identity, he invariably replied, "I'm American. One hundred percent." Pressed further, he would only answer "Romanian!" Among Arabs, it seemed, Friedman's worst apprehension was that he might actually be unmasked as a Jew.

Whenever Israelis violated his liberal precepts, Friedman sharply castigated them for subverting "Jewish" values. ("How could you do this to me, you bastards?" he wondered about Israeli generals. "I always thought you were different. I always thought *we* were different.") "Boiling with anger," as his liberal illusions about Israel were stripped away, he became determined to "nail Begin and Sharon" and "help get rid of them." This rather contorted interpretation of journalistic objectivity was rewarded with a Pulitzer Prize.

Why were American Jewish liberals so uncontrollably angry with Israel? Because the Begin political revolution had challenged the integrity of their Jewish identity in the United States. In 1977, American Jews discovered to their dismay that "Zionism," whose meaning they were certain they understood, was a contested ideology in Israel. Not only was it defined by secular Israelis in the Labor party but by religious nationalists who voted for Likud candidates. There was the Zionism of Jewish integration, which understandably appealed to American Jews, and the Zionism of Jewish distinctiveness, which just as understandably frightened them.

For the first time, American Jews confronted the reality of two Zionisms, one of which was compatible with American liberal values while the other contradicted them at every crucial point. As an unholy alliance of Revisionists and Sephardim, joined by rabbis and settlers, swept into power in Israel, the light unto the nations seemed dimmed by political reaction and religious fanaticism. American Jews found themselves pulled between competing liberal and Jewish values which, until then, had seamlessly converged. Zionism, once a source of American Jewish pride, now became a source of embarrassment and discomfort.

To American Jews, Begin's least forgivable sin—like Shamir's and Netanyahu's after him—was his articulation of a Zionist alternative to liberal Judaism. Liberalism may have cut the knot of dual loyalty for American Jews, assuring them that they were better Jews (and more truly American) the more liberal their politics. But once the Israeli political balance tilted to the right, American Jews experienced the anguish of dual loyalty—not, as *Commentary* editor Norman Podhoretz suggested, "between Israel and America, but between Israel and liberalism."

Begin and his Likud successors forced American Jews to confront an excruciating choice between (American) liberalism and (Israeli) Zionism. The Israeli political culture, between 1977 and 1992, was too religious, too Orthodox, and too nationalistic for the liberal sensibilities of American Jews (and, to be sure, for many secular Israelis as well). No longer was Israel the land of the Hebrew prophets, those revered patron saints of Jewish liberalism who had thundered their timeless jeremiads for social justice. Instead, Israel was where Gush Emunim zealots demanded the Land of Israel for the people of Israel according to the Torah of Israel. As religious nationalism competed with secular liberalism for Zionist supremacy, American Jews reconsidered their relationship to Zionism. Once Israel turned to the right, American Jewish liberals turned their backs on the Jewish state.

The ascendancy of the Israeli political and religious right during the eighties confronted American Jews with repeated wrenching conflicts between their attachment to liberalism and their attachment to Israel. First the war in Lebanon brought down a cascade of criticism upon the Jewish state for its unrestrained military aggression. Then there was the attempt of Orthodox rabbis in Israel to define under Israeli law the answer to "Who is a Jew?"—an insulting rebuke to an American Jewish community increasingly decimated by intermarriage and largely indifferent, if not actively hostile, to *halakhic* standards. Finally, the arrest and imprisonment of Jonathan Pollard for passing classified American military intelligence to Israel evoked, yet again, the nightmare of Diaspora disloyalty.

American Jews who managed, through all this, to remain steadfast in their support for Israel had their patriotic loyalty viciously impugned. During the loan-guarantee imbroglio of 1991, President Bush famously depicted himself as one lonely voice for genuine American interests, standing firm against the hordes of (presumably un-American) Jewish lobbyists for Israel who had descended upon Washington.

Harmony between Israel and American Jewry was not restored until 1992, when Yitzhak Rabin's election ended fifteen years of Likud political dominance. Rabin's victory, abetted and applauded by the White House and the State Department, prompted audible sighs of relief from the American Jewish community. Allegations of Jewish disloyalty subsided. No longer were there complaints from the likes of Patrick Buchanan about Israel's "amen corner" in the United States, or Capitol Hill as "Israeli-occupied territory." The sniping of American Jews toward Israel for betraying liberal values moderated. Once again, American Jews could embrace the Jewish state without compromising their liberalism or their patriotism.

Rabin proved to be the ideal leader for the emerging "post-Zionist" Israel of the nineties—and for an American Jewish community that had been all but battered into silent submission by President Bush and Secretary of State James Baker. The glowing centerpiece of this new era of good feelings between Israel and the United States was, of course, the Rabin-Arafat handshake on the White House lawn, with an approving President Clinton basking in their reflected glory. The 1993 Oslo accords were greeted by their euphoric Israeli sponsors and American Jewish supporters as the harbinger of a "new" Middle East, a veritable Benelux on the Mediterranean. With "peace now," Israel could finally become a nation like other nations, perhaps even a state like the United States.

Rabin's peace policy marked an astonishingly abrupt

reversal for an old hawk who had not only commanded the Israel Defense Forces during the Six Day War, but served as the hardline minister of defense in Likud governments. It sharply polarized Israelis, at least half of whom remained unwilling to jeopardize their own security for Palestinian promises of peace that were repeatedly punctuated by murderous terrorist attacks. But it brought peace of mind to American Jewry, whose comfort in the United States depended upon American government pleasure with Israel. It was hardly coincidental, however, that Rabin's most enthusiastic supporters in the American Jewish community, according to polling surveys, came from Jews who were least knowledgeable about Judaism, least religiously observant, least likely to visit Israel, most tolerant of intermarriage, and most inclined to define Jewishness in liberal American terms.

Rabin's assassination in 1995 as a martyr to peace solidified the bonds of American Jewish unity with Israel. The American media overflowed with comparisons to the assassinations of Kennedy and Lincoln. American Jews, like many Israelis, were comforted by President Clinton's evident sorrow, his presence with other world leaders at Rabin's state funeral (tangible proof of Israel's new respectability among the nations), and his poignant words of farewell, "Shalom, Chaver." American Jews were touched (and reassured) that their president had spoken Hebrew, an implicit validation of their own attachment to Israel.

Yet as Benjamin Netanyahu's unexpected, and undesired, political victory in 1996 demonstrated, "We Are One!" remained a conditional promise from American Jews. An Israel governed by the political and religious right remained anathema, an affront to the American Jewish majority at its most vulnerable point of liberal identity. The allegiance to Israel of these American Jews depended, as always, upon the convergence of Zionism with American norms. Whenever they diverged, as they often did (especially under right-wing Israeli governments) on crucial issues of Jewish identity and Israeli security, liberal American Jews were exposed as fair-weather friends of Israel.

It was not very long, predictably, before Prime Minister Netanyahu was excoriated by American Jewish liberals (and, even more enthusiastically, by their Israeli counterparts). His political alliance with the Orthodox religious parties infuriated them, as though the Labor party had never consorted with rabbis to secure a ruling majority. His initial demands for Palestinian compliance with the Oslo accords, for an end to the give-and-take process by which Israelis gave and Palestinians took, made him appear hopelessly intransigent. Only after Netanyahu capitulated to Palestinian violence and American pressure by surrendering Hebron did their hostility abate, at least temporarily. But there was little else that Netanyahu could do as prime minister to appease his liberal critics, either in Israel or the United States, until his election defeat in 1999.

Just as Rabin's victory over Shamir in 1992 had reassured American Jews that Israel met their liberal requirements, so Ehud Barak's election, which dispatched Netanyahu into political exile, solidified their equation of Zionism and Judaism with liberalism. Not only was Barak cast in Rabin's image as the warrior who would make peace; even more reassuringly, he quickly demonstrated his willingness to defer to Clinton administration policy (even when Clinton casually opined that Palestinian refugees should live wherever they wished, presumably including Israel, or when Hillary Rodham Clinton kissed Suha Arafat following her maliciously false accusations of gas poisoning by Israelis). American Jews were grateful for the respite from acrimony that Barak offered; ever since the Ben-Gurion era, nothing has unsettled their equilibrium as *American* Jews more than evidence of friction between their president and the prime minister of Israel. They depend upon Israeli prime ministers to affirm their self-protective equation of Jewish nationalism with American patriotism and Democratic liberalism.

The more land that Israel has relinquished to the Palestinians, winning presidential accolades as it diminished its own security, the easier it has been—and surely will continue to be—for American Jews to identify with the Jewish state. For their security as Americans, Jews need Israel to be in harmony with the United States, just as they require the convergence of Judaism with American norms. That was the enticing promise of Joseph Lieberman's vice-presidential candidacy, which American Jewry greeted with rapturous enthusiasm. His selection proved to Jews, one more time, that they were genuine Americans. With their insatiable craving for acceptance assuaged yet again, they were, at least for the moment, at one with the United States.

4

Zionism

versus

Judaism

In his anti-Diaspora diatribe, *With Friends Like You*, Israeli journalist Matti Golan castigated American Jews who, from the safety of the United States, hold Israel to unreasonable moral standards (to save themselves from embarrassment) while distancing themselves from the Jewish state. That is not a recent problem. Support from American Jews for Israel always has been contingent, depending in the end upon the conformity of the Jewish state to the liberal values that enable American Jews to feel most comfortably American.

Israelis display their own distinctive pattern of cultural assimilation. Its source, paradoxically, is the venerable Herzlian principle of Jewish normalization. Historically, Zionism meant the national liberation of the Jewish people in their own homeland—free from foreign domination. But there is a fundamental, perhaps irreconcilable, tension between Zionism, a revolutionary political movement in pursuit of normalization, and Judaism, the distinctive faith tradition of the Jewish people—a people, according to the biblical text (which, after all, is the ultimate source of Zionism), destined to dwell alone, set apart from the other nations of the world.

Zionism, by the beginning of the new millennium, was relentlessly propelling secular Jews in Israel from Jewish distinctiveness to full integration into the family of nations. But to qualify for family membership, Israel must become, more or less, like other nations, altering its profile to meet foreign standards. This is a talent that secular Zionism has by now refined with considerable skill. The rapid transformation of Israelis into citizens of the world suggests that Zionism may yet return Jews to precisely the spiritual exile from which Zionism once offered itself as a compelling alternative.

The Zionist movement, at its inception, was compelled to reject religious Orthodoxy. Rabbinic Judaism held the Jewish people together for nearly two thousand years, until the embers of Jewish nationalism were rekindled. But the entrenched rigidities of rabbinical authority in the modern era, grounded in the ferocious determination to resist the encroachments of modernity, left no room for human initiatives that impinged upon divine prerogatives. Zionism, the Jewish alternative to assimilation at one extreme and to Orthodoxy at the other, had no choice but to break free of rabbinical constraints.

Zionists, after all, were Jews who refused to wait for the messiah. They believed in action, now. With extraordinary determination and courage, driven by the confluence of historical events both too horrific and too wondrous to anticipate, they achieved what was historically unprecedented—some might even say miraculous. They actually reconstructed the national identity of a dispersed, powerless, and landless people. Who cannot be awed by the singular majesty of their accomplishment?

But the stunning Zionist achievement was not without its serious blemishes, which are already debilitating and may yet become fatal. This has nothing to do with the politically fashionable indictment of Zionism for its "theft" of "Palestinian" land, or its "oppression" of the Palestinian people. Rarely, if ever, in history has any "conquest" or "occupation" secured so much freedom for its beleaguered victims. (The prolonged encounter between pioneers and American Indians was far more exploitative, brutal, mendacious, and destructive than anything done by Zionists to Palestinians.) It is little wonder that the Palestinian national movement, from its claim of biblical antecedents to its language of ingathering exiles and its obsession with Jerusalem, has faithfully mimicked the very Zionism that it so fervently despises.

The real problem is the abiding and deepening hostility within the Jewish state toward Jews and Judaism. The normalization impulse among secular Israelis, so deeply embedded in their Zionist inheritance, is relentlessly driving Israel from its origins in Jewish nationalism and its pursuit of Jewish freedom. The future is already clearly discernible: Israel as an American cultural outpost in the Middle East, clamoring for admission to the global American village.

To be sure, the Americanization impulse—which has included everything from Big Macs and Levis to the Michaels Jordan and Jackson—has all but become a worldwide stampede. But Israel alone, among the nations, has assumed responsibility for preserving the Jewish people in its own national home. Yet its mission is undermined by the inherent ambiguity of Zionist "normalization." Was Zionism intended to make Jews like everyone else, or to enable them, as Jews, to live normal lives?

The fabled pioneers of the Second Aliya, who emigrated from Russia between 1905 and 1914, were socialist revolutionaries no less than Jewish nationalists. (Political scientist Ze'ev Sternhell perversely, if not maliciously, insists upon calling them "nationalist socialists," thereby suggesting that Jewish self-hatred has become quite normal in Israel.) It is no historical exaggeration to claim, as Ben-Gurion did, that "the socialist principle [was] central in the building of the country" and that "socialist Zionists [were] the most devoted builders of Zionism."

From the earliest Galilee kibbutzim to the proclamation of national independence in 1948, and beyond, socialism and Zionism were inextricable components of Jewish national rebirth. Only "Socialist Zionism," Ben-Gurion insisted with pardonable exaggeration, was "a full Zionism, distilling into itself all the historical contents of the redemption of the Jewish people." Socialism, he claimed, was "the means through which Zionism will be realized."

But where in the Zionist revolution was a place for Judaism? Not many Zionists seemed to care. Along with czars and pogroms, Judaism was what Zionists fled Eastern Europe to escape. It was a self-evident truth, even an article of Zionist faith, that Judaism—the ancient and enduring religious culture of the Jewish people—was a substantial obstacle to the achievement of Zionist goals. Nachman Syrkin, the formidable Zionist ideologue, advised Jewish youth that Judaism "is not a religion but a tragedy, the major impediment confronting the Jewish nation on the road to culture, science, freedom." In the very soul of Zionism is to be found the poison of post-Zionism that corrodes Jewish life in contemporary Israel.

The West—with its culture, science, and freedom—served from the beginning as the Zionist model. Religion, after all, was mindless superstition, the rejected faith of all those parochial shtetl Jews whom idealistic young Zionists left behind. Judaism meant religion; religion meant Orthodoxy; and Orthodoxy was nothing but Eastern European obscurantism, "Orientalism" at its worst. In their insistent condemnation of religious Orthodoxy, early Zionists occasionally sounded like nineteenth-century Reform rabbis, who had also elevated science and reason above faith and observance.

Ben-Gurion firmly believed that *"galut* [exile] means dependence—material, political, spiritual, cultural, and intellectual dependence—because we are aliens, a minority, bereft of a homeland, rootless." Yet when he reflected upon "the Jewish revolution" that he was leading toward its climax in national sovereignty, he conceded that "no parallel exists" for the extraordinary fact that among all the peoples who had suffered exile from their homeland, only the Jews had steadfastly refused to accept the verdict of history. Their steadfastness, of course, was grounded precisely in their ancient faith, undiminished after two thousand years in the *galut* that Ben-Gurion so despised.

If religious faith was all there was to Jewish history in exile (and certainly it was not all), it was hardly inconsequential. For without the unyielding determination of Jews to remain Jews, expressed during so many centuries when Judaism elicited the primal hatred of their enemies, modern Zionism is all but inconceivable. Without the astonishing durability of the religious tradition, ironically, no Jews would have survived to reject Judaism for Zionism.

Only in the barren deserts and infested swamps of Palestine, according to the Zionists, could Jews finally master their own fate. Yet Ben-Gurion, more than most Zionists, appreciated the unbreakable link between modern Zionism and ancient Israel. In 1936, he testified before the Peel Commission, sent to Palestine by the British government during a prolonged spasm of Arab violence. When questioned by puzzled commission members about the source of the novel Zionist claim to the Jewish homeland, Ben-Gurion answered succinctly: "The Bible is our mandate." Nonetheless, he envisioned "a Jewish renaissance on humanistic, Zionist, and socialist"—rarely Jewish—foundations. In his call for "*a socialist Jewish state*," the primacy of his first adjective was not accidental.

When Ben-Gurion needed a patina of Jewish authenticity for the secular Zionist revolution, he—like so many other secular Jews who were disaffected from Jewish tradition—turned to the ancient Hebrew prophets for their message of "social justice, universal peace, and love." The State of Israel, he declared, would be guided "by a political and social vision that we have inherited from our prophets."

Ben-Gurion echoed all the other modern Jews, from Reform rabbis to godless atheists, for whom Amos, Isaiah, and Hosea provided biblical authority for their rejection of biblical faith. It was a historically dubious—if enticing—claim. The translation of ancient prophecy, which rigorously demanded unyielding fealty to divine command, into social justice signified the rejection, not the embrace, of Jewish tradition.

"Our Jewishness and our Zionism were interchangeable," asserted Chaim Weizmann, the first president of Israel. But it never was that simple. The tension between Judaism and Zionism—between religious and national definitions of Jewish peoplehood—was irrepressible. The original promise of Zion to the Jewish people, after all, came from the very God in whom few Zionists believed and whose authority they summarily rejected as a relic of Diaspora powerlessness. Zionists certainly did not intend, in the words from the prophet Isaiah that begin every Torah service, that from *their* Zion, the modern Land of Israel, "shall go forth the Law, and the word of God from Jerusalem."

Arguably, few Jews in the modern era have been less

attentive to the word of God than the Zionist founders of the Jewish state. Seldom did Zionists have a kind word to say about Jerusalem, or its companion holy city (Hebron) from ancient Israel, which they were ultimately quite content to abandon to religious Orthodoxy, or to Arabs. To be sure, it was finally decided, after years of acrimonious debate at the beginning of the twentieth century, that the Jewish national home must indeed be located in Palestine, not in Africa or Argentina. Nonetheless, as a state like any other state, it would be committed to Western notions of freedom and equality under (civil, not Jewish) law. Just as newly emancipated Jews had once rushed to demonstrate their loyalty to France, so Zionists pledged their allegiance to the family of nations.

From its inception, Zionism was a tangled blend of old and new, borrowed and indigenous, Jewish and Western. A more incongruous blend of disparate ideologies and impulses—nationalism and socialism, Judaism and democracy, separation and assimilation—can hardly be imagined. Perhaps, as the literary critic Harold Fisch has suggested in his incisive study of the Zionist revolution, "what unites the Zionist movement as a whole is precisely an unwritten consent to harbour this ambiguity!" Unresolved ambiguities, however, have a way of causing unanticipated problems.

If Judaism without the liturgy of return to Zion is unimaginable, then surely Zionism without biblical and sacred memory at its historical core is inconceivable. From the beginning, however, Zionists were exceedingly hostile to rabbinic Judaism, and their hostility was enthusiastically reciprocated by the rabbinate, who perceived secular nationalism, at best, as another despicable example of modern assimilation, an outrageous turning away from God and Torah. To Zadok Hacohen of Lublin, the revered leader of its Hasidic community, Zionists were "fools and malicious conspirers" who "reject all the commandments and cleave to every manner of abomination."

Zionism posed an acute "theological dilemma" for the Orthodox. Zionists certainly believed in the return of Jews to their holy land, but they sharply repudiated the deep-rooted religious conception that the Jewish people and Torah were indivisible. That was why the Golden Calf of nationalism was an "abomination" to the Orthodox rabbinate. In 1912, fifteen years after the First Zionist Congress, rabbis finally responded to the Zionist challenge by founding Agudat Israel, which appealed to "Jews adhering to the Torah." Zionists, by definition, were excluded.

Zionism, as Shlomo Avineri has observed, marked a "fundamental revolution" in Jewish consciousness, substituting secular for traditionally religious Jewish self-identity. Its younger and more militant activists, Marxists conspicuous among them, were crudely (and cruelly) disparaging of *galut* Jewry. The average Diaspora Jew, according to Hashomer Hatzair, the leftist Zionist organization, was "bleak and mournful," presenting "but a caricature of a man healthy and normal in body and soul. His whole life is but a procession of irregular and unhealthy acts performed to enable him to survive." To any robust young Zionist, boldly forging a revolution, the Diaspora Jew was a "hair-splitting and sophistic" parasite, oblivious to the modern world, obsessed with sacred texts, and preoccupied with mindless ritual.

Yet there always were rabbis who advocated the fusion of Zionism with Judaism. "Jewish nationality divorced from Jewish religion," noted Rabbi Yehiel Michael Pines, who moved to Jerusalem in 1878, is nothing but "an abomination to Jews." He warned that "any other people can perhaps have a national aspiration divorced from its religion but we, Jews, cannot." Rabbi Samuel Mohilever of Poland sent a strong message of encouragement to the "beloved sons of Zion" who gathered at the First Zionist Congress. "The resettlement of our country," he wrote, "is one of the fundamental commandments of our Torah. Some of our ancient sages even say that it is equivalent to the whole Law, for it is the foundation of the existence of our people."

To Rabbi Abraham Isaac Kook, Chief Rabbi of Palestine during the British Mandatory era, the inherent unity of Judaism and Zionism was self-evident. Zionism as mere nationalism was, he thought, "a sterile notion." But Judaism without Zionism was also barren, for "a Jew cannot be as devoted and true to his own ideas, sentiments, and imagination"—to say nothing of God—"in the Diaspora as . . . in Eretz Israel." The land of Israel, for Kook, was "the Land of Holiness, the Land of God—in which all of the Divine commandments are realized in their perfect form."

Just as Zionists were touched by holiness, despite their rejection of sanctity, so religious Jews must be inspired by Zionism. "The hope for the return to the Holy Land," Kook wrote, "is the continuing source of the distinctive nature of Judaism." In other words, as Kook intuited, we are all Jews; we are all Zionists. Neither Judaism nor Zionism could be whole, he insisted, until the people of Israel, the Land of Israel, and the Torah of Israel were reunited and fused.

Kook's Zionism of divine redemption remained a distinctly minority view among rabbis and secular Zionists alike. All the forces released by emancipation, strengthened by the secularism that has defined "enlightenment" in the modern era, converged to separate religion from nationalism. So it has aptly been said that Jews became one people divided by a common identity.

For the Orthodox, exile was an appropriate divine punishment for the sins of the Jewish people; it would end only when God, not godless Zionists, willed it. After visiting a kibbutz during the 1930s, a Warsaw rabbi bitterly condemned a Zionism that "detaches many young people from the To-rah and Judaism and leaves them deprived of any Jewish content." Can Israel, he wondered, "be built on the ruins of Judaism and the Torah?"

Certainly not, according to Agudat Israel, whose anti-Zionism remained virulent. Independent Jewish sovereignty, it declared in 1937, endangered Judaism. Without "recognition of Torah authority in public life," it warned, the sanctity of the Land of Israel would be undermined, posing "a hazard to the lofty role of the Jewish People as a holy nation." In the blunt words of Rabbi Elhanan Wasserman: "The Jewish state is our greatest woe."

For Zionists, of course, the sabra and the kibbutz, not the rabbi and the shtetl, were the shining symbols of Jewish redemption. Exile was a condition of weakness and subservience, inherent in the absence of national sovereignty. Without a state, there was no power, human or divine, that could liberate Jews from their spiritual and physical servitude. Zionists recast two thousand years of Jewish history in the Diaspora as an interlude of humiliation and decay between the once and future eras of Jewish national sovereignty.

The rabbinate, which had defined normative Judaism ever since the destruction of the Second Temple, was hardly prepared to yield its authority to godless socialists in Tel Aviv. It was the Holocaust, finally, that mercilessly shifted the balance of Jewish power to the Zionists. It demonstrated the horrific truth of their claim that without national sovereignty Jews were forever helpless before their enemies. With the shtetl and yeshiva culture of Eastern Europe all but annihilated, the shattered remnant of European Orthodoxy was too traumatized to challenge the brash Zionist claim to supremacy. From Jewish tragedy, precisely as Ben-Gurion had predicted, arose Zionist opportunity.

But the Jewish ambiguities inherent in Zionism were

irrepressible, and they were preserved in the founding text of the new State of Israel. The concluding sentence of the Proclamation of Independence, as Fisch shrewdly observes, delicately balanced Zionist normality with covenantal promise: "Placing our trust in the Rock of Israel, we set our hand and testimony to this Declaration, here on the soil of the Homeland, in the city of Tel-Aviv, on this day, the eve of the Sabbath, 5th Iyar, 5708, 14th May, 1948."

Among the more ambiguous locutions, Fisch suggests, was reference to the "Rock of Israel" (rather than, as religious Zionists preferred, "the Lord of Israel"). *Tsur Yisrael* might signify the divine Father and King, as in Jewish liturgy; or, as secular Zionists claimed, the collective national will. Similarly, the parallel measurements of time suggested that Israel, at the very instant of its birth, lived according to a dual calendar in which traditional Jewish time and modern Western (Christian) time must somehow be reconciled. And "the eve of the Sabbath" might refer to the particular Friday afternoon when independence was proclaimed. But it could also signal the imminence of holy time, with the birth of Israel marking the beginning of Jewish redemption. Only time (but whose?) would tell.

There is a story of the wizened old rabbi who approached Ben-Gurion not long after statehood was proclaimed. He reminded the Zionist leader that when a robust young traveler encounters a weak and weary old man, simple courtesy dictates that the vigorous youth (Zionism) show respect to the frail elder (Orthodoxy). Like other Eastern European Zionists, Ben-Gurion could be touched by Jewish sentiment. Indeed, just before the first session of the Knesset convened, he even went to a synagogue in Jerusalem for a thanksgiving prayer. It was the first time in forty years, he noted in his diary, that he had attended a synagogue service in Eretz Israel.

Symbolic gestures aside (and Zionist iconography easily

absorbed, and transformed, such Jewish religious symbols as the menorah), Ben-Gurion would be guided by the imperatives of governance in a parliamentary system. Precisely those imperatives, it turned out, required a measure of Zionist accommodation to religious Orthodoxy. Democracy and normality were necessary, but not sufficient, for a Jewish state. There remained—and remains to this day—the irrepressible issue of *Jewish* legitimacy in the Zionist state.

Just what that required emerged from negotiations between Ben-Gurion and the religious parties. To form a parliamentary majority, he needed their support, both symbolic and political (as has virtually every Israeli prime minister since 1948). The result was the frequently calumnied Status Quo agreement, which distributed power and divided authority to assure a measure of accommodation between Zionist nationalism and religious Orthodoxy.

There would be state subsidies for (Orthodox) religious education. *Halakha* (religious law) would govern certain symbolic aspects of public life: government business would not be conducted (nor would El Al fly) on the Jewish sabbath or holy days; the dietary laws of *kashrut* would be observed at official functions; all religious women, and male yeshiva students, would be exempted from military service. Matters of family status—marriage and divorce—would fall within the jurisdiction of rabbinical courts.

To be sure, the Zionist founders preferred a completely secular state. Ben-Gurion himself confessed (in 1949): "I want the state to hold religion in the palm of its hand." But given historical, political, and religious imperatives, the idea of a normal Jewish state—a state like any state—was an oxymoron. Golda Meir, as resolutely secular as the other Zionist leaders of her generation, acknowledged that "without our religion we would have been like all other peoples who once existed and later disappeared." Even if Judaism had been little more than a prolonged prelude to Zionism, an absurd proposition that Zionists were fond of assuming, its complete eradication from the Jewish state was more than all but a handful of Israelis, at the Canaanite fringe of Jewish self-abnegation, could tolerate.

Yet what, precisely, did Jewish statehood mean other than a state of Jews? How would Jewishness in a modern Jewish state be defined? And by whom? Disagreement over these issues was rampant, which is why the struggle over Jewish identity within the framework of Jewish national sovereignty has been unremitting. In the early years of statehood, cinema riots erupted in Jerusalem when movie theaters opened before the sabbath ended. They were part of a larger "battle for the sabbath" whose skirmishes—ranging from when the Israel-Transjordan Armistice Commission could convene to when police officers must (or must not) shave—preoccupied the first Knesset interminably. All the confusion inherent in modern Jewish identity, precisely what Zionism meant to resolve, was most vividly on display in the State of Israel.

There was a darker side to this jousting for cultural supremacy, which became evident when Labor party youngsters launched Shabbat raids into Orthodox neighborhoods. More insidiously, secular state schools were established in immigrant absorption centers to eradicate the "obsolete religiosity" of immigrant children coming from the Middle East and North Africa. This relic of Diaspora "decadence" was, after all, an impediment to their successful absorption in Zion. Such blatant educational indoctrination, if not intimidation, amounted in the eyes of religiously observant Jews to nothing less than the forced conversion that Jews had steadfastly resisted throughout their history in exile. Now, it seemed, they were in exile in their own national home.

Most Israelis at the time, according to the popular journalist Tom Segev, "saw themselves as Jews, even if they did not know exactly what they meant by it." Their confusion was understandable. They lived in a Jewish state; yet Zionism, to a significant extent, represented a national rebellion against Judaism. From the beginning, the country was divided into warring secular and religious communities, each insisting on its own freedom from coercion even as it tried to coerce conformity from its opponents.

Nothing in the early years of statehood more painfully illuminated the Israeli identity dilemma than the experiences of two groups of new immigrants, Yemenites and Holocaust survivors. Their arrival affirmed the very essence of Zionist purpose, the ingathering of beleaguered Jews in their promised homeland. Yet both groups of Jews, it turned out, were far too "Jewish" for Zionist comfort. Treated shamefully by government officials and private citizens alike, their suffering was needlessly—indeed, cruelly—prolonged.

Operation Magic Carpet, the fabled airlift that transported nearly the entire community of Yemenite Jews to Israel, earned a deservedly special place in Zionist lore. It exemplified the Zionist determination to rescue even the most scattered and isolated communities of Jews from exile. The Yemenites were every Zionist's favorite immigrant group. Belonging to an ancient tribal culture entirely bypassed by modernity, they could trace their dispersion to the first-century Roman conquest. In Yemen they had patiently waited for two millennia for the messiah to return them to their homeland. Exhausted and emaciated from their trek through the forbidding terrain of the Arabian peninsula, they had climbed trustingly aboard the flying machines that would transport them "on eagle's wings" to Zion.

Once in Israel, like other newcomers, they were confined to immigrant camps until permanent housing was available for them. With appropriate guidance (and, where necessary, coercion), they were expected to transform themselves from Jews into Zionists. "Of the Heavenly Jerusalem they have had quite enough," observed the supervisor of immigrant education. Now they needed "civilization and knowledge of the world"—or, at least, the world of secular Zionism. They might, if they insisted, continue to study the Bible (stripped, of course, of its "archaic quality"). But they "must be taught from the viewpoint of the Land of Israel, as it concerns us today."

The Yemenites, as their Zionist educational supervisor readily conceded, might be "a noble tribe, perhaps the noblest of the tribes of Israel." Nonetheless, they were "very primitive"—which, in translation, meant that they were religiously traditional Jews. It was "the duty of the state," he noted, "not to leave a Diaspora community in its Diaspora condition." Therefore, Yemenite children must be removed from their religious schools, and even from their parents, to special youth camps. There they would receive proper Zionist training in "the wondrous Israeli revolution, whose expression is the state."

Early in this reeducation process, rumors began to circulate that Yemenite boys were forced to cut off their sidelocks, grown by observant Jewish males for religious reasons. These rumors were sufficiently insistent and disturbing to force a government inquiry, which discovered that the "rumors" were, indeed, facts. "You don't need sidelocks in Israel," the youngsters had been told. Married men were instructed to "spill their seed on the ground" (biblical birth control) to contain family growth. "You don't need many children," their Zionist educators advised them. What they did not need was, in a word, Judaism.

It is little wonder that one Knesset member (who had helped to draft the Israeli Declaration of Independence) condemned the treatment of the Yemenites as "oppression and coercion in the spirit of [the] Inquisition against the Jewish faith." It was, he warned, "cultural and religious genocide." It created hostility and resentment that to this day festers in the Yemenite community. Rumors continue to circulate of newly born Yemenite children who were given away for adoption to Ashkenazi families, with their parents informed that their babies had died soon after birth and were quickly buried to prevent the spread of disease.

Then there were the Holocaust survivors. To sabras, they were the living demonstration of the ultimate degradation of Diaspora existence, whose debilities proved the truth of Zionism. Even before they reached Israel, Zionist envoys who visited the displaced persons camps in Europe described them as "human debris." "I thought they were animals," a Zionist agent wrote. The demented misery of the survivors was not solely attributable to their ghastly experiences in Buchenwald or Auschwitz. To Zionist agents, this human "trash" vividly demonstrated the inherent deficiencies of an "Exile mentality," which only Zionism could eradicate. Yet if the survivors came to Palestine, an envoy warned, the country was likely to become "one big madhouse."

After 1945, 350,000 Holocaust survivors arrived in Israel. Leaving the unspeakable horrors of Europe behind, they encountered a Jewish state whose palpable discomfort with them only deepened their suffering. "Israel was apprehensive about them," Segev notes, "and wanted to change them." Seeking nothing more than a normal life, the survivors were perceived by Israelis as disturbingly abnormal.

The survivors were described as subhumans who must be taught "the first concepts of humanity." Appropriately reeducated, they might yet "learn love of the homeland, a

work ethic, and human morals." The behavior of child survivors was especially disturbing. Placed in kibbutzim for
appropriate instruction in Zionist pioneering virtues, they
remained "strange and alien" creatures to their Zionist counselors. "Neither romance nor beauty excites [them]," one
counselor wrote with astounding insensitivity, "neither the
prophet Amos nor the country's landscape."

The Zionist goal, bluntly stated, was to forge "a new
pioneering Jewish personality from elements of chaos, dis-
figurement, and both spiritual and physical castration." All
the "invalid and selfish habits, concepts, and moral norms"
that the survivors brought with them from the Nazi camps—
and from their years in exile—must yield to the "positive
values" of Zionism. To be sure, many kibbutzim struggled
valiantly, often at considerable emotional and financial cost,
to absorb the survivors. But "the quality of human material," one kibbutz objected, simply did not conform to Zionist standards. A youngster who persisted in speaking
Polish surely was "disturbed"; another, who had no interest in kibbutz agriculture, was "strange and alien"; youthful survivors from Germany were described as unteachable
because they displayed "the gleanings of Nazi education."

The army, another pillar of the Zionist elite, was as discomforted as the kibbutzim by Holocaust survivors in its
midst. The participation of survivors in the war of Israeli
independence was actively encouraged; and, for the most
part, survivors responded willingly and served bravely. (Indeed, one out of every three fighters, and one out of three
war casualties, was a survivor.) Yet to the sabras with whom
they fought, they remained foreigners, aliens from the land
of exile who were "difficult, stubborn, and cowardly men."
Their presence was blamed (among others, by the young
commander of the Palmach fighting elite, Yitzhak Rabin)
for demoralizing native-born Israeli soldiers. Some officers,

with commendable sensitivity, warned that survivors must not be made to feel like "cannon fodder"—precisely the term used by bitter survivors to express the disdain with which the army treated them.

The deeper issue, which fed the hostility and resentment of kibbutzniks and soldiers alike, was the arrogant Zionist assumption of moral superiority. Zionists chastised Jewish immigrants for having been too enclosed in ghetto Judaism—where "they fell deaf, and shielded their eyes" from the truth of Zionism. The refugees from Nazi extermination camps, according to poet Natan Alterman, were nothing more than "a huddled and despairing throng" of tailors, cobblers, and money changers. In a 1949 meeting with Prime Minister Ben-Gurion, the poet Leah Goldberg described Holocaust survivors as "ugly, impoverished, morally suspect, and hard to love." To see them as human, she conceded, required "a tremendous effort."

The first generation of Israeli youngsters, recalled author Yehudit Hendel, learned that "the ugliest, basest thing is not the Exile but the Jew who came from there." The new state might desperately need Diaspora Jews, but the very Jews it needed generated extreme discomfort among Zionists. Israelis cruelly referred to Holocaust survivors as *sabon* (soap), the ultimate epithet of degradation reserved for those who had not found a way—because none existed—to prevent the Nazis from annihilating them.

Yet the historical record of the *yishuv*, which at best had been helpless to save European Jews from Hitler and at worst indifferent to their plight, hardly gave Zionists the right to claim moral purity or superiority. Dov Shilansky, a survivor who subsequently served in the Knesset, asked pointedly: "What did our brothers [in Eretz Israel] outside of hell do?" Another survivor answered bitterly, "You danced the hora while we were being burned in the crematoriums."

Even after the war in Europe ended, leaving tens of thousands of Jews barely clinging to life, it still took eight months for a Zionist envoy to arrive in Poland from Palestine. Antek Zuckerman, among the handful of resistance fighters who survived the Warsaw ghetto uprising, remained despairing about this episode of Zionist apathy until his death. He had wanted "only one man" to come to Warsaw in 1945, he reminisced from his postwar home in kibbutz Lohamei Ha-Getaot, just one Zionist "who would bring [us] a word of good will from the Land of Israel. . . . And he did not come."

Surely Zionists must not bear the sole burden of responsibility for the degradation of these immigrant Jews. Life in Auschwitz, or even in Warsaw and Yemen, exacted its toll. Even in Israel, however, they were still berated as Jews who must be stripped of their religious identification and converted to Zionism. It should not surprise anyone that fifty years later, the bitter memories of this mistreatment remain vivid and inspire anger.

Segev has precisely located the fierce ideological core of Zionist uneasiness, not only with the survivors but with the successive waves of new immigrants who emigrated from the Diaspora after 1948. "The yishuv was permeated with a deep, almost mystic faith in its superiority," Segev writes. "The sabra represented a national ideal." But Holocaust survivors, joined in time by other Diaspora Jews from the Middle East and Africa, symbolized the antithesis of this ideal. They comprised "an inferior race," Hendel wrote, "who had some kind of flaw." Their flaw, of course, was that they were Diaspora Jews.

In historical terms, the Zionists were surely correct: Jews desperately needed their own national home. But for religious Jews in Israel, even for religious Zionists, Israel was anything but a refuge. Rabbi Moshe Zvi Neria, a leader of the B'nei Akiva yeshiva, decried the "sins" of militant secularism.

During a *halakhic* debate over the merit of reciting the *Hallel* prayer on Israeli Independence Day, he insisted: "Only when our release from alien yoke is accompanied by deep cognizance of the great and liberating hand of God, leading to an internal experience of faith—then shall Israel sing a song of praise." Reviewing the first years of Israel's history, he concluded: "We must consider ourselves in a Jewish Diaspora— a harsh and bitter exile—until the Heavens have mercy on us."

Israel was the world's only Jewish state, but disagreements over Jewish identity made it difficult even for Zionists to decide who was a Jew. The Law of Return, enacted by the first Knesset in 1950, declared unequivocally: "Every Jew has the right to immigrate to the country." A few years later, the state had to decide whether Oswald Rufeisen, who had become Brother Daniel of the Carmelite order, was a Jew who was entitled to return. Rufeisen, born in Poland to Jewish parents, had been an active Zionist in his youth. Imprisoned by the Gestapo in 1941, he escaped; with identity papers as a German Christian, he provided Jews in the Mir ghetto with information and weapons that enabled many of them to flee. Again arrested, he found refuge in a convent, where he converted to Christianity. In 1945, Rufeisen became Brother Daniel.

In 1958, Brother Daniel's application for an immigrant certificate under the Law of Return was denied on the ground that "only a person who declares in good faith that he is a Jew, and has no other religion," could be registered as a Jew. According to Jewish law, however, the child of a Jewish mother (which Rufeisen indisputably was), even an apostate, remains a Jew. In the Jewish state, according to *halakha*, Brother Daniel, a Carmelite monk, was still a Jew.

In 1962, the Supreme Court of Israel decided Brother Daniel's appeal. It conceded that the question "who is a Jew" must be resolved on the basis of Jewish law, according to which Brother Daniel was indeed a Jew entitled to immigrate to Israel under the Law of Return. The Law of Return, however, was a secular law, which must be interpreted according to "the popular, Jewish meaning of the term 'Jew.'" The State of Israel, the Court observed, "is not a theocratic state, because it is not religion that orders the lives of its citizens but [civil] law." According to "popular" (rather than Jewish legal) understanding, "a Jew who has converted to Christianity is not called a Jew." Therefore Brother Daniel, the Carmelite monk who was a Jew according to Jewish law, was not a Jew.

What was the connection—if any—between Israeli nationality and Jewish religion? If the rabbinical definition prevailed, then Zionism was shackled to precisely the religious conception of Judaism that it was determined to repudiate. But if the secular definition prevailed (to the outrage of Orthodox ministers in the National Religious party, who resigned from Ben-Gurion's ruling coalition), then the Labor Zionist government might fall from power. Ben-Gurion, caught between a Zionist rock and an Orthodox hard place, finally appointed a special committee that referred the issue to scholars in Israel and the Diaspora for their wise counsel. In the end, the *halakhic* definition prevailed.

But the chasm between Zionism and Judaism, and between Israel and the Diaspora (once conversions performed by Reform and Conservative rabbis abroad were rejected by the Orthodox rabbinate in Israel), continued to widen. The Jewish state still cannot decide who is a Jew, or even who is authorized to decide the question, without bringing its government to the verge of collapse. There could hardly be a more revealing or more disturbing measure of how Zionism has confounded, not resolved, the confusion over Jewish identity in the modern era.

Yet during a single week in June 1967, it seemed that Zionism and Judaism had finally converged with stunning synergy. The world had watched indifferently as Israel confronted the terrifying prospect of a second Holocaust. Then Israel struck. Within six days, it routed Arab armies on three fronts. The Arab dream of driving Jews into the sea suddenly turned into a nightmare of defeat and humiliation. For Jews, the impending tragedy of annihilation became, instead, a miraculous moment of ecstasy.

There was more, much more, than overwhelming relief after a perilous escape from national disaster. It was, in Martin Buber's words, "an abiding astonishment" when Israel suddenly confronted Jewish memory and, some would say, its own destiny as a people of the covenant. Even the most resolutely secular Israelis found themselves deeply affected by their unanticipated encounter with Jewish history.

Kol Israel broadcaster Rafi Amir reached the Western Wall with the first wave of Israeli soldiers that swept through the Old City: "I'm not religious and never have been," he said breathlessly, "but this is the Wall and I am touching the stones of the Western Wall!" He did not "talk with the newspaperman's objectivity," one soldier recalled; "he wasn't articulate, he couldn't even control the recording machine he was carrying. That's why we all felt how history was beating its wings." In that instant, "for the first time," an army major remembered, "I felt not the 'Israelness' but the Jewishness of the nation."

That moment of encounter at the Western Wall, which by now is meaningless to most Israelis, touched even the most battle-hardened soldiers. As "well-springs of emotion and stirrings of the spirit" were released, they wept openly. It was "as though by a flash of lightning truths that were deeply hidden" had suddenly been revealed. The speaker of these words later that month was none other than the brusque general who had commanded the Israeli army to its astonishing victory, Yitzhak Rabin—a man not known for his spiritual stirrings.

Nor was the Western Wall, or even Jerusalem, the entire story. As the Jordanian army fled from Judea and Samaria, Israel returned to the most ancient holy places in the biblical homeland of the Jewish people. A kibbutznik instantly grasped the meaning of this encounter with biblical history: "The whole of the Promised Land is ours." The "sense of salvation and of direct confrontation with Jewish history," expressed by one soldier, was unmistakable to others—and, for many, overwhelming.

In the months following the Six Day War, staunchly secular soldiers, kibbutzniks all, repeatedly expressed their new sense of Jewish identification. The paratroopers who touched the Western Wall that June day, one recalled, instantly confronted "the whole history of the Jewish people." "I felt it," conceded Avi from Kibbutz Mishmar Hasharon. "I became one with the House of David, the Kingdom of Solomon, and the Temple. I feel as if a curtain has suddenly lifted and the very letters of the Eternal Book have sprung to life, familiar and immediate. I am no longer a stranger. . . . Suddenly I am a son of my people. . . . The Land of Israel, the Land of our Fathers becomes a reality."

Such feelings of Jewish identification instantly bridged the divide between secular Israelis and religious Jews. An Israeli paratrooper, an Orthodox Jew who fought in the decisive battle for Jerusalem, recalled: "I felt as if I had been granted the great privilege of acting as an agent of God, of Jewish history." Watching other soldiers weep at the Western Wall, he knew that his army friends, "kibbutz-educated toward an attitude of scorn for traditional religious values, [were] now overwhelmed by a feeling of holiness, and as elated and moved as I was." There is "in all of us," he concluded, "in the entire Jewish people, an intense quality of Jewishness that is neither destroyed by education nor blurred by foreign ideologies and values."

Suddenly, and finally, Israelis had discovered that they were, at bottom, Jews. Zionism was transformed. The return to Jerusalem, to the Western Wall, to Rachel's Tomb, and to Machpelah in Hebron was not merely a return to ancient holy places but an encounter with "the formative roots of the Jewish People." As secular Israelis found their buried Jewish identity, religious Jews discovered the hidden promise of Zionism. In an astonishing moment of reconciliation, Israelis and Jews encountered each other, inside themselves.

But that passionate moment of Jewish unity, when personal identity converged with national destiny, was short-lived. The counterpoint, from the secular left, was articulated by an aspiring young writer whose first novel was nearing publication. Born in Jerusalem in 1939, he had grown up at the seam between the Jewish and Arab sectors of the city. His parents, the Klausners, were European refugees who had fled to Palestine to escape Hitler. Young Klausner attended "a Hebrew school with strong National Religious leanings, where I was taught to yearn for the glory of ancient Jewish kingdoms and to long for their resurrection in blood and fire." Instead, he was destined to become "a plain tough Israeli, fair-haired and free from Jewish neuroses."

At age fourteen, two years after his mother's suicide, the boy fled from Jerusalem, which he remembered as "a lunatic town" filled with dreamers and zealots. In Kibbutz Hulda, where the Jewish indoctrination of his childhood yielded to the socialist indoctrination of his adult years, Klausner was reborn as Amos Oz. On the kibbutz, he studied "the origins of the Jewish disease," learning how to liberate his own children from "certain Jewish and Jerusalemite afflictions that tormented my parents and their parents and me myself."

With his personal transformation, the Jerusalem of Klausner's boyhood became "an alien city" to the adult Oz. Located at the end of the road at the edge of the state, it was "not within the State of Israel, but along side it; Jerusalem as opposed to Israel." Returning after the Six Day War had reunified the city, Oz experienced intense isolation and despair. Not only was he estranged from the defeated Arabs, who "hate me, wish me dead." His trepidation over the implications of the Israeli victory deprived him of the exultation that surged among his compatriots. "I was not born to sound the trumpet or liberate lands from foreign yokes," he wrote (more than once) with evident anguish.

For Oz, as for the secular left whose most eloquent spokesman he became, 1967 meant Jewish tragedy, not triumph. It was a lost possibility (for peace now), not a precious opportunity (to reconcile Zionism and Judaism). The increasingly violent Israeli-Palestinian struggle over disputed land was merely "a clash between right and right." (Oz had learned at Kibbutz Hulda that the Palestinians "not only had a point of view, but a fairly convincing one at that.") Indeed, it almost seemed to Oz like a trivial disagreement; "nothing but a dispute over property: whose house?"

Had not the use of force, Oz wondered in a spasm of guilt, negated the right of Jews to their ancient homeland? But why, he was asked incredulously, should Israel regret having won a war that it had never wanted, "almost as if winning was a catastrophe?" Was Zionism invalid because the Palestinians, with bombs and guns and knives, belatedly asserted a counter-claim? Oz replied: "I think it's all a tragedy . . . when both sides are a hundred per cent in the right." He was quite willing "to visit the Western Wall as a tourist, just so long as there's peace. . . . It doesn't matter a

fig to me if in order to [pray there], [Jews] have to get a Jordanian stamp." The dreary Tel Aviv suburb of Holon, where
Oz first fell in love, was a far more important part of his
"homeland" than Hebron.

Oz's response is a most revealing expression of the deep
malaise of secular Zionism, so hopelessly remote from Jewish tradition, culture, and identity. Oz would plead for his
right, as a Jew, "to decide what I will choose from this great
inheritance" of Judaism; indeed, "to 'import' and combine
with my inheritance what I see fit," yet still call it Judaism.
Enlightenment and emancipation had encouraged the rendezvous between Judaism and the West, which was "a fateful one, formative, constitutional, irrevocable." Nobody, Oz
concluded, "will force us to choose . . . between our Judaism and humanism."

There may be no more eloquent statement of the tragedy of Zionist assimilation. The notion that Judaism is infi-
nitely malleable, comprising any "import" that an individual
Jew may select for inclusion, is historically absurd. Judaism
never meant, and could hardly mean, anything a Jew wants,
or does. This may describe how a Jew behaves in a shopping
mall, but it fails abysmally to define a culture so richly en-
dowed by history, language, text, memory, and ritual, as well
as some time-honored processes for determining where lines
may, must, or must not be drawn. The notion that one must
choose between "humanism" and "Judaism" demonstrates
an astonishing ignorance of the humanistic precepts that
have been deeply embedded in Judaism ever since Sinai.

So it was, during a single fateful week in June 1967,
that the internal contradictions of Zionism, suppressed during twenty years of struggle to create and secure the Jewish
state, were propelled to the surface of Israeli consciousness.
Soon there were Zionists for whom the return to Judea,
Samaria, and Jerusalem, to the very heart of Zion, might

yet infuse the Zionist revolution with Jewish content. Then the Zionist revolution could spread beyond the Hula swamps and coastal orange groves, beyond Tel Aviv, even beyond Oz's beloved Holon and Kibbutz Hulda. It would finally penetrate the Samarian and Judean hills, all the way from biblical Shechem to Hebron, where Jewish history in the Land of Israel began.

After 1967, Israel confronted an extraordinary opportunity to fulfill its destiny as a Jewish state. Not as a theocracy, a *halakhic* state ruled by rabbis. Rather, a state in which the convergence of Zionism and Judaism could finally repair the serious fissures in Jewish identity that had opened with emancipation and deepened, with Zionism, in the modern era. But the Six Day War, which gave Israelis the opportunity to become Jews, turned out to be a squandered opportunity that may never return. Nineteen sixty-seven was the turning point that did not turn, the historical moment when Zionists could have tapped the most ancient and enduring sources of Jewish—and Zionist—inspiration, but failed to seize the opportunity.

Why, in the end, did it not turn? Because Jews who had already submitted to the enticements of emancipation were helpless to reverse the process. Too many Israelis believed that Western culture (the very culture whose defenders had done so much to decimate Jews and eviscerate Judaism) offered the best escape from the excruciating burdens of Jewish history.

Yet there actually were Jews, called "settlers"—a badge of Zionist honor back when kibbutzniks wore it—who seized the historical moment after 1967. Endlessly vilified ever since as fanatical zealots who would drag Israel into a holy war with Arabs or a civil war between Jews, they remain an uncomfortable reminder of lost Zionist opportunity.

The settlers were Zionists who rejected the fateful

synthesis between Judaism and Western modernity for an older, deeper Jewish synthesis of religion and nationalism. They grasped the future settlement of Judea and Samaria as a defining moment for the Jewish people, the outcome of which might, finally and decisively, determine the character and fate of the Zionist experiment.

Zionism, as a Jewish settler in Ofra once reminded Amos Oz, "has always stood up against overwhelming odds, on the brink of lunatic daring." Yet the daring of this new generation of settlers, who adopted all the classic Zionist techniques of settlement—"another stake, another goat, another acre"—has already been shunted beyond the pale of Zionist legitimacy.

Secular Israelis speak bitterly, even maliciously, about the newest wave of Zionist settlers, while simultaneously touting themselves as paragons of enlightened opinion. Were their comments made anywhere outside Israel, they surely would be accused—and rightly so—of anti-Semitism. Indeed, of late there is far more seething hostility toward rabbis, religious Jews, and Judaism in the Jewish state than anywhere else in the world.

A Jewish state that finally fused Zionism with Judaism, modern Israel with the biblical Land of Israel, might have truly enlarged and fulfilled the Zionist revolution. Instead, the inner contradictions of that revolution wrench Zionism and Judaism, Israelis and Jews, ever further apart.

5

The Return

to the

Biblical

Homeland

More than any other issue since 1967, Jewish settlement in Judea and Samaria, formerly the West Bank of the Kingdom of Jordan, has sharply polarized Israeli domestic politics and vastly complicated its foreign policy, especially its diplomatic relations with the United States. Understandably so, since the settlements raise some of the most tormenting questions of Jewish religious and Israeli national identity and, indeed, the ultimate meaning of Zionism. Their fate is likely to determine whether the movement for Jewish national liberation becomes yet another form of Jewish assimilation in the modern era.

The most controversial settlement has always been Hebron, where, ironically, the Jewish people has its ancient historical roots in the Land of Israel. Hebron is deeply intertwined with the biblical narrative of the Jewish people.

Abraham's purchase of the Machpelah caves as tombs for Sarah and their descendants gave the Jewish people its first legal title in the Land of Israel. Many centuries later, David was anointed king of Israel in Hebron and established his kingdom there. The Jewish claim to Hebron is, if anything, more venerable than the claim to Jerusalem.

An argument against Jewish settlement in Hebron, as elsewhere in Judea and Samaria, might as readily be turned against Zionist settlement in any land claimed by Palestinians for their own national home, which includes virtually all of Israel. The Jews in Hebron are surrounded by a large Arab majority; but the first Zionist settlers in Palestine also were vastly outnumbered by Arabs. (Indeed, the biblical text records that when Abraham entered the promised land, the Canaanites were already there.) By slaughtering Jews in 1929, Hebron Arabs made the city *judenrein*. But when has a hostile majority (with Jewish blood on its hands, no less) ever nullified either divine promise or a Zionist claim? Too casually dismissed by their political enemies, both in Israel and the United States, as "zealots for Zion," Hebron's Jews still carry the Zionist torch, at considerable personal and communal risk of Arab hostility and Israeli betrayal.

On Independence Day 1967, just weeks before the outbreak of war, Rabbi Tzvi Yehuda Kook, head of the Mercaz HaRav yeshiva in Jerusalem, spoke at a celebratory gathering of his students. Rabbi Kook, the only son and revered disciple of the renowned Chief Rabbi of Mandatory Palestine, Abraham Isaac Kook, who had struggled valiantly to fuse Judaism and Zionism, recounted the biblical holy places that still lay outside the borders of modern Israel. Nearing the end of his list, he inquired sorrowfully: "Where is our Hebron? Do we let it be forgotten?"

Within a month, Hebron, along with Jericho, Shechem, Shiloh, and the entire Old City of Jerusalem, belonged to

Israel. As the Six Day War ended, with the area around the Western Wall secured, a military jeep was dispatched to Mercaz HaRav to bring the elderly Rabbi Kook to the holiest site of the Jewish people, now restored to Jewish hands for the first time in nineteen centuries. In a ceremony at the ancient Jewish cemetery on the Mount of Olives, Moshe Dayan, who had commanded the battle for Jerusalem, proclaimed: "We have returned to the cradle of our people, to the inheritance of the Patriarchs. . . . We have returned to Hebron." Israel, that is, had returned to Jewish history.

But the heart of biblical Israel was, and had long been, without Jews. Not only were Jews prohibited by Jordanian law from living anywhere in the kingdom; it was (and still is) a capital offense under Jordanian law even to sell property to a Jew. When Dayan spoke with such evident feeling about the Jewish "return," not a single Jew lived anywhere in Judea and Samaria, nor in the Old City of Jerusalem—across what came to be known as the "Green Line." But the relationship between Zionism and Judaism, as many Israelis discovered that June, was irrepressible.

Rabbi Moshe Levinger, a recent graduate of the Mercaz HaRav yeshiva, remembered Rabbi Kook's poignant prewar question about Hebron. Levinger was an ascetic loner who had worked for a time as a shepherd on a kibbutz near the Syrian-occupied Golan Heights. After the war, he met with Elyakim Haetzni, a German-born lawyer in Tel Aviv. Haetzni was active in the new Land of Israel movement, comprising mostly secular Israelis (many from Labor party circles) who believed that the State of Israel must include the historic Land of Israel within its borders. Levinger and Haetzni drafted a newspaper advertisement, seeking Jews who might be willing to resettle the biblical homeland.

Meeting at Haetzni's office or in a café in north Tel Aviv, they planned settlement strategy. Their primary objective was Hebron, the city of the patriarchs and matriarchs of the Jewish people where virtually no Jews had lived since the massacre of 1929, when scores were slaughtered by marauding Arab mobs. Failing in attempts to buy apartments in the fiercely Islamic city, they decided to rent the Park Hotel for the Passover holiday.

On April 4, 1968, a dozen Jewish families arrived in Hebron to celebrate Passover. The celebrants included many future leaders of the settlement movement: Moshe and Miriam Levinger, Rabbis Eliezer Waldman and Haim Druckman, *Ma'ariv* journalist Yisrael Harel, Benny Katzover, and Rabbi Shlomo Aviner (who would subsequently lead Jews back to abandoned Jewish properties in the Old City of Jerusalem). When the holiday ended, they announced their intention to remain in Hebron.

The Hebron contingent, for the most part, comprised religiously observant Jews. But as even their most hostile critics have conceded, "they also spoke in the name of the very right upon which the Zionist claim to Eretz Israel has always been founded"—the right, that is, of Jews to live within the borders of their historic homeland. Embracing Zionism, they nonetheless offered a radical revision of it. Their purpose, explained one of their rabbis, "is not the normalization of the people of Israel—to be a nation like all other nations—but to be a holy people, a people of a living God."

Amid persistent efforts to delegitimate the settlers, it is often forgotten that the Levinger group received significant assistance from Israeli government officials who surely recognized familiar Zionist principles in the new settlement movement. Successive prime ministers from the ruling Labor party, first Levi Eshkol, then Golda Meir and Yitzhak Rabin, gave at least tacit support. Yigal Allon, the deputy prime minister, explicitly encouraged the return to Hebron. Shimon Peres supported it. Once Jews were there, defense minister Dayan canceled expulsion orders. Former prime minister David Ben-Gurion, the aging lion of Jewish statehood, had written to Levinger at the Park Hotel: "Hebron is still awaiting redemption, and there is no redemption without extensive Jewish settlement."

There was, for a time, reason to believe that a new synthesis between Zionism and Judaism could emerge from settlement efforts in Hebron. Surely the governing Labor elite would not have offered support to a renegade band of misguided religious fanatics. Perhaps the Hebron settlers, brimming with energy and determination, reminded them of their own youthful Zionist zeal, now dimmed by age and political expediency. Certainly they knew that Zionism was not merely a mandate for Jews to return to the coastal plain once inhabited by the ancient Philistines. They may even have realized that Rabbi Levinger was a Zionist with a *kipa*, no more and no less. Settlement of the Land of Israel, after all, was what Zionism had always claimed to be about.

The Levinger group was unrelenting. Relocated from the Park Hotel to the military governor's compound, its members remained obdurate. After four months, the Israeli cabinet finally permitted them to open a yeshiva near the Machpelah tombs, where they insisted upon their right to pray. That fall, during the holiday of Succoth, hundreds of Jews came to Hebron for the first time in more than three decades to worship at the ancient shrine. Outside Machpelah, as they awaited entry to the burial chambers (from which Moslems had barred them for seven centuries), a hand grenade was thrown in their midst. More than forty Jews were seriously wounded. The Israeli cabinet quickly responded by authorizing a new community, Kiryat Arba (the name of biblical Hebron), to be built on a hill overlooking the city.

Levinger remained a leader in search of followers. Except

for Kiryat Arba, and the tiny bloc of restored Jewish settlements in Gush Etzion, near Jerusalem, the pre-1967 boundaries continued to separate Israelis from their ancient
homeland. But the devastating shock of the Yom Kippur
War, six years later, changed everything. The carefully co-
ordinated Egyptian and Syrian attack, on the holiest day of
the Jewish year, punctured the bubble of Israeli invulner-
ability and severely weakened the hold of the ruling Labor
party.

The postwar political disarray sparked the emergence
of a new movement. Gush Emunim (Bloc of the Faithful),
an offshoot of the National Religious party, recruited actively among graduates of the Mercaz HaRav yeshiva. Its
manifesto, blending political Zionism and Orthodox Judaism, called for "a grand movement of reawakening within
the people of Israel in order to fulfill the Zionist vision in
its entirety." Kiryat Arba became its model for settling Judea
and Samaria.

Gush Emunim sharply challenged the Herzlian assumptions that had first inspired and then inhibited Labor Zionism. The idea of Zionist normalization was anathema to
Gush settlers, who wanted Israel to fulfill its destiny as a
holy people, not become a nation like other nations. "We
have not settled here to look for peace and quiet," insisted
Rabbi Meir Yehiel; "we have come here despite the sound
and fury, in order to fulfill the Lord's command."

In the waning years of Labor party rule between 1974
and 1977, Gush leaders capitalized upon government weakness and internal division. It skillfully played off rival politicians to secure support for its settlement activities from
Prime Minister Rabin and his cabinet. Menachem Begin's
stunning electoral victory in 1977 emboldened Gush
Emunim to intensify its pressure on the government to open
Judea and Samaria to Jewish settlement.

Hebron, just down the hill from Kiryat Arba, still ranked highest among Rabbi Levinger's priorities. Although the geographical balance of holiness in Judaism had long since tilted toward Jerusalem, Hebron remained one of the four holy cities of Israel. Jews had lived there and prayed outside the ancestral tombs until the murderous Arab terror in 1929 drove them away. Among the abandoned Jewish properties in Hebron was Beit Hadassah, a decrepit old medical clinic building in the city center, just a short walk from Machpelah.

One night in the early spring of 1979, Miriam Levinger and a small group of women from Kiryat Arba, accompanied by their children, suddenly moved into Beit Hadassah. Mrs. Levinger, the American-born daughter of Hasidic refugees from Hungary, was a mother of eleven who was about to become a formidable political activist. The women refused to leave or relinquish their children. Hebron, she insisted, "will no longer be *judenrein*."

The tactics honed by the Levingers in Hebron were applied to settlements in Sebastia, Kedumim, Elon Moreh, and Shechem. Small groups of settlers, taking the military and political authorities by surprise, would establish a temporary presence near an ancient biblical site. Then they refused to leave, finally accepting the "compromise" of a yeshiva. Acquiescing in their temporary evacuation to a nearby military base, they waited months, even years, until the government finally wearied of the stalemate and granted permission for a permanent community.

Except for their religious commitment, the Gush Emunim activists followed the classic Zionist settlement formula. Like the *halutzim* who had drained the swamps and tilled the rock-strewn terraces of the Galilee, they reclaimed the Land of Israel "dunam by dunam." Their new outposts in Judea and Samaria resembled nothing more than the old Zionist "watchtower-and-stockade" settlements that had once dotted the northern Galilee and the Jezreel Valley during the heyday of Zionist pioneering.

Israelis have struggled to reconcile the settlements with, or distinguish them from, their pioneering Labor Zionist antecedents. More evocatively than any other Israeli writer, Amos Oz has confronted the settlement issue. Drawn to and repelled by them, he has engaged with the settlers only to castigate them for daring to reconcile Zionism with Judaism. Oz's book *In the Land of Israel* offers a remarkable glimpse of secular Zionist agony—and fury—as the torch of Zionist passion passed to a new generation of religious Zionists. Deeply troubled by the spasm of religious ecstasy that Israel experienced after the Six Day War, Oz understood that the future of Jewish settlements would fatefully define Israel and Zionism for generations to come. The struggle, he realized, was over nothing less than "the nature of Zionism and even the meaning of Jewish destiny."

In Ofra, Oz listened as Yisrael Harel, editor of *Nekuda* (the settlers' newspaper) and chairman of the Council of Jewish Settlements, described "the major barricade" in Israel "that divides the Jews from the Israelis." Jews, Harel insisted, were guided by Torah, but Israelis yearned to become "a satellite of Western culture." Zionism, he noted, had always stood "on the brink of lunatic daring"; but now, among ordinary Israelis who craved normal lives, its meaning had been diluted into "pleasure-seeking and personal gratification"—a Zionism, that is, of "spiritual desiccation."

Oz's response, his "Argument on Life and Death," has lost none of its urgency or eloquence. It is an impassioned credo of secular Zionist hostility to the infusion of Zionism with religious meaning. It also bears witness, more than Oz might have cared to acknowledge, to the remarkably impoverished Jewish content of secular Zionism.

The Jewish religion, for Oz, was a debilitating sickness

for which Zionist normalization was the only cure. Unending conflict with Arabs, now fed by land claims grounded in biblical sources, was "pushing us back into our 'hereditary' depression, into the neuroses, the atavistic tribal madness from which we were trying to escape." This language of pathology suggested that for Oz, religion still remained hopelessly enmeshed in painful childhood memories of his mother's mental illness.

Oz ruefully conceded that the emergence of Gush Emunim settlers had struck "a blow to the ego of the youth in the kibbutzim and the Labor movement." These Zionist exemplars—the Zionist "firstborn"—had been "swindled" (a pointed reference to the biblical Jacob story) by religious nationalist upstarts. Suddenly, in Judea and Samaria, there were "people who were masquerading in *their* sloppy army jackets, running around on hilltops with submachine guns and walkie-talkies, who had adopted the mannerisms and the slang of the kibbutz." It was, to Oz, "as if here were the heirs of the pioneering spark that had dimmed." His sense of Zionist displacement was palpable—and entirely justified.

But it was Harel's distinction between "rootless Israelis" and "authentic Jews" that stung Oz most deeply. It provoked his fervent defense of the modern "marriage" between "the Jewish heritage and the European humanist experience." Rejecting any "'purist' return to the sources," Oz raised only to dismiss the rather striking parallel between the Zionist embrace of Western culture and the fateful attraction of ancient Jews to Hellenism. The modern rendezvous of Judaism with the West, for Oz, was "formative," "irrevocable"—and an unequivocal blessing.

As a modern Jew who responded to the siren song of emancipation, Oz perceived "certain astounding genetic similarities" between Judaism and Western humanism. Judaism, he noted proudly, had "assimilated" with Western

humanism in the modern era. It was all the more imperative, therefore, that it resist the "dangerous threat" of religious nationalism, which would transport Israel from its
convergence with modern liberalism back to "fanatical trib-
alism, brutal and closed."

To Oz, Judaism meant little more than an assortment
of personal choices from the vast cornucopia of Western
possibilities. "I am free to decide what I will choose from
this great inheritance," he insisted. Rejecting "ritual" for
"creativity" (a false but convenient polarity between ossi-
fied Judaism and exuberant Zionism), Oz defended the in-
trusion of "outside influences" from the West upon Jewish
culture in Israel.

Exalting the convergence of Judaism with freedom of
choice, Oz vividly illuminated its dangers. His metaphor of
"marriage"—in reality, the intermarriage of Zionism with
Western culture—was no less revealing than his choice of
"assimilation" to describe it. For it was precisely the Zionist longing for intermarriage and assimilation with the West
against which the Jews of Judea and Samaria had rebelled.

Oz's irritation was evident. The Ofra settlers, after all,
were not *haredim*, ultra-Orthodox Jews whose unyielding
theological opposition to Zionism made them anathema to
virtually every Zionist. These were, quite obviously, impassioned and committed Zionists. They joined the elite
units of the army, served longer than necessary, and then
invested themselves in Zionist settlement—precisely as
kibbutzniks had done after the War of Independence. Even
Oz seemed to concede that they were more than deserving
of the Zionist birthright.

Oz was not immune to the magical allure to Jews of
their ancient biblical homeland. He acknowledged "the elusive cunning of the Biblical charm of this landscape"—the
weathered hills and stone terraces, the fig trees and grape

arbors, the flocks of sheep and goats that grazed near deep cisterns like those once dug by Abraham and redug by Isaac. To Oz, however, there was nothing Jewish about it. The charm was "Arab, through and through."

Israelis could continue to gaze upon Judea and Samaria from afar—or, at least, from across the Green Line—but, like Moses at Moab, they were fated not to enter it. "For if you should enter," Oz warned, "the Biblical charm will fade like a dream. The penetration will not be one of harmony, but of occupation and capitulation and destruction." His peroration expressed precisely the argument against the Zionist penetration of Palestine made by Arabs—and by anti-Zionist Jews—ever since the first Zionist settlers arrived a century earlier.

In Hebron and Kiryat Arba, as in Ofra and Ariel, Israelis were not persuaded. They came; they outwitted the government; they stayed; their numbers increased; they defied their Arab enemies and Zionist critics alike. "The Levingers told me they would never move," recalled the Israeli military commander of Hebron. The only Jews in a city where they were surrounded by hostile Moslems, amid wretched surroundings and with minimal provisions, they held firm.

In the end, Miriam Levinger and her band of women and children from Kiryat Arba stymied the Begin government. It would not evict Jews from one of the four holy cities of Israel; but neither would it sanction their presence among one hundred thousand Arabs. Calculating that the primitive living conditions and Arab hostility would drive the women back to Kiryat Arba, the government merely instructed the army to prevent Rabbi Levinger and the other husbands from joining them. "There might be bloodshed here," responded Sarah Nahshon, "but we won't leave Beit Hadassah." She was correct on both counts.

After several months of negotiations with the Begin

government, and the murder of a young yeshiva student near Beit Hadassah, the government finally granted permission for several families to live in the abandoned building. That December, Hanukkah candles flickered in the windows of Beit Hadassah for the first time in fifty years. It was not an easy life. Jews were stabbed, stoned, and shot; their homes were fire-bombed. To many Israelis, however, they deserved what they got for giving Israel such a bad name in the editorial pages of Western newspapers.

On an early May sabbath in 1980, a group of Kiryat Arba yeshiva students left evening prayers at Machpelah to recite *kiddush* at Beit Hadassah before returning to their dormitories. Along the way, they sang a verse from the Book of Jeremiah: *"V'shavu banim l'gvulam"* (your children shall return to their country). Passing the spot where the yeshiva student had been murdered just three months earlier, they continued along King Faisal Street toward Beit Hadassah.

It was an especially tense time in Hebron. The head of the Kiryat Arba municipal council had warned the Israeli military governor that the security situation had deteriorated, but the army officer reassured him. Jews were the daily targets of Arab hostility, but Defense Minister Ezer Weizman counseled restraint. Israel, he explained to the Knesset, must respect "world opinion."

Just as the yeshiva students began to cross the footbridge leading to Beit Hadassah, they were caught in a murderous crossfire of grenades and bullets from four Arabs stationed on nearby rooftops and in doorways. Six young men (including an American winner of the Congressional Medal of Honor in Vietnam) were killed; sixteen were injured. The slaughter outside Beit Hadassah was neither the beginning nor end of Arab terror in Hebron. On a July morning in 1983, Aharon Gross, an eighteen-year-old yeshiva student, was brutally stabbed to death in the Hebron casbah. The toll of terror victims steadily mounted.

The Israeli government was trapped in a dilemma of its own making. It would neither evict Jews from Hebron nor adequately protect them. Soldiers were under tight restraining orders. "I thought I'd be put in jail if I opened fire," one soldier explained. "Better one of your people than one of ours," an army commander responded after a yeshiva student was murdered. Rabbi Levinger reported conversations with soldiers who assured him, "If we get the right order, we'll solve the problem." The right order never came.

The Hebron Jews persisted. Slowly, they rebuilt their community in the neighborhood founded by Rabbi Malchiel Ashkenazi after his expulsion from Spain in 1492. The Avraham Avinu Synagogue, the religious center of Jewish life in Hebron for nearly five hundred years until it was razed by the Jordanians in 1948 and replaced with a goat sty and public urinal, was restored. The Machpelah tombs, closed to Jews by the Moslems for seven hundred years, were open to daily Jewish prayer. On the Tel Rumeida hilltop, a caravan of mobile homes became the nucleus of a new community.

The stereotypical Hebron settler was easily identifiable in the media by his knitted *kipa*, dangling *tzitzit*, and cocked uzzi. The reality was more complex; indeed, the Hebron Jewish community comprised a virtual microcosm of the country itself: a rabbi whose parents had fled the Nazis; a secular Israeli from Tel Aviv; an aging (female) veteran of the Stern Gang; a lawyer who often represented Arabs in Israeli courts; and modest young women, variously named "Rutie" or "Etty," who extended home hospitality to visitors while young children played at their feet.

In 1984, several prominent residents of Hebron and Kiryat Arba were arrested, tried, and convicted for terrorist activities. They belonged to a Jewish underground, which had planted car bombs that seriously injured the Arab mayors of Nablus and Ramallah, launched an attack on the Islamic College in Hebron that killed three students and wounded three dozen, and plotted to bomb Arab buses in Jerusalem to avenge the deaths of Jews. For some members, who located their plans at the outermost edge of destructive fantasy, the ultimate goal was destruction of the Dome of the Rock in Jerusalem in order to hasten the building of the third temple where its predecessors had once been located.

Israelis were stunned by the exposure and arrest of the underground. Many of its members not only came from yeshivas and settlements, widely assumed to be breeding grounds for violence, but from mainstream Zionist institutions like the army and kibbutzim. There were as many war heroes as yeshiva graduates; Golan settlers and Jerusalemites were arrested along with residents of Hebron. Among the convicted were members of elite army brigades, graduates of the Mercaz HaRav yeshiva, and a son-in-law of Rabbi Levinger.

Several rabbis from Kiryat Arba and Hebron, including Levinger, had been consulted by members of the underground. The implication of rabbis, at least in the planning stages, suggested that terrorism "was not marginal but central" to religious Zionism. Critics—the underground had few defenders, even among settlers—attributed this disturbing display of Jewish "extralegalism, vigilantism, . . . and finally, indiscriminate mass terrorism" to the misguided religious messianism of the settlers, which had finally festered into fanatical zeal.

The author of this impassioned accusation, which became the accepted academic indictment of the Jews of Judea and Samaria, was political scientist Ehud Sprinzak. He was galvanized by the Gush Emunim underground (and by the election of the right-wing rabbi Meir Kahane to the Knesset soon thereafter) to study—and harshly condemn—what he branded Israel's "radical right."

The "radical right" was an American conceptual import dating from the mid-fifties. It had been used to explain—but mostly to condemn—the political ascent of Senator Joseph R. McCarthy and his anti-Communist crusade. Employed by American social scientists, the "radical right" was less an analytical concept than the ascription of paranoia and pathology to the political enemies of liberal intellectuals.

What all this had to do with Israeli political culture, as even Sprinzak conceded, was not readily apparent. But the "radical right" did offer a useful rubric for tarring Israeli settlers with the brush of messianic fanaticism. Suddenly, Zionist history was clarified: from Jabotinsky's Revisionists in the pre-state era through Begin's Likud, and beyond Gush Emunim to the outermost fringe of Rabbi Kahane's tiny Kach movement, the entire Zionist right wing was implicated in a sustained conspiracy to undermine Israeli democracy.

The Israeli "radical right" might envision itself as "perfect Zionists, the true inheritors" of the *halutzim* and fighters for Israeli independence. But this, to Sprinzak, was "a paranoic" delusion. It fed a "conspiracy mentality" that combined "ultranationalism, militarism, ethnocentrism, and religiosity" into a frightening mix of fanaticism and terror.

Yet precisely these pejorative labels—except for "religiosity"—had once been used by anti-Zionists to besmirch Labor Zionism. Only religious commitment—the firm identification of Zionism with Judaism—can explain the sharpness of Sprinzak's critique of the entire settlement movement. For Sprinzak, Gush Emunim was a "religious raid into the heart of secular Israel." Its "Judaization" of

Israel was an alarming prospect. It simply made no sense to a secular Israeli academic that Zionism and Judaism might have valid historical reasons for convergence.

The problem of violent Jewish retaliation deeply embarrassed Israel in the eyes of a disapproving West. Yet "most acts of settler vigilantism," even Sprinzak conceded, "were triggered by Arab harassments." Especially in Hebron, however, "harassment" was an astonishingly mild word for the incessantly violent assaults directed against Jews. The "intense paranoia" that Sprinzak attributed to Jews in Judea and Samaria was, by his own admission, solidly grounded in the realities of daily life for Jews living among hostile Arabs.

For Sprinzak, as for his Labor Zionist predecessors, the Labor Zionist tradition was the only true Zionism. The very idea of legitimate political opposition had always seemed self-evidently contradictory to the Labor Zionist elite. Ben-Gurion, after all, brought Israel to the brink of civil war at the very moment of its founding to crush, with military force, his right-wing political opponents. He long refused to refer to Menachem Begin by name in Knesset debate, lest this imply recognition of Begin's political existence. (To Ben-Gurion, Begin was merely "the gentleman next to Mr. Bader.") To Sprinzak, the challenge from the Israeli right wing was not an example of democracy at work, but "a serious indication of the decline of Israeli democracy."

Jewish settlers were relentlessly demonized by American Jews, who had no desire to be implicated in Israeli behavior that offended liberal precepts, media pundits, or American presidents. American analysts of these "Zealots for Zion" (as journalist Robert I. Friedman labeled the Jews of Judea and Samaria) expected the Jewish state to be a miniature United States. They judged it harshly when it failed to comply with American standards.

Friedman, a *Village Voice* reporter, located Jewish settlements within Israel's "colonial pursuits" and "sins of occupation." Settlement activity made Israel "a right-wing apartheid state-in-the-making." His indictment of a Zionism "debased by the zealots" recycled virtually every anti-Israel cliché in the arsenal of the political left. Nothing was more troubling, of course, than the damage done by settlers "to Israel's image as a democracy." For that, of course, every American Jew might be held accountable.

To Professor Ian Lustick (then of Dartmouth College), Jewish "fundamentalism" violated conventional American assumptions about "what Israel and Israelis are all about." The problem was less the damage that religious zealots might inflict on Israel than their potential for undermining American strategic interests in the Middle East. The Jews of Judea and Samaria were driven by an "uncompromising, dogmatically based, and comprehensive" ideology of redemption that drove them to reject the natural, rational (and characteristically American) preference for pragmatism. If unrestrained, they would "plunge the Jewish state into a true Kulturkampf" that could undermine its "social democratic tradition."

Lustick was deeply troubled, as were other American Jews, by the settlers' synthesis of Orthodox Judaism and Zionism. Their preference for an authentically Jewish government in Israel, rather than for a "Western-style liberal democracy," was inexplicable, and unforgivable. Such a "highly parochial brand of Jewish redemptionism" sharply contradicted "Western liberal/democratic values." The task for policy-makers, in Israel and the United States, was to "undermine the attractiveness of the fundamentalist message." Indeed, a liberal democratic government in Israel must be prepared "to use tough, possibly ruthless methods" against its Jewish opponents.

Lustick justified ruthlessness in pursuit of liberalism (a venerable Labor Zionist tactic) because a fundamentalist Israel "would destroy the special relationship" between the Jewish state and the United States. American interests in the Middle East would be jeopardized by right-wing rabbis in Israel no less than by Moslem mullahs in Iran. The United States must make it clear to Israel that financial and military aid depended upon shared "democratic, libertarian, and universalistic values." It was in American interests "to divide, isolate, and defeat" religious fundamentalist ideology wherever it appeared. Coercion in the name of freedom was entirely appropriate.

At the core of the disagreement over Jewish settlement in Judea and Samaria was the nagging dilemma of Jewish modernity: would Jews finally become "normal," all but indistinguishable (except, perhaps, for a few quaint customs) from their Gentile neighbors? American critics of the settlers, like their Israeli counterparts, demanded Zionist normalization. That invariably implied accommodation to American norms as the overriding Zionist priority.

Yet certain Jewish settlements remained above reproach. The legitimacy of Gush Etzion, the Labor Zionist cluster of kibbutzim overrun by Arabs in 1948 and rebuilt after the Six Day War, was widely accepted across the Israeli political spectrum. Gush Etzion, a sentimental favorite, preserved a cherished link to the glorious pioneering days of Labor Zionism in the pre-state *yishuv*.

In time, Ariel and Efrat also became palatable. In appearance, at least, they were an extension of Israeli suburbia. With their tile-roofed villas, verdant lawns, barbecue grills, tennis courts, and swimming pools, they symbolize affluence, moderation, and civility, not religious zeal. Similarly, Ma'ale Adumim, in the Judean hills between Jerusalem and Jericho, could be justified for security reasons. But

Hebron and Kiryat Arba, where the most unyielding religious Zionists live, remained beyond the pale of Zionist legitimacy.

In 1994, when Dr. Baruch Goldstein of Kiryat Arba massacred twenty-nine Moslems at prayer in Machpelah, all the Jews of Hebron and Kiryat Arba—and, indeed, throughout Judea and Samaria—were routinely, and recklessly, demonized. Despised in Israel and abroad, they were denounced as Hamas terrorists wrapped in *tefillin*, poised to shed innocent blood, sabotage Middle Eastern peace, even plunge Israel into civil war. Jewish settlers were the only Jews, anywhere in the world, whom it was permissible to loathe and revile without being accused of anti-Semitism.

But the Shamgar Commission, appointed to investigate the Goldstein massacre, confirmed the angry allegations of settlers that the government of Israel had not adequately protected them. Ever since the outbreak of the Palestinian *intifada*, five years earlier, all Jews living in Judea and Samaria had become vulnerable to Arab terrorist attacks. According to the commission's statistics, there had been more than 150,000 reported instances of rock-throwing, 5,655 firebomb attacks, nearly 3,000 assaults and knifings, 821 shooting incidents, and 256 hand-grenade attacks. In five years, 64 Israelis were killed and nearly 4,000 were injured.

In portions of its report that received little public attention, the commission noted that "the [Israeli] authorities' helplessness in enforcing the law was apt to make residents feel abandoned, encouraging them to take the law into their own hands." To assure stability and security, the commission concluded, the (Labor) government must "end the attacks against Jews." This, however, the government would not do, lest a policy of toughness toward Arabs antagonize American presidents or offend world opinion.

In Hebron, the agreement between Israel and the PLO signed on the White House lawn in 1993, followed by the Oslo II accords two years later, marked days of infamy. The government of Israel, in the end, had betrayed the claim of the Jewish people to their own homeland. And, despite its democratic pretenses, the Labor government had done so without anything remotely resembling a popular mandate from Israeli voters. Indeed, by Oslo II, that government, which clung to power by one seat, could not even command a Jewish majority in the Knesset. Hebron Jews could not understand how the biblical city could pass to foreign hands—not because it was conquered in war, "but because a Jewish government gave it away."

At a conference in Kiryat Arba, rabbis declared that "giving parts of the Land of Israel to non-Jews is strictly forbidden" according to Jewish law. Even by democratic principles, the Rabin government lacked the authorization of a popular mandate to cede land. For Hebron Jews, the Rabin-Arafat handshake signified a covenant with terrorists: "Never before has any Israeli government or kingdom been willing to hand over parts of Eretz Israel to our enemy." To the rabbis, this signified "a spiritual crisis, a break from our roots."

The Hebron community was stunned: "everything has been turned upside down." Suddenly, "the enemy has been turned into the brother and the brother has been turned into the enemy." When the Oslo II accords foreshadowed the ultimate transformation of Judea and Samaria into a Palestinian state, Hebron Jews issued a "Declaration of Intent," proclaiming their determination to remain in place. "The citizens of Hebron," it declared, "will not leave the city of their own free will under any circumstances or for any reason." Jews, it asserted, "have an inalienable right to live in Hebron, the City of the Patriarchs." The inevitable with-

drawal of the Israeli army from Hebron, the Hebron community warned ominously, "will be regarded as an act of
treason and betrayal against the people of Israel and specifi-
cally against the Jewish residents of the Hebron region."

In the spring of 1996, Hebron Jews received a brief respite when a wave of horrific Palestinian terrorist attacks
in Jerusalem and Tel Aviv abruptly halted the Oslo process.
Benjamin Netanyahu, the Likud nominee for prime minister, offered political hope. "We are in Hebron by right," he
proclaimed. "We will not forfeit our rights, nor the force to
defend our rights." During his campaign, he reassured the
settlers that Hebron would remain under the exclusive control of the Israeli army. As prime minister, however, Netanyahu's confident campaign assurances quickly evaporated
under renewed Palestinian violence, accompanied by relentless diplomatic pressure from the United States. Unable or
unwilling to resist, Netanyahu consented to Israeli rede-
ployment from Hebron. What had happened, Hebron Jews
wondered, to all those proud Zionist claims that never again
would Jews be abandoned to their enemies before an indifferent world?

When the last Israeli officer handed over the keys to the
Hebron Military Compound to his Palestinian counterpart,
Hebron Jews were returned, by tacit consent of the government of Israel, to the ghetto. Barricades and chain fences,
erected by the Israeli army to separate them from Palestinians, confined them to their isolated neighborhoods (but
Palestinian rocks, firebombs, and gunshots continued unabated across the barriers). In a stunning radio interview, an
Israeli army reservist bitterly recounted how soldiers in
Hebron "have been transformed into cannon fodder" by
political constraints. Regardless of Palestinian provocations,
he noted, "it is forbidden to react. If [soldiers] react, they
are liable to be put on trial." In Hebron, "peace" meant that

Arabs were unrestrained by the Palestinian police while Jews were unprotected by the Israeli army.

By the end of the nineties, 180,000 Jewish settlers in Judea and Samaria were outnumbered by more than a million Palestinian Arabs. Yet even that ratio was considerably more favorable to Zionists than it ever had been during or after the first and second *aliyot*, those fabled earlier epochs of settlement in Palestine before World War I. At the time, no Zionist had argued that an Arab majority preempted Jewish settlement.

But the terms of debate in contemporary Israel had been deflected from Zionist and Jewish imperatives to liberal principles. It was argued that Israel would lose its character as a Jewish state if it were to absorb the large Arab population in the territories, a point most frequently argued by Jews who were least amenable to the idea of a *Jewish* state. And if Israel did absorb large numbers of Arabs, while refusing to extend the full rights of citizenship to them, then it no longer would be a democratic state.

Settlers never concealed their discomfort with democratic principles (nor did secular Zionists reveal theirs, lest they undermine the historical legitimacy of their own earlier settlement efforts). In a truly Jewish state, settlers responded, conflict between democratic and *halakhic* principles must be resolved according to Jewish law. "If democracy means that authority is derived from the public," conceded Rabbi Yehuda Hankin, "then Judaism, as is the case with most religions, is not democratic."

According to lawyer Elyakim Haetzni, "Even if 100 percent of the Jewish inhabitants of Israel should vote for its separation from the Land of Israel, that 'hundred percent consensus' would not have any more validity than the 'hundred percent consensus' that prevailed within the people of Israel when it danced around the golden calf." To the settlers, any government that ceded portions of the biblical homeland, regardless of its popular mandate, instantly squandered its legitimate authority.

Zionist legitimacy, they insisted, is not derived from popular will. The Land of Israel, Hanan Porat explained, "is a land of destiny, a chosen land, not just an existentially defined homeland." The linkage between the people of Israel and the Land of Israel ultimately rests upon the covenant between God and the Jewish people. The Land of Israel "is the land of the Jewish people by virtue of God's command." In the words of Rabbi Tzvi Yehuda Kook: "We are commanded both to possess and to settle. . . . We cannot evade this commandment."

If settling the land is commanded by Torah, or grounded in ancient history, then Western democratic norms present a problem, not a solution. For Hebron Jews, the ultimate source for the return of Jews to Zion is not a constitutional text, or a plebiscite based on what "we the people" have decided. "The Torah took pains to explain to us God's motive in taking a land from one people and making it the home of another. There is no problem here of 'being in the wrong,' or being in the right." For the believing Jew, wrote one settler, the source of Jewish settlement was "the command of God." Even Ben-Gurion, after all, had conceded, "The Bible is our mandate."

Every new Zionist settlement, from Rishon l'Tzion in 1882 to Hebron in 1968, was nourished by the identical dream of returning to Zion. But after 1967 settlers discovered, to their dismay, that Zionist rules had changed. New settlements were prohibited or obstructed by the government; their legitimacy was challenged; and settlers were blamed for doing what Zionists had always done. In the nineties, for the first time in Jewish history, relinquishing the Land of Israel, not settling it, came to define Zionist purpose.

The question of democracy, however, nags at Zionist history. Zionists were always trapped between their Zionist and democratic commitments (as were American Zionists, between the world wars, who supported Jewish statehood despite the Arab majority in Palestine). The only way to be a Zionist and a democrat during the pre-state years, when Arabs vastly outnumbered Jews in Palestine, was to assume that in the long run Zionist numbers would finally converge with democratic principles. Without the mass exodus of Arabs in 1947–48, that convergence would have been indefinitely postponed, perhaps forever. If current democratic standards had been applied to Zionist settlement policy throughout the twentieth century, Zionism would have been largely confined to the sand dunes of Tel Aviv.

In Hebron, where biblical metaphors still resonate with undiminished intensity, democracy is irrelevant. Hebron Jews speak another language, which can easily be mistranslated by their critics as "self-destructive messianism" and demented "fanaticism." Rabbi Levinger, "a black-bearded zealot willing to martyr himself for the right of Jews to rebuild an ancient civilization" on Palestinian land, was instantly recognizable as "Israel's Ayatollah Khomeini." (Substitute white hair for black beard, however, and it might also describe A. D. Gordon in Degania, during the formative era of Labor Zionism.) Levinger seems preposterous, indeed dangerous, because he actually believes that it was "God, and not Herzl, who was the first Zionist."

Hebron Jews, who remain attentive to God's covenantal promise to the Jewish people, are casualties of the conflict between Jewish memory and Zionist yearning. They proudly describe their "link in the eternal chain, bonding the People of Israel to the Land of Israel, according to Jewish law and tradition." They know that Hebron "is where it all started—the roots of the Jewish People in the Land of

Israel." They endure unremitting hostility and danger because they see themselves as "a living link in the history of our people, in the city of Abraham." They are Zionists who remain determined to validate the most ancient Jewish claims in the Land of Israel.

Hebron Jews are anathema to modern secular Jews precisely because they have rejected, unequivocally, the terms of emancipation. Indeed, they are living reminders of the renunciation of Judaism that emancipation required. They refuse to consign Judaism—the traditional religious culture of the Jewish people—to the periphery of their existence. Rather than separate Zionism from Judaism, as emancipation demands, they have integrated religion and nationalism in an effort to revive a very ancient Jewish synthesis. For that, more than anything else, emancipated Jews cannot forgive them.

Nowhere does Jewish memory extend further back in time than Hebron. Abraham, the Bible recounts, did not steal this piece of land, least of all from Palestinians. Or occupy it. Or settle it. He purchased it for the full asking price of Ephron the Hittite, who most assuredly was not Yasir Arafat's ancestor. Hebron Jews, who often rely upon historical analogies to defend their community, have occasionally compared their struggle to a struggle in the hill country near Jerusalem more than two thousand years ago, when a small band of Jewish zealots (by any definition) rebelled against the ravages of Hellenism. When the officers of King Antiochus arrived in Modi'in to command Jewish fealty to foreign rule, Mattathias objected: "I and my sons and my brethren walk in the covenant of our fathers. Heaven forbid that we should forsake the Law." The revolt of the Maccabees had begun.

For Mattathias and his sons, their war against Antiochus was simultaneously a Jewish civil war. Not only the Temple, but the Hellenized soul of Judaism, had to be cleansed. The very first casualty of their rebellion was a Jew who had stepped forward to worship idols. In every generation, Hebron Jews argue, Hellenized Jews are prepared to surrender covenantal Judaism for promises of peace, prosperity, and normality.

It may be the fate of Jews to be perennially tempted by foreign enticements. Hellenism, urbane and international, enjoyed widespread favor in the ancient Mediterranean world. In modern times, Greek theater has yielded to VCRs; the *gymnasium* has been supplanted by shopping malls; and young Israelis have transformed Michael Jackson and Madonna into the cultural equivalents of Greek gods. The problem of "Hellenism," the allure of foreign culture, seems destined to endure in Zion.

Since 1967, Jewish settlers have been the most faithful defenders of the Zionist revolution. They may be the last, best hope for reconciling Zionism with Judaism, a necessary synthesis if the State of Israel is not to be torn apart by its own internal contradictions.

6

The Zionist

War against

the Jews

The old "watchtower-and-stockade" settlements of the Mandatory era, constructed literally overnight by bold and dedicated *halutzim*, were built in violation of government policy—but it was British rule, the policy of a foreign government, that Zionists violated. Once there was a Jewish state and Jews governed themselves, it is argued, the heroic pre-state tactics of subterfuge, evasion, and disobedience could no longer be justified. In a modern nation-state, after all, the rule of law is supreme.

But not every issue can be resolved with abstract legalisms. Least of all in a Jewish state (or even a state of Jews), where sacred and secular legal authority, variously aligned with Jewish or democratic principles, compete for legitimacy. From the beginning, settlements have divided Israel because they touch the deepest and most sensitive nerve of Jewish statehood, the relation between Zionism and Judaism.

The founding text of political Zionism, Herzl's *Der*

Judenstaat, was ambiguous on this crucial point of Zionist identity. Herzl dreamed of a Jewish state, but it was a Zion with little Jewish content. Argentina was an acceptable location; an "aristocratic republic" offered a worthy constitutional model; and Switzerland's "federation of tongues," Herzl believed, was preferable to a Hebrew-speaking nation.

Within fifty years, precisely as Herzl had predicted, Israel was born. The fragment of the Jewish people that was pulled by destiny or driven by catastrophe to its ancient homeland succeeded in creating a sovereign state. Yet now, fifty more years after Jewish national independence secured Herzl's reputation as a prophet, Israel stands at the brink of fulfilling his assimilationist vision. Perhaps it is time to reconsider all those claims, ever since 1948, of Zionist superiority over the Diaspora. They are, by now, slightly suspect.

It was easy enough, in the bleak aftermath of the Holocaust, for Zionists to argue that Diaspora Jews were eternally frightened, passive, helpless, and spiritually impoverished. They were good for little but martyrdom, it seemed, or for aliya. Yitzhak Baer, the eminent Israeli historian whose *Galut* was published on the eve of Jewish statehood, described the Diaspora as "the abolition of God's order," a status of "political servitude, which must be abolished completely." Not long afterward, Ben-Gurion denigrated the Diaspora as "a sad, wounded, limping, and impoverished existence." Only in the State of Israel, he insisted, "is a full Jewish life possible."

Such Zion-centered assertions of superiority were occasionally challenged by a diminishing band of defenders of Diaspora Jewish vitality. Simon Rawidowicz, the American scholar to whom Ben-Gurion addressed his scathing indictment, vigorously rejected any notion that a Jewish state was "therapy" for the presumed debilities of "*galut*." Dismissing "every tendency of monopoly and hegemony" claimed by Israel, Rawidowicz insisted upon the full equality of homeland and Diaspora, each sharing responsibility with the other "for all aspects of Jewishness, for the yoke of Torah and commandments, old and new." With the revival of Jewish sovereignty, he claimed, "Israel" once again meant Jerusalem *and* Babylon.

After 1948, however, Diaspora Jews found it exceedingly difficult to challenge the swelling proclamations of Zionist triumphalism. A besieged Israel, clinging to the precipice of survival after the Holocaust, infused the Zionist claim with special moral urgency. Among Diaspora Jews, there was an uneasy defensiveness and deference to Israel, which lingers to this day. Who, after all, would prefer a spiritually impoverished "exile" to life in a spiritually exalted "home"?

But the sharp dichotomy that so many Diaspora Jews took for granted fifty years ago, and internalized as a measure of their inferiority to the real Jews—Zionists in Israel—no longer exists. As Israelis become ever more hostile to religious Judaism and addicted to American cultural fashion, the venerable Zionist contrast between Israel and *galut* evaporates like a desert mirage. Nor should this be surprising. Exile and home, we were once reminded by Jeremiah (whose landscape for prophetic denunciation did not even include Tel Aviv), are places of spiritual depth, not fixed geographical locations.

The Zionist return to Eretz Israel was, of course, a movement of radically secular Jews. The *halutzim* celebrated nationalism, Marxism, socialism, and assorted varieties of secular utopianism. Now that many of these enthusiasms have receded into historical oblivion, Zionists have turned as avidly to Western individualism and consumerism. Hardly a secular Zionist today would affirm Ben-Gurion's explanation for the success of Zionism: "I believe that the inspiration of the Bible sustained us, returned us to the land,

and created the State." How quaint—or, perhaps, subversive—this would sound in contemporary, "normalized," Israel.

To be sure, a century ago Zionists were energized by their liberation from religious tradition for their onerous tasks of state-building. To revive Jewish nationalism, they were required to dismiss Judaism as the dying ember of the Diaspora they despised. The most that religiously observant Jews could expect from brash and confident Zionists was condescending pity. Orthodox Jews in the *yishuv* were treated as rather unwelcome guests at an obligatory family gathering. Zionism, after all, proclaimed itself the boldest expression of Jewish faith in the modern era. Few Zionists, during the early decades of statehood, stopped to consider whether a Jewish state might also require a Jewish state of mind. Otherwise, why return, of all places, to Zion?

Hostility to Judaism—toward Diaspora Jews and their religious culture—guided Zionists and critics of Zionism alike. Even before statehood, the Canaanite critique of Jewish statehood vigorously—and often viciously—attacked Judaism as the expression of a demented Diaspora mentality that threatened to stifle the emergence of a secular Hebrew nation. Yonatan Ratosh, the poet-philosopher who was the movement's theoretician, decried the "sick culture of immigrants and pilgrims" and "the stupor of the ancient Jewish poison" that was already polluting life in the *yishuv*.

The Canaanites never were more than a handful of the disaffected, located at a remote edge of Israeli culture. With statehood, they quickly vanished into political oblivion. But their critique, with its negative images of Diaspora Jews and Judaism, lingered. During the early years of statehood, antireligious stereotypes in Israel occasionally bordered on anti-Semitic caricature. Israelis described "typical" Jews from the Diaspora with cruel distortions of their physical characteristics, financial avarice, physical cowardice, and "savage" primitivism. The best that Ben-Gurion could bring himself to say about Eastern European Holocaust survivors was that they were "hard, evil, and selfish."

For a time, at least until recently, such vulgarisms receded from Israeli public discourse. But the secular Zionist dismissal of religious Judaism as a Diaspora malady has remained deeply embedded in Zionist ideology. Just a few years ago, the veteran leftist Akiva Orr, conceding the "unbridgeable chasm" between Zionism and Judaism, complimented Israelis for becoming "Hebrew-speaking Gentiles" rather than "Jews." To this day, on the fashionable Zionist left (Leah Rabin was a good example), Israelis can more readily contemplate peaceful reconciliation with Arabs in keffiyahs than with Jews in *kipot* and *tzitzit*.

The split Zionist vision—a Jewish state depleted of Jewish content—is nowhere more vividly on display than in the Israeli rendition of a tale of two cities. Long before Zionism, of course, there was "Zion." Jerusalem, as decayed and barren as it might be in reality, remained the spiritual centerpiece of return. Even today, for all the garish excesses of its modern architecture—-the obtrusive glass towers and ponderous public buildings—Jerusalem still turns Jews inward upon their own history as a people. The twisted alleys of its shtetl neighborhoods, transplanted from the decimated Eastern European centers of Orthodoxy, lure visitors from modernity into a maze of Jewish memory that winds all the way back to the Second Temple and beyond, to King David's ancient city.

Isaiah's prophecy proclaimed that the word of God would go forth from Jerusalem. This unique city of myth and metaphor demands fidelity to Jewish history, religion, tradition, and memory. Yet the literature of modern Zionism, virtually from its beginning, displayed what has aptly been called a resentful "demystification" of the holy city. Among Zionist writers for nearly a century now, the "irrelevance" of Jerusalem has been a persistent theme.

From Leo Pinsker and Ahad Ha'Am (who, despite his yearning for a cultural center for Judaism, preferred to live in Tel Aviv), through Chaim Nahman Bialik and Yosef Chaim Brenner, into the era of statehood and down to our own time, the Zionist literary imagination has remained hostile to Jerusalem as the repository of Jewish memory. Even among contemporary Israeli writers—once again, Amos Oz comes conspicuously to mind—Jerusalem is little more than a dismal symbol of Jewish "national deformity and impotence," a wandering ground for demented religious mystics and zealots.

Zionist political leaders displayed similar indifference to Jerusalem. The Knesset, the seat of government power, was located there but Ben-Gurion commuted from Tel Aviv. During Golda Meir's years in office, the prime minister's residence in Jerusalem rarely was occupied. Only in 1967 did Jerusalem begin to assume the spiritual and emotional centrality in Zionism that it had always enjoyed in Judaism. The city that Ben-Gurion would not fight for in 1948 became, twenty years later, the city that Israel would never abandon.

Even today, despite its high-rise apartment and office buildings, luxury hotels, and state-of-the-art shopping mall, Jerusalem still stands slightly apart from modern Israel. Astride the hills of Zion and Moriah, at the end of the road from Tel Aviv, it remains too Jewish to fit altogether comfortably into a Zionist state. Secular Israeli visitors often seem uncomfortable in Jerusalem, where they are surrounded by too many Jews whose very presence is an "encroachment." Even Jerusalem residents are prone to complain bitterly about the "takeover" of the city by "black hats," as though ultra-Orthodox Jews constitute an invading foreign army.

Tel Aviv, by contrast, is the consummate Zionist city, brashly asserting Israeli normality. Its very existence repudiates Jewish memory. Built early in this century on the shifting sand dunes (both real and metaphorical) that covered all traces of the Jewish past, it literally turned its back on the geographical cradle of Jewish history. Facing away from the Samarian hills, it focuses Israeli longing toward the Mediterranean and beyond, to the glittering West. Its most distinctive historic architecture is the cluster of Bauhaus buildings in the old city center. A Western import, they were as definitively modern as they were unambiguously foreign.

Tel Aviv is the secular, liberal, hedonistic fulfillment of Herzl's dream, a magnet for Israelis who crave relief from spiritual yearning, historical claims, and divine command. Here Yom Kippur can be just another (holy) day at the beach, a fast day that is as likely as not to prompt a lavish meal behind discreetly closed shutters. So insulated are Tel Avivians from Judaism by their cosmopolitanism that they have occasionally been stunned, whether by scud missiles or terror bombings, into the astonishing realization that to enemies of the Jews they, too, are the Jewish enemy.

In the current post-Zionist era, even Zionist memory—for so long the source of national cohesion—seems to have become an unwelcome encumbrance. Here may be the ultimate Zionist irony: Israelis, who proudly leapt backward over two thousand years to resume a golden age of national sovereignty, now routinely denigrate the very heroes of antiquity who once inspired the Zionist struggle.

The pioneering iconoclast of post-Zionist historiography was Yehoshafat Harkabi, a retired army general who taught international relations at the Hebrew University. In a furiously debated 1983 book, Harkabi explored and denounced "the Bar Kokhba syndrome" that he found embedded in Israeli culture. He defined the syndrome as an excess of nationalistic zeal, which had once condemned the Jewish people to national suicide and would surely do so again if religious nationalism was not eradicated from Zionist ideology and Israeli politics.

Bar Kokhba ranked high in the pantheon of ancient Zionist heroes. The leader of the second-century revolt against Roman rule, during which his ally, the revered Rabbi Akiva, was martyred for the cause of national liberation, Bar Kokhba had waged the last, desperate struggle for Jewish national survival for two thousand years. The fall of his outpost at Betar, merged in Jewish tradition with the destruction of the First and Second Temples, was commemorated on the fast day of Tisha b'Av.

Long a revered Zionist symbol of national pride, Bar Kokhba returned to life for Israelis in 1960. Archeologist Yigal Yadin, the army chief of staff during the Independence War, dramatically informed Israeli president Yitzhak Ben-Zvi: "I am honored to be able to tell you that we have discovered fifteen dispatches written or dictated by the last President of ancient Israel eighteen hundred years ago."

The discovery of the Bar Kokhba letters was a source of immense national pride. Israelis felt instantly reconnected to their ancient warrior-hero. In a state burial ceremony, soldiers carried coffins with the bones of Bar Kokhba's warriors to their final resting place in the Judean desert. Yadin himself personified the fusion of military daring and archeological passion through which Zionism could reconnect Israel to its ancient homeland.

Harkabi's book, published two decades later, measured the waning of secular Zionist passion and purpose. *"By admiring the Bar Kokhba Rebellion, "* Harkabi insisted, *"we*

*Israelis enmesh ourselves in the predicament of reverenc-
ing our people's destruction and rejoicing in an act of national suicide.*" Harkabi was astonished that "a rebellion
that brought calamitous results, nearly the extinction of our
national existence, would suddenly be converted into a symbol of revival." The Bar Kokhba rebellion, rooted in false
messianism, was nothing less than "a catastrophe" for the
Jewish people from which it had taken nearly two thousand
years to recover.

The meaning of the Bar Kokhba revolt, to be sure, had
long been vigorously contested in Jewish texts. Bar Kokhba
(son of a star) was also known in Jewish history as Bar Koziba
(son of a lie) for his messianic pretensions. But modern Zionists had found inspiration in Bar Kokhba for their own
heroic struggle against overwhelming odds. With the rise of
religious nationalism after the Six Day War, however, religious Jews began to use him for their Zionist purposes. Suddenly, Bar Kokhba was a problematic hero.

Harkabi's plea for "a realistic approach" to political,
military, and strategic calculations was a thinly veiled critique of Likud policy and the settlement movement. "A return to realism in our national thinking," he insisted, offered
the only alternative to "the pits of unreality and fantasy."
Harkabi's analysis was designed to "counteract the trends
within Israeli society that reject realism." He sharply condemned what he perceived as devotion to "a cultistic rever-
ence for suicide and death."

Harkabi's epilogue ("Is Current Israeli Policy Realistic?")
made his linkage explicit. For more than a decade, Harkabi
had urged Israeli concessions to the Arabs, recognition of
the PLO, acceptance of Palestinian national self-determi-
nation (leading inevitably to statehood), and Israeli withdrawal from Judea, Samaria, Gaza, and the Golan Heights.
Any policy to the contrary suggested a pathological "syn-

drome." For Harkabi, "international considerations"—
especially the need for American diplomatic and financial
support—defined political realism in the modern age. A "realistic" Israel must transcend Jewish history and Zionist
mythology to take its place among the normal nations of
the world.

Harkabi could not entirely escape from history or myth,
but he could try to convert them to his own political uses.
Jewish settlements, he wrote, exemplified "the primiti-
vization of political thinking" in Israel that was manifested
in "demagogic leadership" and accompanied by "chauvinism and national boasting." In the twentieth century as in
the second, a "bankrupt ideology" threatened Israel with
national destruction. Any resemblance between Bar Kokhba
and Begin, between Betar and Kiryat Arba, between the war
against Rome and Israel's war in Lebanon was, for Harkabi,
purely intentional.

The issue is not whether Harkabi analyzed an ancient
rebellion with even a modicum of fidelity to the sparse sur-
viving evidence. ("I am not a historian," he conceded.) Nor
is it the utility of historical analogies, which is always de-
batable. (Harkabi disclaimed historical analogies even as he
repeatedly asserted them.) Nor is it even a question whether
"realism" (which, in Harkabi's definition, bore a remarkable resemblance to Israeli surrender to Arab demands) is
preferable to messianic zeal.

Rather, as various Israeli critics suggested, Harkabi's plea
for "realism" was a transparent surrender of Zionist will,
the "disintegration of values . . . in the name of pragmatism."
Yadin, one of Harkabi's milder critics, responded: "There
are things that are measured not by lost territories but by
lost values." When, after all, had "realism" ever been the
criterion for Zionist struggle? If Zionists had not abandoned
"realism" for tikva (hope), there never would have been a

Jewish state at all.

Bar Kokhba's revolt was not the only venerable Zionist symbol to be tarnished by Begin's critics on the left. In heroic Zionist lore, no place in Israel was more deeply revered than Masada, the Judean desert fortress where nine hundred Zealots had committed mass suicide rather than be taken into Roman slavery. Masada, the last Jewish outpost to fall during the first-century war against Rome, symbolized—along with the Maccabees and Bar Kokhba—an ancient struggle of the Jewish people for freedom and national independence from which modern Zionists had drawn inspiration.

To Zionist youngsters, whose daring pre-state pilgrimage to the remote wilderness site of Masada was an important rite of passage, the besieged Zealots epitomized precisely the "active heroism, love of freedom, and national dignity" that a new generation of Zionists wanted to emulate. Hardly a tourist in Israel could avoid an impassioned defense of Zionist zeal from a guide who proudly located modern Israel within the spiritual walls of the ancient fortress.

Yigal Yadin's extensive archeological excavations at Masada explicitly linked modern Zionists to their first-century forebears. A state funeral (which became the ceremonial model for Bar Kokhba's slain warriors) paid homage to the Zealots as the precursors of the Israel Defense Forces. Thereafter, new army recruits would take their oaths of allegiance to the Jewish state atop the mountain fortress, where they affirmed that Masada would not fall again.

Precisely because Masada had so fired the Zionist imagination, it became a sharply contested symbol once the pendulum of Israeli historiography swung to the revisionist left. To Yadin, who not only supervised but popularized the excavations, the defenders of Masada remained "Zealot Jews who fought for freedom," deserving of the supreme honor that a grateful nation could bestow. After Begin's election, however, such displays of Zionist zeal were brusquely discredited. Just as the secular left complained about a Bar Kokhba "syndrome," so it decried the Masada "complex."

During the 1980s, the revisionist indictment of Zionist mythology carried the day. The proliferation of Jewish settlements, an increasingly unpopular war in Lebanon, and the eruption of the Palestinian *intifada* convinced secular Israelis that Zionist militancy—now that they had abandoned it—signified a national psychosis. If unabated, it led to mass suicide, national self-destruction, and assorted messianic disorders that passed, as though by genetic inheritance, from first- and second-century Zealots to Menachem Begin's Likud government.

Simultaneously, the rewriting of modern Israeli history further sapped Zionist legitimacy. According to a cluster of revisionist historians, who borrowed the language of the most hostile Arab opponents of Jewish statehood, Israel was hardly the "pure and innocent" Jewish state that Zionists had once proudly proclaimed. Instead, concluded Benny Morris, Israel was "born tarnished, besmirched by original sin." The sin, of course, was the willful dispossession of Palestinian Arabs from their land. Indeed, a yearning to "transfer" Arabs from Palestine, the explicit goal of almost no Zionist then or since (except for tiny groups on the right-wing fringe of Israeli politics), was inserted by Morris into mainstream Zionist theory and practice. In post-Zionist Israel, ironically, the transfer impulse is confined to Zionists on the left, who have long and vigorously advocated the removal of Jews from their settlements in Judea and Samaria.

This "new history," as one of its foremost practitioners acknowledged, was designed less to reconstruct the past accurately than to "serve the purposes of peace and reconciliation" between Israelis and Arabs. Such highly politicized history was popularized in Israel by *Ha'aretz* journalist Tom Segev, whose twin exposés of Zionism during the formative years of statehood became instant best-sellers. Researching *1949*, his account of the first year of Israeli national sovereignty, Segev had discovered that "the founding fathers of Israel were much less idealistic and more cynical than was commonly assumed. 'The good old days' were not so good after all."

Indeed, by the pacifist standards of the new Israeli left, they were very bad days indeed. Israel was blamed by Segev, as by Benny Morris, Avi Shlaim, and their acolytes, for ignoring the (presumed) Arab willingness to make peace. Israeli society, Segev concluded, was "less pioneering and heroic," and "less enlightened, less idealistic, less altruistic" than Israelis had always imagined. Rather, from its birth, Israel had promised "neither justice for all, nor equality for all, nor peace."

Segev's 1991 sequel, *The Seventh Million*, his study of Israelis and the Holocaust, appeared at a time when Israel was even more tormented by Zionist self-laceration than it had been a decade earlier. Accordingly, Segev's politics were more explicitly on display. By the nineties, the Holocaust itself had become a somewhat tarnished symbol in Israel. Segev researched his book while Israel brought to trial John Demjanjuk, a Ukrainian implicated in the murder of 870,000 prisoners, mostly Jews, at Treblinka. Unlike the intense drama surrounding the earlier trial of Adolf Eichmann, the Demjanjuk trial was mired from the start in Israeli doubt and Zionist recrimination.

Whether Demjanjuk truly was the "beast" of Treblinka, as his accusers claimed, or merely a murderous guard at Sobibor, as his defenders insisted, became all but irrelevant. For Segev, the misguided centrality of the Holocaust among Israelis was the central issue. The Holocaust, after all, had molded "the collective identity" of Israel. "As a justification for the State of Israel," he noted, "the Holocaust is comparable only to the divine promise contained in the Bible." After half a century of statehood, to Segev's dismay, the Holocaust still remained deeply implicated in "a fierce struggle over the politics, ideology, and morals of the present."

Israel, Segev wrote, "was isolated, set apart from its [Arab] surroundings. Its religion, culture, values, and mentality were different. It lived in insecurity." Why? Because, he argued, Israelis still clung to the Holocaust as a link to their Jewish past. Memories of the Holocaust, Segev complained, actually encouraged Israelis "to express their connection to Jewish heritage." This, he implied, was a seriously misguided digression from the proper Zionist striving for normalization. Consciousness of the Holocaust, after all, encouraged "insular chauvinism," attentiveness to national-security needs, "oppression" of Palestinians, and insensitivity to "moral imperatives, including respect for human rights." The lessons of the Holocaust, Segev concluded, set limits to the willingness of Israelis "to take the risks involved in a compromise peace settlement."

As long as Jews clung to their insular Holocaust memories, Segev insisted, Israel could not become a normal nation. Memory, he warned the people whose very national existence was anchored in memory, was dangerous. Israelis must strip the Holocaust of its Jewish content, Jewish tragedy, and, indeed, Jewish meaning. For normal Israelis, the true function of the Holocaust must no longer be to activate Jewish memory but to serve as a summons "to preserve democracy, to fight racism, and to defend human rights."

Just a year later, with Yitzhak Rabin's election as prime minister, historical revisionism converged with post-Zionist political reality. Supported by the Bush administration in Washington, which actively opposed Prime Minister Yitzhak Shamir, Labor managed to cobble together a razor-thin coalition, resting upon Israeli leftist and Arab parties whose Jewish consciousness was roughly equivalent. Led by Rabin, the first native-born prime minister of Israel, the new government exemplified the Jewish shallowness of Israeli secular culture.

By 1992, Israelis were delighted to relinquish the burdens of Jewish history for the blessings of McDonald's and malls. Of these post-Zionist Israelis, it could aptly be said (precisely as sociologist Nathan Glazer had written of American Jews during the 1950s): "Less and less of the[ir] life . . . is derived from Jewish history, experience, culture, and religion. More and more of it is derived from . . . American culture." What American Jewry had been in the 1950s, Israelis had become in the 1990s.

Rabin personified the vast chasm that separated Zionism from Judaism in the Jewish state. He was raised in a doctrinally severe socialist Zionist family and his formal education was largely confined to agricultural training school. Until he launched his political career in the 1970s, his entire adult life was spent in the military. Rabin's soldiering virtues might still evoke a bygone Zionist era of self-denial and state service. But as secular Israelis broke free of old Zionist constraints, those values had become all but obsolete.

Gruff in his warmest moments, crudely blunt to his critics, and brutal toward Palestinian insurgents during the *intifada*, Rabin had campaigned as Israel's "Mr. Security." He had repeatedly promised never to recognize the PLO or "come down" from the Golan Heights. No one looked to Rabin for expansive Zionist vision or radical change. A crusty veteran of Israel's foreign and domestic wars, with an undistinguished record during his brief term as prime minister during the seventies, he had endured in politics as a useful adjunct to hard-line Likud policy whenever it needed Labor support.

Foreign Minister Shimon Peres, by contrast, had no trouble articulating his own expansive Zionist vision, with its severely atrophied Jewish content. The most striking aspect of Peres's conception of a "new Middle East," which ultimately became the foundation of Labor party foreign policy, was its paucity of references to Jews, Judaism, or a Jewish state. Beyond a ritualistic gesture of respect to his birthplace of Vishniva, once "a center of Jewish spiritual life" that was converted by the Nazis into a Jewish cemetery, Peres all but obliterated Judaism from his Zionist dream. He yearned for Israelis to transcend nationalism, to embrace "a supernational identity" as "citizen[s] of the world." Ever attentive to the latest gossip in the global village, he borrowed foreign ideas indiscriminately. Even *The New Middle East*, the title of his futuristic fantasy, was a phrase taken from a letter written by one of Yasir Arafat's aides.

Peres struck a familiar Zionist pose, contrasting a proud Zion with the miserable *galut* of "oppression and suffering." But his distinction floated on a haze of wishful clichés about "a new sort of cooperation" in "a regional community of nations," modeled on a foreign import, the European Community. In the Middle East, the site of the most ferocious tribal warfare of modern times—with Arabs repeatedly slaughtering Jews, Christians, Copts, Kurds, and each other—Peres actually envisioned one united people, "without regard to origin, religion, nationality, or gender." Without, that is, Judaism or Jews.

The Rabin government is best understood as the political expression of all the post-Zionist forces that had coalesced in protest against Likud ascendancy. The historical and moral clarity of 1967, when Israel was momentarily reconnected to Jewish history, had become politically murky by 1992. The return of the Labor government to power expressed a weariness with Zionist struggle. The older challenges of settlement and state-building, combined with the military daring that had once inspired Zionist legend, seemed to embarrass members of Israeli cultural and intellectual elites. A younger generation of Israelis preferred to gyrate in Tel Aviv discos and explore cyberspace. Their heroes were not Herzl or Ben-Gurion, to say nothing of Jabotinsky or Rav Kook, but punk pop stars Aviv Geffen and Gidi Gov.

On the left, political passion was reserved for denouncing religious Jews, Orthodox rabbis, settlers—anyone beyond the pale of secular liberalism. Indeed, nowhere in the world during the nineties were Jews subjected to such venomous verbal abuse as in Israel. To the maverick Hebrew University professor Yeshayahu Leibowitz, a guru to the left (although not himself a secularist), Jewish settlers were "murderers" and the soldiers who defended them were "Judeo-Nazis." A world-traveled kibbutznik expressed his eagerness "to shoot at settlers, preferably between the eyes, like one shoots at kangaroos in Australia." Only "with force and a willingness to enter into a civil war," declared an academic historian, could the "fascism" of the settlements be curbed. According to his Hebrew University colleague, "the Torah is more dangerous than *Mein Kampf* and the children of the Jews who live in Hebron are like Hitler youth."

Not only Jewish settlers, but Jews as Jews were routinely defamed in the Jewish state. During the Gulf War, an Israeli journalist openly yearned to take Jews from the various religious parties, "tie all of their beards together and light a little match." Whenever he saw religious Jews, declared Yigal

Tumarkin, the internationally acclaimed Israeli sculptor, "I understand the Nazis." In the mass-circulation *Yediot Achronot*, Ora Shem Ohr confessed: "I am sick and tired of seeing them with their long coats full of aged oil and their fur hats as if they are still in their [Eastern European] villages." Religious Jews would be lovable, wrote a *Davar* journalist, "if we locked them on reserves and charged tourists money to see them."

In post-Zionist Israel, Zionism—together with Judaism—was anathema. Israel had been berated for so long in the court of world public opinion that Israelis seemed finally to have internalized the malicious censure of their most implacable enemies. The respected novelist Aharon Meged, a veteran Labor Zionist, sparked an Israeli firestorm in 1994, two years after the Rabin government came to power, when he identified "a subconscious suicidal drive" that was propelling Zionism to self-destruction. Meged recalled the (suddenly prophetic) poem by Natan Alterman, in which Satan asks: "How will I conquer this beleaguered one? He possesses courage, ingenuity, resourcefulness and tools of war." Satan concludes: "This I'll do—blunt his mind, till he forgets his cause is just."

Meged was astonished by the unparalleled "emotional and moral identification by the majority of Israel's intelligentsia with people openly committed to our annihilation." For two or three decades, he wrote, Israeli academics, authors, artists, and journalists "have been working determinedly and without respite to preach and prove that our cause is not just." Not only was Israeli occupation of the West Bank immoral, and the birth of Israel lodged in the "original sin" of Palestinian displacement; but Zionist settlement in the Land of Israel, dating back more than a century, was an injustice. How, Meged wondered, could such "pathological" self-laceration be explained?

Zionist pathology is even more astonishing if one re-
members that Jews, as Ruth R. Wisse observes, "have more
concurrent rights to their land than any other people on
this earth can claim: aboriginal rights, divine rights, legal
rights, internationally granted rights, pioneering rights, and
the rights of that perennial arbiter, war." Yet in the nineties, Israelis seemed acutely embarrassed lest any assertion
of Zionist rights incur the censure of the West or the hostility of their avowed Arab enemies.

When has any nation, including those (such as "Palestine") with far shakier rights of national legitimacy than
Israel possesses, so recklessly squandered its own claims?
Even in the United States, where historic sins against minorities are now compulsively revisited, such spasms of
national recrimination have been slight by comparison.
Something deeply embedded in Zionism has elevated national self-flagellation, at times bordering on anti-Semitism,
into a cultural reflex.

More than anything else, the Rabin-Arafat handshake
on the White House lawn finally propelled all the unresolved
issues of Jewish identity and Zionist legitimacy to the surface of Israeli politics. By 1993, the Rabin government was
floundering, with the narrowest of Knesset majorities—-and
not even a Zionist majority at that. Yet without anything
remotely resembling a popular mandate for recognition of
the PLO or major territorial concessions, Rabin signed an
agreement that all but relinquished Israel's claim to its biblical patrimony.

Israelis who had taken Rabin at his hawkish word in
the election campaign were stunned to discover the enor-
mity of his policy reversal. In a democracy, to be sure, a
one-vote majority (precisely what Rabin enjoyed in the
Knesset) is legally sufficient to do anything. But a wise leader
will tread carefully, and with consummate sensitivity, when

an issue of the most fundamental national import may be so narrowly decided. Rabin, however, was prepared to redraw Israel's boundaries (with biblical Judea and Samaria largely outside them), as though he enjoyed a sweeping popular mandate for the most consequential territorial and political decision in modern Israeli history. In the process, he split the nation into warring camps.

Rabin's territorial concessions—first Gaza and Jericho, which most Israelis could easily live without, and then most of Judea and Samaria—drove a wedge through the Zionist heart of Israel. Suddenly, "Zionism" had come to mean the relinquishment of Jewish claims to the historic homeland of the Jewish people. As *Ha'aretz* columnist Yoel Marcus wrote, "While the Arabs have remained faithful to their ideology of the holiness of the land, . . . Israel is ready lightly to withdraw from those lands that were the cradle of Judaism." Israel was prepared to return its own Jews to exile in their own homeland.

The Oslo agreement was surely not, as President Clinton exuberantly exclaimed when Rabin and Arafat shook hands, "a peace of the brave." Rather, it was a peace of the weak in which two ideologically exhausted adversaries leaned upon each other in desperation to avoid collapse. By then, the Palestinians were spurned, if not mocked, throughout the Arab world. Arafat, isolated and marginalized in Tunis, had become a globetrotting parody of a national leader. The autocratic dispenser of financial largesse to his loyalists, he lagged far behind the very people in "Palestine" whose interests he claimed to represent.

Zionism, driven by the logic of its craving for Jewish normality and Western approval, was hardly more robust. Indeed, Rabin and Peres confronted impending political oblivion. (At the time, Rabin was trailing Benjamin Netanyahu in public opinion polls.) With popular support waning, the Rabin government seemed to possess no Zionist vision beyond relinquishment of Israel's historic homeland to its most implacable enemy—in return for hesitant, convoluted, and (as the next seven years amply demonstrated) hollow promises of peace from the most notorious murderer of Jews since Hitler. The peace initiative with the Palestinians, in sum, was the culmination of a prolonged Zionist surrender process. It was the acknowledgment that Israel had lost the will to defend its own historic homeland.

Perhaps, more than anyone suspected at the time, Rabin shrewdly grasped the new post-Zionist reality: Arabs might cling tenaciously to every dunam of land, and Moslems would fight to the death for their mosques (especially those built over Jewish holy sites), but secular Israelis had long since exhausted their Zionist energy. Rabin may have intuited that Israelis had lost their will to continue the struggle. Peace advocates, after all, were insisting that no territory (except, perhaps, Dizengoff Square in Tel Aviv) was worth a single drop of soldier's blood, nor even "one tear" from a worried mother. With Rabin's military career as their fig leaf, normal Israelis were prepared to surrender and call it "peace."

The Oslo accord fractured Israeli society at its most vulnerable point, the ideological rift between secular Israelis and religious Jews. In Judea and Samaria, residents tore their clothes in mourning for a Zionism that had "died of its own will." It was, they lamented, a Zionism that "has given up on itself." Rabin seemed more than eager to rub salt into their wounds. Whenever the validity of his mandate for such sweeping concessions was challenged, he simmered with fury. His own blunt words of delegitimation—branding settlers "crybabies," "spinning propellers," and "not real Israelis"—indicated how deeply their allegations stung. In a cruel twist of Zionist irony, a government that was prepared to make peace with Palestinian terrorists seemed ready to declare war against Jews.

It was not long before perceptions of Zionist betrayal led to Zionist catastrophe. In the early spring of 1994, Dr. Baruch Goldstein, a Brooklyn-born resident of Kiryat Arba, murdered twenty-nine Moslems in prayer at the Machpelah shrine in Hebron. (Goldstein himself was killed by enraged Arabs.) The hideous massacre triggered a firestorm of Israeli fury toward Hebron settlers. Amid ugly spasms of shame and blame, Israeli outrage quickly turned against all settlers, indeed against all Orthodox Jews. They were reviled with a ferocity rarely matched in a political culture notorious for its demonization of political opponents. The Israeli left—in the name of liberal values, no less—held all settlers guilty by association with the murderer, demanded collective punishment, and urged a population transfer of Hebron Jews.

Every settler became "Goldstein," a racist murderer. Prime Minister Rabin angrily denounced Goldstein "and those like him": "You are not part of the community of Israel. . . . You are not partners in the Zionist enterprise. You are a foreign implant. You are an errant weed." Jewish settlers, Rabin proclaimed, were not "real Israelis." According to Foreign Minister Peres, all the residents of Judea and Samaria were "gun-toting bearded men with yarmulkes."

The most "liberal" Israelis, it seemed, harbored the most repressive impulses. Peace Now advocate Amos Oz, in an outburst of militant fury, advocated suppression of "racist and bloodthirsty agitations" with "an iron first." He demanded that Rabin outlaw "extremist" groups and crush "Jewish terrorism." Jews like Goldstein, after all, were nothing more than "Hezbollah in a skullcap." Ze'ev Chafets, the American-born *Jerusalem Report* columnist, was even less restrained. To Chafets, Goldstein symbolized the "religious irrationality" of "a segment of Israeli society that is beyond the range of reasonable words and enlightened policies." He warned: "It's us or them, our values or theirs, reason and civil authority or religious frenzy and the rule of a junta of holy men and a mob of morons."

In post-Zionist Israel, there was no place for religion or rabbis. The newspaper *Ma'ariv* complained about American parents who send "their lunatic children" to Israel. Goldstein's "brethren from Brooklyn" (according to the Israeli immigration minister) were aliens in the Jewish state. Orthodox Jews from the United States, the only Americans who made aliya in significant numbers, suddenly were pariahs in Israel.

With Palestinian terrorism intensifying, and with Israeli criticism of Oslo becoming ever more strident, the Rabin government sharply escalated its own hostile rhetoric. The prime minister refurbished charges of treason and rebellion that had not been heard in nearly fifty years. Like Ben-Gurion before him, he accused his political enemies of seeking "to topple the government through violence in the streets," and harboring plans "to try to violently take over the government offices."

When prominent rabbis called for conscientious objection in defiance of any orders that might be issued to evacuate settlers, Rabin was outraged. With the characteristic venom that he displayed whenever his authority was challenged, he labeled them "ayatollahs" and bluntly insisted that "whoever calls for conflicts with soldiers does not belong to this people anymore."

Although "Brooklyn Jews" were pariahs in Israel, just about everything else American was avidly absorbed into Israeli culture. The most important Zionist story by the mid-nineties, according to *The Jerusalem Report*, was "the Americanization of Israel." When a McDonald's opened in Rishon l'Tzim, the very first Zionist settlement, an Israeli exulted: "This is America, but better. . . . Now we have it all." In Herzliya (named to honor the Zionist prophet), Chinese take-out and pizza were available in a sparkling new shopping mall, where a country-and-western band was booked for Texas Jack's on the sabbath.

The "fast-food invasion" of Israel—not only the requisite McDonald's but Burger King, Pizza Hut, and Kenny Rogers' Roasters—stimulated the appetite of Israelis for rampant American-style consumerism. Tel Avivians could hardly contain their delight with Tower Records, the Gap, and Toys "R" Us. Prosperous Israeli suburbanites took time away from their villas and swimming pools to shop at Ace Hardware and Office Depot. By 1995, the newest status symbol no longer was a VCR, or even a computer, but the ubiquitous cell phone. With cable TV, Israelis could move beyond *Dallas* to a wider range of American sitcoms. That December, to heighten holiday cheer, shops in Tel Aviv displayed Christmas decorations.

The younger generation of Israelis was all but indistinguishable from its American counterpart. Children tested their roller blades on Yom Kippur, when the streets were empty of heavy traffic. Teenagers in designer jeans flocked to the Hard Rock Café. At the Hebrew University, where courses in business and Asian studies were oversubscribed, the Institute of Jewish Studies, for decades the intellectual core of the university, confronted an enrollment crisis. As the head of the Hebrew literature department explained sorrowfully, "There is an alienation from everything connected to Judaism."

The author of the *Jerusalem Report* survey, Stuart Schoffman, himself a transplanted American Jew, admitted to conflicted feelings of pride and dismay. The "homogenized consumer culture" of shopping malls, tennis clubs, and computerized fitness machines seemed somehow inspiring. Consumerism, after all, "implies choice, opportunity, a sense of openness and freedom." Indeed, "with any luck Israel will become much more Americanized." Yet Schoffman could not help but wonder, "What becomes of tradition, Judaism, self-sacrifice—of Zionism itself?" Might the "ugly Israeli," he mused, fulfill both definitions of *goy*, the Hebrew word that not only means "nation" but "Gentile"?

If secular Israelis exulted over *normaliut*, defined as Americanization, Israelis with Zionist memory despaired. The "rising tide of self-doubt" among Zionist intellectuals, Aharon Meged concluded, had finally encouraged Israelis to doubt "our right to be here." Post-Zionist normalization, added Yoram Hazony, a young political analyst in Jerusalem, meant "the end of Zionism." The Rabin government could divest Israel of its biblical homeland because the "near-total collapse" of Zionist ideology had prepared the way. Western cultural imports were merely symptomatic of the Zionist malaise; the debilitating malady that sapped Zionist vitality was the loss of Jewish memory and the evisceration of Jewish identity.

The Rabin government seemed dedicated to expunging any lingering Jewish content from Israel. The minister of education, Shulamit Aloni of the Meretz party, criticized school trips to Auschwitz for encouraging "nationalist" feelings. Her deputy minister proposed that the text of "Hatikva" be changed for the benefit of "citizens who are not Jews." The new chairman of curricular reform for the Education Ministry was the Hebrew University historian who had recently compared the Bible to *Mein Kampf*. The character of Israel as a Jewish state, along with the biblical origins of Jewish history, all but disappeared from new textbooks. No longer was it "a subject of primary importance," the historian explained, for Israeli youngsters to learn about the Jewish people and the State of Israel.

In the same spirit, the Israeli army revised its list of "values" and "basic principles" to exclude mention of the Jewish state, the Jewish people, and the Land of Israel. After the Goldstein murders, the Jewish Agency considered introducing a "fitness" test for Jewish immigration, which the Law of Return had always assured to all Jews worldwide (including Brooklynites). The Law of Return itself, the foundation law of Israel as a refuge to world Jewry, was reconsidered. The Foreign Ministry lobbied actively abroad for financial assistance, not for Israel but for the PLO. Visiting dignitaries were no longer taken to the Golan Heights or Masada, lest attention to these sites reinforce a spirit of national strength and determination. "Israel's next goal," Foreign Minister Peres declared, "should be to become a member of the Arab League."

By 1995, despite two years of "peace" with the Palestinians, Israelis in unprecedented numbers were being blown apart in hideous terror bombings inside the populated heart of the country. The Rabin government seemed oblivious to the dire consequences of its own policies, plunging recklessly forward without an electoral mandate on an issue of deepest national consequence. "Much of Israel," wrote the respected essayist Hillel Halkin (a dedicated Labor party voter), "felt like passengers on a ship that had been hijacked by its own captain and crew, . . . with the consent of half of those aboard, toward an unrevealed and perhaps calamitous destination."

Under unremitting political attack, the Labor government vilified its opponents as "enemies" of peace as if they were an isolated lunatic fringe, rather than half the Israeli electorate. Rabin openly proclaimed his indifference to the plight of the settlers, who were under constant Palestinian siege with minimal Israeli military protection. After all, he said dismissively, they comprised merely 2 percent of the population—and he claimed to represent everyone else. Rabin never seemed to understand that his banishment of political critics beyond the pale of Israeli legitimacy not only stoked their rage but severely compromised his own political authority.

Throughout the summer and fall of 1995, left and right, Israeli and Jew, were locked into a macabre and embittered political dance. Each demeaned the patriotic loyalty and political legitimacy of the other. The government acted legally, its defenders insisted, because it had been duly elected. It was not a legitimate Jewish government, responded its detractors, because it was prepared to relinquish the sacred homeland without even the support of a Jewish majority. The deep fissures that had been exposed within Zionism after 1967—above all, the irrepressible conflict between secular Zionism and religious Judaism—were splitting the country apart.

With Rabin's assassination by a right-wing Orthodox Jew, the political conflagration spread out of control. Labor government ministers instantly grasped the opportunity to demonize anyone outside the government peace consensus. Everyone from rabbis to Likud leader Netanyahu to the most demented celebrant of Rabin's death was transformed by the left into a virtual co-conspirator in the assassination. Meretz Knesset member Yossi Sarid, blaming Netanyahu, said, "There may have been one assassin but many inciters." Shulamit Aloni urged "emergency measures" to suppress "the right's incitement." Ehud Barak, about to become foreign minister in the new Peres government, demanded that right-wing extremist groups be "pulverized."

The prime minister's widow, Leah Rabin, converted

personal anguish into calculated political revenge. Like the old Palmach soldier she was, she struck swiftly at her enemies. Just one day into *shiva*, the intensely private period of Jewish mourning, she appeared on television to excoriate Netanyahu and other Likud Knesset members for creating the climate of hate that had incited the murder of her husband. Before the week was out, she received Yasir Arafat in her home and expressed a preference for her children to be "Arabs rather than Orthodox Jews."

Few Rabin supporters cared to distinguish between speech and incitement, between incendiary language and murder. In the name of democracy, the Israeli left jettisoned the fundamental democratic freedoms of speech and political association. Even Shimon Peres, who succeeded Rabin as prime minister and remained commendably aloof from the frenzy within his own government, stumbled over these distinctions. In a cabinet meeting two days after the assassination, he defended "freedom of expression" while reiterating his determination "to use all measures against people who incite, lead astray, and shoot"—as though these were indistinguishable.

To be sure, such vituperative rhetoric was hardly novel to Israeli politics. Indeed, the issue of political legitimacy had festered during sixty years of Zionist history. As far back as the assassination in 1933 of Chaim Arlosorov, a rising star in the Labor party, the delegitimation of the right had served as an instrument of Labor power. During the early months of statehood, the pattern repeated itself. Ben-Gurion, imagining an imminent civil insurrection, all but fulfilled his own foreboding by ordering the Haganah "holy cannon" to be fired on the Irgun ship *Altalena*. Fourteen Irgun members were killed; others were shot by Haganah soldiers as they swam desperately to shore. The Palmach commanding officer on the Tel Aviv beach, who believed that he was suppressing "a military *putsch*," was a young officer named Yitzhak Rabin.

Thereafter, the Labor party assumed that it alone was entitled to rule. Not only were right-wing opponents misguided; they were disloyal. Menachem Begin, the Irgun leader, was banished to the political wilderness. When the right finally came to power, thirty years later, the left reflexively tarnished it with allegations of "fascism." The political alliance of Likud with the religious parties (which had previously aligned themselves with Labor) prompted malicious cartoons depicting hawk-nosed, fanged Orthodox Jews rarely seen since the Nazi era, except in Arab newspapers. Responding to Begin's victory in 1977, Amos Oz had urged "sane" Zionists to prepare to fight in the streets against the new "tribalist" regime.

So it was, yet again, following the Rabin assassination. Once Rabin's assassin was identified as an Orthodox Jew, secular Israelis launched their own holy war against Jews, Judaism, and the rabbinate. Ze'ev Chafets described Yigal Amir, the son of a Torah scribe, as "a faithful product of the present culture of religious Orthodoxy." Hebrew University philosopher Moshe Halbertal traced Amir to "the Gush Emunim settler movement," to Likud, and to "the rabbinical establishment." Poet Yair Garboz pointed "an accusing finger . . . at the entire political right, without any exceptions, all of them."

American Jewish liberals, on cue, were quick to parrot Israelis with their own renditions of guilt by association. Anthony Lewis of the *New York Times*, long a hectoring critic of Israel, erroneously described Rabin's assassin as a "settler," the better to blame all the Jews of Judea and Samaria. His colleague Thomas Friedman concocted a "connection" between Amir and Netanyahu. Michael Lerner of *Tikkun* contrived something called "Settler Judaism" (located, perhaps, in Amir's hometown of Herzliya) to denounce. And Leon Wieseltier, literary editor of the *New Republic*, could hardly wait until the "trigger-happy saints of the right . . . really are crushed."

Rabin's assassin, to be sure, had claimed religious sanction for his deed. Amir cited the *halakhic* principle of *rodef*: a "pursuer" who intends to kill a Jew may be killed to save the intended victim's life. "According to Jewish law," he declared, "the minute a Jew gives over his people and his land to the enemy, he must be killed." As misguided and appalling a justification as Amir offered, it hardly warranted the malicious indictment of Orthodoxy, settlers, rabbis, Likud, and everyone else against whom the left nurtured a political grievance.

In the wake of the assassination, the government launched a sweeping investigation into patently spurious allegations of rabbinical sedition. After the police minister announced that Amir "drew on *halakhic* rulings made by rabbis," police rounded up an array of religious authorities who were suspected of declaring Rabin a *rodef*. Under the glare of publicity, more than a dozen rabbis were brought to police headquarters for interrogation for "inciteful" and "inflammatory" statements. The evidence, such as it was, proved insufficient to indict anyone.

The round-up, according to the mass-circulation newspaper *Yediot Achronot*, signaled a "hunting season for rabbis" (a pointed analogy to the "Season," back in 1944, when the Haganah had turned over Irgun members to the British). It is difficult to believe that any other country would have dared to humiliate and intimidate rabbis as Israel did following Rabin's assassination.

Amid the waves of anguish and grief that swept over Israel after Rabin's death, the shared responsibility of the left for the rancid Israeli political climate was conveniently overlooked. But "the Labor party that Rabin led," Hillel Halkin wrote, "cannot walk away from all responsibility for the anger, born of frustration and a sense of being lied to, that seethed in much of the nation" in the months preceding the assassination.

Rabin, after all, had identified Likud as "a collaborator with Islamic Jihad and Hamas," while branding rabbis who disagreed with him as "ayatollahs" and dismissing settlers as "crybabies." His own vicious language, no less than the malevolent accusations of treason that his political enemies hurled at him, constituted fighting words of political malice and slander.

In death as in life, Rabin symbolized the Zionist rejection of Jewish tradition, symbols, and memory. At the solemn state funeral of the first sabra prime minister, it seemed somehow appropriate that his son, standing at his father's grave, would demonstrate his own evident unfamiliarity with the language of Jewish mourning. Israelis seemed excessively impressed by the number of foreign dignitaries who attended Rabin's funeral, as though Israel depended upon foreign validation even at its most intimate moment of grief and mourning. In the days following the assassination, groups of saddened Israeli teenagers incessantly gathered in public to express their sorrow. Their heart-felt poems, songs, graffiti, and candle-lighting struck more than one curious observer as a pagan parody of Jewish mourning ritual. Secular Israelis loved Rabin so much because he had succeeded in liberating them from the stifling enclosures of Jewish history and identity. As one Israeli observed proudly after Rabin's death, he "took us out of the ghetto."

Rabin's Oslo policy became a national commitment once Netanyahu implemented it in Hebron. To Rabin and Peres, Hebron was an Arab city with a few Jewish troublemakers; to Netanyahu, it was merely a bargaining chip to be exchanged for American approval. All of Netanyahu's confident campaign assurances in 1996 about standing firm against Arafat quickly evaporated under Palestinian violence, American diplomatic pressure, and a deepening loss of Zionist will that cut across party lines. Netanyahu's surrender scenario would be repeated four years later when Prime Minister Barak displayed his willingness to relinquish Israeli sovereignty over an undivided Jerusalem and control over the Temple Mount, for two thousand years the holiest Jewish site in the world.

The Zionist revolution, from the beginning, had contained within it a powerful assimilationist impulse, which finally reached fruition in the nineties. Zionism, as journalist Boas Evron conceded, was one expression of the "alienation from Jewish historical consciousness" experienced by so many modern Jews. It represented "a rejection of historical Judaism" by those very Jews whose new nation, while building on ancient Jewish memory, was nonetheless intended to repudiate two thousand years of Jewish history.

So it was, within barely two generations of the rebirth of Jewish statehood, that the flood tide of Zionist passion had yielded to the ebb tide of Western normalization. The more longingly that Israel yearned to become a nation like other nations, the more rapidly that Zionism transformed itself into yet another virulent expression of Jewish assimilation in the modern era. It had reached the point where a new immigrant could sharply contrast Jewish apathy and ignorance in Israel with the Jewish vitality of his own Diaspora community—in Syria!

In her fine study of Zionist collective memory—and its dilution in recent years—Yael Zerubavel describes how Zionism "turned away from traditional [Jewish] memory." In the process, rabbinical Judaism, which had held Judaism together for two millennia, yielded its primacy to the exu-

berant nationalist zeal of Zionists. By the Rabin era, however, the very Jewish freedom fighters whose militancy Zionists had once celebrated—the Maccabees and Zealots,
even Trumpeldor at Tel Hai—had become Zionist pariahs.
The Zionist return to the "deep-rootedness" of Jewish history in the Land of Israel had become, in the end, a flight
from the Jewish past.

Some Israeli intellectuals, to be sure, still reflexively
proclaim the dated maxims of Zionist triumphalism. In his
bleak musings about the future of Diaspora Jewry, historian David Vital has suggested that "the more conscious
Diaspora Jews are of their special identity and ancestral roots
and the more highly they value them, the more powerfully
Israel saps at the foundations of their communities." With
Diaspora Jewry decimated by assimilation and intermarriage, Vital insists, only Israel can maintain and transmit
Jewish identity to future generations.

Written just a decade ago, Vital's words sound hollow
today, when Israel's ability to transmit Jewish identity to
its own children is severely diminished. Perhaps, within a
decade or two, Israelis will as likely send their youngsters
to the United States to learn how to be Jews as American
Jews will send their children to Israel. For some time now,
the standard Zionist tours—to Masada, a kibbutz, the Western Wall, Yad Vashem—have offered excursions to an Israel
that exists largely in the minds of tour guides. Visits to these
Potemkin villages of Jewish history deflect American youngsters from the living reality of post-Zionist Israel, where
little attention is paid to historical memory or holy space
except to denigrate them.

If "the name of the malaise" of post-emancipation Jewish life is secularism, as Vital's colleague Robert Wistrich
insists, then the conventional Zionist remedy—national
sovereignty and Hebrew literacy—has doomed itself to

failure. For the overwhelming majority of contemporary Jews, wherever they may live at the beginning of the twenty-first century, neither Diaspora individualism nor Israeli post-Zionism can for long sustain the collective memory of the Jewish people, upon which Jewish identity must in the end depend.

Only Orthodox Jews are likely to remain immune to the debilitating loss of Jewish memory from which secular Zionism suffers. Their lives are structured to remember what most Jews have conveniently chosen to forget: that Jewish culture, deprived of nourishment from religion, *halakha*, history, or any other source external to the subjective self and modern fashion, will as quickly wither in Tel Aviv as in Los Angeles.

The pursuit of Jewish normality may once have been the glory of Zionism, anchoring it to the ennobling tasks of ingathering Jewish exiles and state-building. For most contemporary Israelis, however (as for most Diaspora Jews), the prospect of belonging to a distinctive people who dwell alone in a covenantal relationship with God is slightly embarrassing, if not altogether unappealing. Encouraged by their politicians, public intellectuals, entertainers, journalists, and writers, they yearn for Israel to become the chic Mediterranean vacation spa, consumer paradise, and hi-tech center of a "new" Middle East.

In the Diaspora, it took nearly two centuries for emancipation to eviscerate Jewish life. In Israel, however, fifty years of statehood has sufficed. As Israel becomes a nation like other nations, the Zionist dream is fulfilled—yet Zionism becomes increasingly indistinguishable from Jewish assimilation. Israelis may (or may not) be spared the Diaspora plague of intermarriage, but Israel's cultural intermarriage with the West already seems all but irreversible.

By the end of the nineties, the signs of Zionist disintegration were everywhere apparent. Slouching toward its fiftieth birthday in the spring of 1998, Israel could hardly bring itself to celebrate its own Jubilee. Never had the country been more despairing over its history, identity, or destiny. Rejecting the heroic "founding myths" of Zionist achievement against seemingly insurmountable historical odds that had once inspired so much struggle and sacrifice from so many, secular Israelis yearned for little more than a culture of self-gratification modeled on American hedonistic norms.

Two highly touted books by Israeli academics offered post-Zionist variations on this familiar theme. Ze'ev Sternhell, analyzing "the founding myths of Israel," brusquely dismissed "the sanctity of the Jewish heritage" (so much for Judaism) and "the mystique of the land" (so much for Zionism). In *Rubber Bullets*, Yaron Ezrahi celebrated the emergence of Israeli individualism, finally liberated from the encumbrances of Jewish memory, religion, and nationalism. Seeking nothing less than "a retreat from Jewish history," Ezrahi avidly embraced "the private values of the self."

Such signs of Zionist exhaustion were reaffirmed by some astonishing statements from Israeli public officials. Not long before the Jubilee, Labor party leader Ehud Barak told a television interviewer that had he been born a Palestinian, he probably would have "joined a terrorist organization." Killing Jews, in other words, is a legitimate Palestinian activity. (Just days later, a Hamas terrorist, on trial for killing eleven Israelis, took the cue and justified his murderous actions by quoting Barak.) Shlomo Gazit, the former head of army intelligence, compared the knitted *kipot* worn by religious soldiers to the Nazi swastika. Judaism, in other words, is fascism.

What does it say, after fifty years of statehood, that respected Israeli leaders cannot distinguish Zionism from

terrorism or Judaism from Nazism? Or that academic lumi-
naries at the university in Jerusalem that once was a symbol of the revival of Jewish culture are mesmerized by life
in *galut*? It says, sadly, that secular Zionism, the Zionism
of Jewish normalization, has reached a dead end. For once
Zionism is depleted of Jewish content, it bears an uncanny
resemblance to Diaspora materialism, consumerism, and
individualism. Well might another Josiah mournfully proclaim: "Great is the wrath of the Lord that is poured out
upon us, because our fathers have not kept the word of the
Lord, to do according to all that is written in this book."
This time, however, "the book" is *The Jewish State*, not
the Torah; and Zionists have faithfully obeyed Herzl's urgent command that Jews become a normal people.

7

Altneuland

Revisited

A Journey
to Palisdan

The days when *halutzim* tilled the land by day, danced the hora all night, and won astonishing military victories the next morning were long ago in Israel's youthful past. As the formative era of Jewish statehood fades into history, Israelis have clearly wearied of the Zionist struggle. "Enough is enough," the mother of a soldier recently conceded. "We don't have the strength for this anymore." Who cannot sympathize with the fear of a parent for her child's safety? But how can a nation, or an ideal, survive once parental fear is their measure?

Israel, more than ever before, has become polarized into Zionist and Jewish extremes. Among secular Zionists, there is an evident readiness to capitulate—whether to its Arab enemies or to the tawdriest temptations of Western culture hardly matters. Who, after all, would not prefer promises of peace to threats of war, or glitzy shopping malls to bomb shelters?

Then there are the *haredim*, ultra-Orthodox Jews whose insular religiosity and dense shtetl culture remain a standing rebuke to the Zionist revolution. They will not sing "Hatikva" or stand for a moment of silence on Memorial Day. Their children do not serve in the army. Their disdain for the state and its leaders, symbols, and ceremonies (but not for its funding) infuriates Israelis. And all this, of course, in the name of God. They are, in the end, a living reminder of everything Jewish that Zionists assumed they had defeated in their struggle with the rabbis for Jewish cultural supremacy in the modern era.

There are also the settlers of Judea and Samaria, who are just a notch above the *haredim* in secular Zionist demonology. They are Zionists to the core of their existence, but secular Israelis fear that these zealots, in their determination to dwell in the biblical homeland of the Jewish people, will drag Israel into a holy war with the Palestinians or the Syrians, Hamas, Hezbollah, or some other deranged enemy of Jewish statehood. Challenging the authority of the state, the settlers seem willing to override, by force if necessary, the strenuous objections of the vast majority of Israelis who could not care less whether Jews live in Ofra, Eli, Kiryat Arba, or, least of all, Hebron. To a secular Zionist, anyone who even defends the settlers belongs to the "Sikharim," those most murderous of ancient zealots who sabotaged Israel from within while Jerusalem was besieged by Roman legions.

Jews in Israel have become a people divided against themselves. The decisive turning point may have been the Rabin assassination, just when the Oslo peace process had all but blown up in the wake of Israeli outrage over repeated Palestinian terrorism. Under withering, often vicious, criticism, settlers and their rabbis began to search their souls over their own responsibility for *sinat hinam*, the groundless hatred that had finally spilled over into political murder. It was an important, indeed urgent, step toward national reconciliation.

The left, however, refused to engage in political introspection of its own. Arguably, Rabin's greatest achievement was to have initiated peace with the Palestinians. But his tragic failure—and the failure of his most avid supporters, before and after his death—was the venom directed toward all religious Jews, especially the settlers, who opposed his policies. Sadly, there was more than enough groundless hatred in Israel to cross party lines.

But no soul-searching on the left seemed necessary. Rabin's one-vote majority in the Knesset, it was argued, was sufficient for any policy initiative, no matter how extreme—even if that policy was precisely what tore Israel apart so tragically that assassination was its terrible culmination. Blame for the festering hatreds in Israel, the left insisted, rested entirely upon the religious right. It could not comprehend how the malicious and incessant delegitimation of rabbis, religious Jews, settlers, and right-wing critics of Rabin policy contributed to—and continues to poison—Israel's malevolent politics.

In the end, peace with the Arabs may cause a war between Jews, if a majority of Israelis should decide to ratify a decision to sever the biblical homeland from the state, or to divide Jerusalem and relinquish sovereignty on the Temple Mount. And even then, if only thirty-six Jewish zealots claiming to hear God's word should oppose such a cruel partition, their anguish should not be denigrated, nor their commitment to Zion maligned. The permanent loss to the Jewish people of the ancient homeland, to which all Jews are connected by the umbilical cord of our history as a people, would be no less devastating if it were felt by so few Jews. The overwhelming majority of Israelites who worshipped the Golden Calf did not, after all, carry the day in Sinai—nor did they prevail in our historical narrative.

A Jewish democrat may continue to insist that an elected majority in the Knesset, even if it is not a Jewish majority, is enough. Israel must move toward peace now, with undiminished determination. Nothing can deflect it. Not terror attacks, nor the assassination of a prime minister. Not repeated and orchestrated eruptions of Palestinian violence. Not the waves of malice that sweep over the country. Not even the risk of a Jewish civil war. There will be no retreat from the brink of peace, no hesitation or searching of souls, or reconsideration whether Oslo can be so good for the country if so many Israelis remain so vehemently opposed.

Then, however, the left—the self-designated "beautiful" and "enlightened" Israel—bears as much blame as those it vilifies. For if all Israel, caught as it is in a tragic web of malice, slander, and mutual demonization cannot collectively say *hatanu*, *We* have sinned, then there is no hope that this ominous schism within the Jewish people can possibly be healed.

But that may be expecting too much. For all its achievements of state building, the historical record of Labor Zionism contains some terrible blemishes of intolerance, betrayal, and military aggression toward its Zionist enemies. The very party leaders who, at the first words of criticism of their peace policy, incessantly condemn "incitement" by the right have themselves participated in political demonstrations where Menachem Begin and Ariel Sharon were branded as "murderers" and "war criminals." Why are not these inciters on the left also "errant weeds" to be "spit out" from the Jewish people, just as Rabin advocated for settler extremists?

Consider statements like the following: ultra-Orthodox Jews "suck from the same sinister passions which nurtured the Nazis" (Minister Aloni). "Exterminate the haredim at birth" (wall posters in the lovely town of Kfar Saba). Religious Jews are variously characterized as "black ants," "humming locusts," "backward barbarians," "soul-snatchers," and "parasites," whose activities are discussed on Israeli radio by "experts in contagious diseases." Israeli liberals have voiced concern over Judaism as "a threat to Israel." Bluntly called by its proper name, this is vicious anti-Semitism; or, at best, virulent Jewish self-hatred.

Among secular Israelis, political scientist Yaron Ezrahi writes (proudly), identity has increasingly become "an act of improvisation." But Ezrahi's yearning for a liberal, individualistic culture in Israel (which is well along toward fulfillment) has little to do with traditional Jewish—or Zionist—sources, despite his effort to locate it there. In the post-Zionist era, the "self-indulgent hedonism" and "egoistic materialism" that once were banished from Zionism in order to build and defend a Jewish state have become Zionist virtues. Zionism has become what liberalism long has been for American Jews: a strategy of assimilation. As Hillel Halkin has astutely observed, "In many ways, indeed, post-Zionism *is* the Americanization of Israeli life."

It is sadly evident that the modern tragedy of Jewish assimilation is not confined to the Jewish Diaspora. For Zionists, no less than for Diaspora Jews, emancipation continues to pose a stark choice: integration or isolation; normalization or distinctiveness. All modern Jews, wherever they may live, confront the identical dilemma: whether to assert their Jewish distinctiveness and remain a people apart; or relinquish it and submerge themselves in the dominant culture. Torah, after all, is hardly the founding text for freedom of choice and liberal politics.

Jews in the United States rapidly abandoned Jewish tradition lest they seem insufficiently American. These children of European immigrants, Barry Rubin writes, "rushed to escape a world that meant to them, at worst, a stigma setting them apart and, at best, a sentimental memory that had no future." It is insufficiently understood, however, that Zionists in Israel, like Jews in the Diaspora, must also confront the fundamental dilemma of emancipation: whether to be, or not to be, Jews. Israelis, quite like the Diaspora Jews whom Zionists always despised, clearly prefer to be like everyone else. The deadly Canaanite impulse toward dejudaization, refurbished in the trendy language of post-Zionism, has finally triumphed.

Secular Israelis have all but abandoned any aspiration to develop an indigenous Jewish culture in the Jewish state. Finally cast aside, revisionist historian Benny Morris writes with evident relief, are "the chains of [Zionist] ideology" for "a more open, liberal, capitalist, and democratic world view," in which Judaism clearly has no place. The fervent Zionist embrace of American culture has blunted, if not obliterated, the very distinctions upon which Zionism once triumphantly asserted its claim to Jewish supremacy.

The Jewish self-abasement that has come to characterize post-Zionism demonstrates the very attributes of "ghetto" Judaism that Zionists once ferociously despised. No one has made this argument more persuasively than Ruth Wisse, professor of Yiddish literature at Harvard. Faced with unending Arab hostility for more than a century, Zionists have finally wearied of resistance. So, she notes, they have revived the survival strategy that Jews long ago refined when they lived in exile amid hostile Moslem and Christian majorities: try to accommodate to others, Jews learned—but when they still hate you, blame yourself. There can be no peace in the Middle East, Professor Wisse warns, until Arabs finally learn to relinquish land and Jews become determined to hold on to it.

It might have been otherwise. In 1967, with the return to Judea and Samaria, Israel encountered a fork in the road of Jewish destiny. As Zionism was reinvigorated with Jewish content, Israelis confronted a fateful choice. Their preference is now quite clear. As journalist Ze'ev Chafets recently exulted: "Twenty years ago, Israel shut down on the Sabbath and holidays. Now you can shop on Saturday in suburban malls, see a movie on Friday night (even in Jerusalem) and get a cheeseburger on Passover (with or without bacon)." Fulfillment of the Zionist dream has become a Jewish nightmare.

The experience of Nathan Englander, a fine young American Jewish writer, is revealing. Englander grew up in an Orthodox community on Long Island that he labeled "a shtetl with strip malls all around it." After years of yeshiva education, he yearned for exposure to the liberal arts. During his junior year abroad in Israel, he experienced "cultural shock" when, for the first time, he encountered secular Jews. Inspired by the Israeli example, he removed his *kipa*, let his hair grow, and left religious Judaism behind to study world literature. What does it say about a Jewish state that it teaches Jews how to abandon Judaism?

Israeli children who are reaching school age will learn new truths about Zionism. "We are getting rid of certain myths," explains an Israeli educator who wrote a new post-Zionist textbook for Israeli youngsters. Among these myths: the "myth" of a unique Jewish nationality (to be replaced by something called "universal history"); and the "myth" of the importance of the biblical narrative, Zionism, Israel, and the Holocaust (which now must yield to worthier subjects such as decolonialization in Algeria, new trends in art, and United States history from the Kennedy assassination to Watergate).

The result, as a member of the Education Ministry's

curriculum committee (yet another university historian) conceded, is that the "Zionist narrative has disappeared." Even Ben-Gurion's picture has vanished from the new textbooks; only Israeli statesmen who can be shown shaking hands with Arab leaders at peace-treaty signings are included. Israel as a Jewish state has been written out of the new post-Zionist texts. Why not, novelist Aharon Meged has inquired bitterly, "just translate the Palestinian books for our children and be done with it?"

Secular Zionists (like secular Diaspora Jews) yearn for "a naked public square: politics without God, without myth and fantasy, without eternal enemies, without sacred causes or holy ground." Without—not to put too fine a point on it—Judaism. Their newest hero is Chief Justice Aharon Barak, who is determined to use vigorous judicial activism, in the name of worthy liberal causes borrowed from American jurisprudence, to mold a state of all its citizens, not a Jewish state. Barak has rejected the very idea of a "Jewish" state, instead insisting that Israel's values "are those universal values common to members of a democratic society." To reach its goal, the Barak court is prepared to impose what its leader has arrogantly called "the views of the enlightened community in Israel," whose values are "universal [and] progressive." Here is judicial post-Zionism with a vengeance, sounding the death-knell for Zionism as a Jewish national movement.

In their own distinctive ways, American Jews and Israeli Zionists have finally eluded the vibrant Jewish culture that their ancestors developed and preserved for two thousand years. For most Jews of modernity, who absorb every passing Western fashion and call it Judaism, it hardly matters any longer whether they live in Israel or the Diaspora. *Galut*, despite Zionist claims to the contrary, is not, in the end, merely a geographical location. It is also a state of mind, a barren interior landscape no less pernicious among Jews in Israel than in the United States. To the enlightened modern Jew with universal and progressive values, Judaism is either irrational fundamentalism, to be consigned to historical obsolescence, or pallid universalism, to be consigned to the fringe of contemporary irrelevance.

The transition in Israel from Zionism to post-Zionism is troubling enough to anyone with a sense of Jewish history. Worse yet is the incessant denigration of those Jews who actively resist the alarming Zionist descent into normalization. "That a Jew feels pain upon recognizing Israel's weakness and decay," writes Yoram Hazony, "is a sign of a still-living national consciousness, the essential achievement of Zionism." That so few Israelis seem troubled by the atrophy of Zionism may signify the greatest Zionist failure of all.

A visceral hostility to Jewish religious tradition, which was always latent in Zionism, has cascaded into a torrent of Jewish self-loathing. With astonishing speed and indifference, Israel has traded its Jewish birthright for a mess of post-Zionist pottage. It is already being described—by Russian Jews, who surely know about such things—as the former Jewish state. In the humane, enlightened, progressive, modern homeland of the Jews, nothing is alien except Judaism.

A sad example of Zionist disarray, couched as a Zionist victory, was the chaotic, final flight of the once proud Israel Defense Forces from southern Lebanon in May 2000. With soldiers commanded to leave tanks and *tefillin* behind in their rush to safety, here was a vivid demonstration that the peace process begun at Oslo would inevitably lead to abject Israeli surrender. It was bad enough that the Israeli army was finally defeated by a rag-tag band of Hezbollah guerillas, no more than five hundred full-time fighters. Worse yet was its abandonment of its South Lebanese Army allies, who had stood loyally by Israel for twenty years. But worst of all was the probability that this humiliation would not be the last such Zionist defeat. The demoralization of Israelis that led to the debacle in Lebanon was bound, sooner or later, to culminate in the return to what diplomat Abba Eban had derisively labeled "Auschwitz borders": Israel without Judea and Samaria and with only a tenuous hold on Jerusalem.

For Lebanon was only the beginning of the end. Yasir Arafat could hardly be expected to accept less for the Palestinians than Egypt and Lebanon received, or than Syria demanded. Before long, the insidious logic of appeasement will require the final relinquishment of any Zionist claim to the biblical homeland of the Jewish people. It is little wonder that Israeli-American journalist Yossi Klein Halevi, writing from Jerusalem after the Lebanon fiasco, should confess: "I am beginning to feel my country unraveling."

The ultimate surrender, already clearly foreshadowed, will come in Judea and Samaria, and Jerusalem, where the last strongholds of Zionism will be abandoned by the government of Israel to "Palestine." Then Israel will relinquish any lingering and feeble connection it may still retain to Jewish national history, to the very taproots of Zionism itself. To be sure, Israel's humiliation will be marked by a splendid signing ceremony on the White House lawn, choreographed to celebrate an American president's legacy of peace in the Middle East. And the overwhelming majority of American Jews will cheer, for their yardstick for Israeli leaders remains—as it always has been—compliance with American demands.

Even if Prime Minister Barak could not have his way on territorial concessions, secular Zionist efforts to deplete Israel of Jewish content were likely to continue. Coinciden-

tally, amid Israeli peace talks with the Palestinians, a co-
hort of Israeli archeologists challenged biblical accounts of
David, Solomon, and the first Jewish Commonwealth. Their
revisionist reports were gleefully received by Palestinians
who were only too eager to undermine Jewish claims to the
Temple Mount. Indeed, Palestinian tenacity over Jerusalem,
amid Barak's willingness to divide control over the Old City,
suggested that "If I forget thee, O Jerusalem" had become
the motto of the Palestinian national movement.

Barak, in his fury with religious Jews who opposed his
peace policy, retaliated with proposals for a "civil revolution." Challenging Ben-Gurion's Status Quo agreement,
which had preserved a modicum of peace between secular
and religious factions for half a century, he advocated abolition of the religious ministry, termination of rabbinical authority over marriage and divorce, and the initiation of public
transportation and El Al flights on the sabbath. Whether
negotiating with the Palestinians or attacking the religious
parties, Barak's agenda was driven by the same impulse: to
remove Judaism to the margins of Israeli culture. The inner
logic of secular Zionism, permitted to run its course, would
all but denude Israel of Judaism.

The folly of it all, and with it the unraveling of the peace
process, was tragically demonstrated as Jews welcomed the
new year of 5761 in the fall of 2000. A visit to the Temple
Mount by Likud leader Ariel Sharon "provoked" waves of
calculated, carefully orchestrated, Palestinian violence. At
the very moment when Israel had indicated a previously
unimaginable willingness to partition Jerusalem, the Palestinians demonstrated with stones and bullets their implacable hostility to any sharing of holy sites with Jews.
Encountering the unprecedented withdrawal of Israeli soldiers in the face of Arab violence, Palestinians seized and
destroyed Joseph's Tomb in Nablus (biblical Shechem). As

Israeli Arabs and Jews fought each other in Jaffa, Haifa, and Nazareth, the ineradicable tribal animosity between Moslems and Jews gave the lie to any delusions of peace. Oslo was a mirage of peace, not a peace process. Israel had offered the Golan Heights to Syria, relinquished its security zone in Lebanon, withdrawn from portions of Judea and Samaria, and was prepared to divide Jerusalem while disclaiming sovereignty over the Temple Mount. For this, it received waves of renewed Palestinian violence and virulent Arab hostility. The seven-year Oslo strategy of surrender had finally unraveled.

A century ago, the overwhelming majority of Jews who left Russia, Poland, and Romania came to the American *goldene medina*. Only a tiny fraction went to Palestine to rebuild Zion. Now, in one of the curious twists of Jewish history, their circuitous paths have finally converged. Most Jews in Israel and the Diaspora (except for their small Orthodox minorities) stand united in their rejection of Jewish religious tradition and their embrace of Western secularism. "Hatikva," once the Zionist anthem of hope, now expresses the irrepressible yearning of Israelis to achieve the American dream. Finally, Israel and the Diaspora are "one."

What might an American Jewish visitor to Israel find in 2023, a century after the time of Herzl's *Altneuland* and seventy-five years after the declaration of Israeli independence proclaimed, without embarrassment, "a Jewish state in the land of Israel"?

———

It had been a long time since Jacob had visited Israel. With its fateful decision to squander the covenantal legacy of the Jewish people, Israel had relinquished its claim upon his allegiance. He stopped following news from the Middle East. For thirty years, he did not return. But in 2023, when he was past eighty, he reconsidered. Despite his undiminished disillusionment with Zionism, Jacob felt an irrepressible urge to visit the homeland of the Jews one more time. In preparation, he reread *Altneuland*, Herzl's fantasy of the Jewish state in the distant future of 1923.

Herzl's utopia, predictably, was a Jewish Vienna. "We only had to take the inventions of the Western world and use them," explained David Litwak, Herzl's prototypical Israeli, to a foreign visitor. In *Altneuland*, Litwak continued, the "inherited dead-weight" of the Jewish past had finally been lifted from the Jewish people. Here, in the "New Society," Jews were governed by the laws of "all civilized European countries." Arabs and Jews lived together harmoniously, indeed indistinguishably. No embarrassing questions of identity intruded "about anyone's race or religion." Symbolized by "All Nations Square" in Haifa, there was "a new feeling of brotherhood" in the land.

Lingering traces of a vestigial Judaism managed to survive in *Altneuland*. But they were well concealed, and Herzl had little to say about them. A great new Temple (singularly bereft of Jewish content) had been built in cosmopolitan Jerusalem, which—like Herzl's Vienna—was a modern city of boulevards, institutes, and "splendid public buildings and places of amusement."

The Temple, Herzl's modest gesture to Jewish parochialism, was more than balanced in splendor by a nearby "Peace Palace." The squalid Old City, once inhabited by religious Jews, had become "an international centre which all nations might regard as their home." Litwak's visitor was impressed with *Altneuland*. Here Judaism no longer was "ashamed of itself," and Jews were "proud and free"— if indistinguishable from everyone else. *Altneuland* was "a free commonwealth in which [Jews] could work for the good of mankind."

Herzl had once imagined that the Jewish Question, the place of Jews in modern society, could be solved by the mass conversion of Jews to Christianity. *Altneuland* suggested that Zionism had become his preferred instrument of transformation. But the result was the same. Zionism would complete the process of assimilation that emancipation had begun a century earlier.

Jacob feared that Israel had fulfilled the assimilationist dream of its prophetic founder. With considerable trepidation, he decided to see for himself.

"Welcome to the New Middle East," read the flashing strobe-lit sign at the Palisdan International Airport. Inside the terminal, which resembled a Giza pyramid, Jacob was bewildered by the array of unfamiliar local destinations: Palisdan-by-the-Sea. Canaan. Palestine Province. Bedu-Negev. Galilee Autonomous Zone. Judah. He spotted an enormous map, labeled "Palisdan," which looked suspiciously like Israel, Judea, Samaria, and Jordan—even parts of Lebanon and Syria—all merged together. Could it be, Jacob wondered in astonishment, that Israel had finally found a way to reverse its slide into Jewish oblivion and regain its biblical patrimony?

Interrupting his reverie, a young woman in uniform identified herself as an international guide to Palisdan. She led him to her desk, clicked on her computer for a detailed map of the region, and asked Jacob where he wished to travel. When he replied "Israel," she seemed bemused. In the New Middle East, she explained gently (for she had considerable experience with elderly American Jews who still used archaic place names from their youth), the former Israel had merged into the confederation of Palisdan—uniting Palestine, Israel, and Jordan—which was about to celebrate its twentieth birthday.

Perhaps, she continued solicitously, Jacob would permit her to suggest an itinerary. Fatigued by his journey, already dispirited, and confronting the labyrinth of unfamiliar place names, he readily consented. He might go north, she told him, but not beyond Safed, which marked the international border with Lebanon. How, Jacob wondered aloud, could the border have moved so far south? It had been a small price for Israel to pay, she replied, for peace now in the north.

Nor, she reminded him, could he visit the Golan Heights without a Syraqi visa. While she would not presume to inquire into his race or religion, he should know that Jews were not welcome there. Furthermore, all traces of Jewish history and habitation had been obliterated after Israel had relinquished the Golan and transferred its Jewish residents.

Indeed, she continued, he might even find it a bit uncomfortable in the Galilee Autonomous Zone, stretching from Afula to Safed. Jacob was confused; could it be that the fertile Galilee, once home to so many flourishing Zionist kibbutzim, no longer was part of Israel? That, his guide explained, exemplified Israel's commitment to democratic principles. For once Israel had granted the right of return to Palestinian refugees, which post-Zionist logic required, there no longer was a Jewish majority in the Galilee. According to democratic precedent, by which Judea and Samaria had been relinquished back in 2003, the Galilee Arab majority also enjoyed the right of self-government. There remained, however, one mixed Israeli-Arab city, Kfar Kalkilya, where modest traces of pre-Palisdanian Israeli culture could still be found.

For anything more than that, the guide suggested helpfully, Jacob should visit Canaan, surrounding old Tel Aviv on the Mediterranean coast. Its fine restaurants, luxurious resort hotels, fashionable boutiques, enticing gambling casinos, and computerized work-and-play centers gave the

Palisdan-by-the-Sea district of Canaan international renown. Its people, too, were most unusual: the grandchildren of Israelis, they were proud of their identity as Hebrew-speaking Gentiles, insisting upon the right to dwell apart and be called Canaanites.

There was also Bedu-Negev, stretching from Beer Sheva south to Eilat. The Bedu-Negevians had gained autonomy under the Indigenous Peoples Resolution, sponsored by Israel in return for some gestures of international approval from the United Nations. They were a most engaging people, who welcomed visitors to their hospitality villas. There, volunteers fondly reminisced about the enlightened Zionist government that had severed the Negev from Israel to enable Arabs to build a land bridge that stretched all the way from Gaza to Baghdad. It was, the government had insisted at the time, a small price to pay for peace.

Jacob's guide strongly recommended a brief stopover in Jerusalem, on his way to the desert reserve of Husseinia beyond the Jordan River. He would marvel at its transformation from the provincial capital of Israel, inhabited mostly by Jews, into the multi-ethnic, transdenominational United Nations City. There he should be sure to visit the magnificent Raperfat Peace Center—named, of course, in recognition of the exemplary cooperation, back in the nineties, between Rabin, Peres, and Arafat, the foundation for the New Middle East with Palisdan as its keystone.

A forlorn Jacob asked whether, anywhere in Palisdan, he might still find any Jews. His guide hesitated, before recalling from her training program that an occasional Jewish tourist might still ask that embarrassing question. Certainly, she responded; at the Peace Center, he could obtain a one-day visa to Judah, located by the terebinths of Mamre in biblical Hebron. There, some ten thousand Jews still lived according to Jewish law in the Jewish homeland, as though Zionism had never happened.

Jacob was tempted. Before the collapse of Zionism he had frequently visited their communities, where he had always been inspired by the strength of their Jewish commitment. They were, he believed, the last true Zionists, whose undiminished attachment to the Land of Israel might somehow inspire other Jews to defend their historic homeland. Abandoned by the government of Israel, they resolutely declared autonomy, renaming their ghetto Judah to commemorate the last stronghold of Jewish national independence in the First Temple era.

But Jacob could not, in the end, bear to witness the humiliation of this proud and ancient community of Jews. He remembered the story of the elderly European rabbi who had finally met the obligation incumbent upon Jews to return to Zion. Landing at Jaffa, he had stepped ashore and paced the four els required to fulfill his *halakhic* obligation. Then, to the astonishment of his students, who could hardly contain their eagerness to guide him to Jerusalem, he returned to his ship to await its departure to the Diaspora.

Thanking his guide for sparing him a wrenching encounter with Palisdan in the New Middle East, Jacob boarded the next flight home. As his plane crossed the Mediterranean, he sorrowfully pondered the remarkable rise—and astonishing collapse—of Zionism in his own lifetime. Once a revolutionary ideology of Jewish renewal, Zionism had reduced itself to a whimper of Jewish normalization. Within seventy-five years of the birth of Israel, assimilation was as rampant in Tel Aviv, the first Zionist city, as anywhere in the American Diaspora. Everywhere, Jews lived in *galut*.

Had Zionism, Jacob wondered, been fatally flawed from the outset? The Zionists, after all, rejected the religious faith that alone could explain why Jews must rebuild their national home in Zion, and only there. So avidly did secular Zionists repudiate Jewish history, memory, and ritual that even their claim to Jewish land finally proved too onerous to defend. Palisdan gave the lie to the incessant claim of secular Israelis, at the beginning of the twenty-first century, that they could have it all: give land to the Arabs, make peace, join the New Middle East, and still retain their own distinctive national identity. Instead, they had won the argument—and lost the Jewish state. What newly emancipated Jews had wanted as individuals—freedom from Judaism and integration into Gentile society—the State of Israel had finally assured to all its Jewish citizens.

"We Are One!"—the resounding slogan of American Jewish unity with Israel—may once have been a proud boast. But it had always disguised a lurking fear, for trapped inside their dual identity American Jews remained vulnerable to insinuations of divided loyalty. Only a normal Jewish state, where Zionism was indistinguishable from Americanism, offered a safe commitment. For most American Jews, therefore, as for most Israelis, Palisdan fulfilled their dreams of normalization—and the Jewish state was only a memory.

Jacob realized, with a sigh of sorrow, that the journey of modern Jews, from emancipation through Zionism to assimilation, was over.

Acknowledgments

Longer ago than I care to recall, the National Endowment for the Humanities awarded me a College Teachers Fellowship that enabled me to begin work on the project that ultimately became this book. Near the end, in a time of intellectual weariness, a grant from the Littauer Foundation encouraged me to complete it. If the form and content are somewhat of a surprise to them, so they also are to me. But this was the book that demanded to be written, and I am deeply grateful for their assistance at crucial times. I appreciate my sabbatical leaves and research grants from Wellesley College; as so often during the past thirty years, Wellesley's generous support of my scholarship, once again, was vital.

Librarians at the Central Zionist Archives in Jerusalem, the David Ben-Gurion Library in Sde Boker, the American Jewish Committee in New York, and the American Jewish Historical Society in Waltham, Massachusetts, were extremely helpful. I am grateful to Robert Bleiweiss, former editor of *Jewish Spectator*, and to his son Mark, who succeeded him, for their willingness to publish essays that other editors, for avowedly political reasons, had declined. *Jewish Spectator* and *Midstream* kindly granted permission to reprint material that originally appeared in their pages.

Several scholar-friends provided encouragement and assistance along the way. Jonathan Sarna, Stephen Whitfield, and Edward Alexander were especially generous with their efforts on my behalf, and I am deeply grateful to all of them. Allon Gal's invitation to participate in a 1993 conference at Beer Sheva University gave me the opportunity to offer my heretical historical interpretation in public for the first time. Joseph Diamond's invitation to deliver the 1999 Dora and Leo A. Diamond Memorial Lecture at Congregation Rodeph Sholom in New York was especially welcome for the re-union with dear friends from long ago that accompanied it.

I am immensely appreciative to David Myers of Rutgers University Press for his understanding of what I was trying to do, his willingness to let me do (most of) it, and his valu-able suggestions along the way. Eric Schramm went beyond skillful copyediting to significantly improve the manuscript with his pointed queries and thoughtful guidance. With skill and tact, Marilyn Campbell guided the manuscript, and me, to publication. Melissa Luce expertly, and expeditiously, prepared the index.

In the end, books matter less than friendship and fam-ily. Here I am truly blessed. "The Fathers," as our group of six has collectively identified itself, has banded together for more than a decade to provide support, encouragement, and nourishment of various kinds, in good times and bad. My thanks to Les Fagen, Irle Goldman, Len Lyons, Allen Spivack, and David Strauss. Over the years, Bill Novak and I have talked our way through endless miles of walking together. Bill, an impeccable critic, had the good judgment to alert me to some problems with my manuscript long before I was willing to acknowledge them.

It is stunning to realize that I now have friends who span half a century. Michael Rosenthal, Stanley Fisher, and Michael Meltsner have offered the abundant joys of friend-ship in ways that perhaps only an only child can ever fully appreciate. Haggai Hurvitz has been extraordinarily generous and supportive since we met at Lod Airport, nearly thirty years ago. Despite his deep disappointment with what I now have to say about Israel, he has never permitted our disagreements to weaken the indissoluble personal bonds between us. For that, even more than for all that he has taught me about Israel, I am deeply grateful.

I have no doubt that the members of my family long ago wearied of this book. Jeffrey, already a historian and author of distinction, offered shrewd comments that were unerringly thought-provoking. Pammy, the fine lawyer that I never could have become, illuminates the road not taken with her remarkable energy and talent. If the test of being Jewish no longer is whether your grandparents were Jews, but whether your grandchildren are, my Jewish future has been assured by Cole, Dalia, and Jonah. Shira and Rebecca both grew from delightful little girls into wonderful young women while this book was being written. Even as they dutifully remind me of my deficiencies, they continue to fill me with love and joy. Susan, who has always been there for me during the past twenty years, is the love of my life.

J.S.A.
Newton, Massachusetts
December 2000
Kislev 5761

Bibliographical Essay

This essay is not intended as a comprehensive survey of the voluminous literature about American Jewish history, Zionism, or the State of Israel. Rather, it highlights some of the especially engaging or provocative sources that stimulated my own thoughts about modern Jewish history.

For readers wishing to survey these subjects in breadth, the following may be helpful. For American Jewish history, there is Henry L. Feingold, ed., *The Jewish People in America*, 5 vols. (Baltimore: Johns Hopkins University Press, 1992); Howard M. Sachar, *History of the Jews in America* (New York: Vintage, 1992); Jack Fischel and Sanford Pinsker, eds., *Jewish-American History and Culture* (New York: Garland, 1992); and Jonathan D. Sarna, ed., *The American Jewish Experience*, 2d ed. (New York: Holmes & Meier, 1997).

For a comprehensive survey of Jewish history, see H. H. Ben-Sasson, ed., *A History of the Jewish People* (Cambridge: Harvard University Press, 1976). The best single-volume history of Israel is Howard M. Sachar, *A History of Israel from the Rise of Zionism to our Time*, 2d ed. (New York: Knopf, 1996). David Vital's history of the Zionist movement, beginning with *Zionism: The Formative Years* (New York: Oxford University Press, 1988), is detailed and comprehensive.

Many of the significant Zionist documents appear in Arthur Hertzberg, ed., *The Zionist Idea* (New York: Atheneum, 1975), a fine anthology with an excellent introduction.

My understanding of the prophet Jeremiah was informed by Yehezkel Kauffmann, *The Religion of Israel* (New York: Schocken, 1972) who sees Jeremiah as an obscure seditious visionary; J. A. Thompson, *The Book of Jeremiah* (Grand Rapids, Mich.: Eerdmans, 1980); and Robert P. Carroll, *From Chaos to Covenant* (New York: Crossroad, 1981) and *Jeremiah* (Sheffield, Eng.: JSOT Press, 1986). David Biale, in *Power and Powerlessness in Jewish History* (New York: Schocken, 1986), pays tribute to Jeremiah as the precursor of rabbinical accommodation and cites his letter as the foundation for Jewish communal life in the Diaspora. Elias Bickerman's *From Ezra to the Last of the Maccabees* (New York: Schocken, 1962) and *The Jews in the Greek Age* (Cambridge: Cambridge University Press, 1988) explore the early history of Jewish Diaspora-homeland relations. W. D. Davies, *The Territorial Dimension of Judaism* (Berkeley: University of California Press, 1982) examines the historical "contradiction" between the powerful connection of Jews to their homeland and their lengthy and creative sojourn outside its boundaries. Zionist hostility toward the Diaspora as "exile" can easily be detected in Yitzhak F. Baer, *Galut* (New York: Schocken, 1947). Ben Zion Dinur, *Israel and the Diaspora* (Philadelphia: Jewish Publication Society, 1969), offers a useful contrast between Diaspora "centers of authority" and "centers of influence," with Babylon exemplifying the former and Spain, Germany, Poland, and—presumably—the United States symbolizing the latter. For one modern example, among many, of the justification of the Diaspora in Jeremiah's terms, see Milton R. Konvitz, "Zionism: Homecoming or Homelessness," *Judaism* 5 (Summer 1956): 210–211.

The basic documents for emancipation appear in a fine collection of primary sources: Paul Mendes-Flohr and Jehuda Reinharz, eds., *The Jew in the Modern World* (2d ed., New York: Oxford University Press, 1995), which also has an excellent selection of Zionist, and anti-Zionist, material. Some early Zionist texts—those of Pinsker, Herzl, and Ahad Ha'Am on the European side and Gottheil and Brandeis on the American—are excerpted in Hertzberg, *The Zionist Idea*. Ernst Pawel, *The Labyrinth of Exile* (New York: Farrar, Straus & Giroux, 1989) is a fascinating exploration of Herzl's troubled soul; the best biography of Ahad Ha'Am is Stephen M. Zipperstein, *Elusive Prophet: Ahad Ha'Am and the Origins of Zionism* (Berkeley: University of California Press, 1992). For brief but cogent analysis of an array of Zionist thinkers and doers, see Shlomo Avineri, *The Making of Modern Zionism* (New York: Basic Books, 1981).

For American Jewish history, the Reform movement and German-Jewish acculturation have been thoughtfully explored in Leon A. Jick, *The Americanization of the Synagogue, 1820–1870* (Hanover, N.H.: University Press of New England, 1976); Naomi W. Cohen, *Encounter with Emancipation* (Philadelphia: Jewish Publication Society, 1984); and Michael A. Meyer, *Response to Modernity* (New York: Oxford University Press, 1988). There is useful information, if an exaggerated emphasis on American preoccupations with the Jewish state, in Peter Grose, *Israel in the Mind of America* (New York: Schocken, 1984). The history of American Zionism, from the perspective of a liberal enthusiast, can be tracked in Melvin I. Urofsky, *American Zionism from Herzl to the Holocaust* (New York: Anchor Press/Doubleday, 1975) and *We Are One! American Jewry and Israel* (New York: Anchor Press/Doubleday, 1978). Louis D. Brandeis, the consummate Zionist as American, has inspired more biographies (and hagiographies) than all other American

Zionists combined. Philippa Strum, *Louis D. Brandeis: Justice for the People* (Cambridge: Harvard University Press, 1984), the best of these, nonetheless affirms Brandeis's stature as a liberal icon; Yonathan Shapiro, *Leadership of the American Zionist Organization, 1897–1930* (Urbana: University of Illinois Press, 1971), is more critical, from an Israeli perspective; Allon Gal, *Brandeis of Boston* (Cambridge: Harvard University Press, 1980), explores the formative years of Brandeis's career. Brandeis's own Zionist development, which was rarely introspective, can be examined in Melvin I. Urofsky and David W. Levy, eds., *Letters of Louis D. Brandeis*, vols. 3–5 (Albany: State University of New York Press, 1973–1978); Naomi W. Cohen, *The Year after the Riots: American Responses to the Palestine Crisis of 1929* (Detroit: Wayne State University Press, 1988), is an exemplary monograph that underscores the docility of American Zionists and Jews in response to an overseas crisis for Jews, an ominous foreshadowing of subsequent events. The first book to finally reject Jewish liberal pieties about American Zionism is Rafael Medoff, *Zionism and the Arabs: An American Jewish Dilemma, 1898–1948* (Westport, Conn.: Praeger, 1997), a perceptive analysis of American Zionists trapped between their divergent Jewish and democratic commitments.

For insight into other prominent American Zionists, especially Judah L. Magnes and Henrietta Szold, see Arthur A. Goren, *Dissenter in Zion* (Cambridge: Harvard University Press, 1982); Marvin Lowenthal, *Henrietta Szold: Life and Letters* (New York: Viking, 1942); and Michael Brown, "Henrietta Szold's Progressive American Vision of the *Yishuv*" in Allon Gal, ed., *Envisioning Israel* (Jerusalem: Magnes Press, 1996). In the same volume, essays by Jonathan D. Sarna, Arthur A. Goren, Stephen J. Whitfield, Chaim I. Waxman, and Jack Wertheimer imaginatively explore dilem-

mas of American Jewish acculturation. For a somewhat revisionist account of American Orthodoxy and Zionism,
emphasizing pre-World War II Orthodox sympathy for the
movement, see Jeffrey S. Gurock, *American Jewish Orthodoxy in Historical Perspective* (Hoboken, N.J.: Ktav, 1996).
It is more than astonishing that there is still no adequate
biography of Rabbi Solomon Schechter, who steered the new
Conservative movement to its embrace of Zionism, and
refused to compromise on the unity of Jewish law and Jewish nationalism. For the transition from Jewish to American law as part of the acculturation process, see my *Rabbis
and Lawyers: The Journey from Torah to Constitution*
(Bloomington: Indiana University Press, 1990).

The Central Zionist Archives in Jerusalem contains a
wealth of important material on American Zionism, including correspondence of Americans for Haganah, Hashomer
HaDati, Mizrachi Youth, Avukah, Mercaz Habonim, and the
Zionist Youth Organization. There I also found the letters
of Bill Bernstein from the *Exodus*; see Jerold S. Auerbach,
"Lost Letters of a Yankee Relate Voyage of Exodus," *Forward*, September 4, 1992. For the reminiscences of members of Habonim, the Labor Zionist Youth Group, see J. J.
Goldberg and Elliot King, eds., *Builders and Dreamers* (New
York: Herzl Press, 1993). The earliest travel guide to the
new State of Israel, as far as I could discover, was prepared
by the Zionist Organization of America, *"So You're Going
to Israel": A Concise and Handy Guide for the American
Tourist* (New York: Zionist Organization of America, 1949).
I located it in the Archives of the American Jewish Historical Society, which have since been relocated from Waltham,
Massachusetts, to Manhattan. See also Ruth Gruber, *Israel
Today* (New York: Hill and Wang, 1958), for another good
example, a decade later, of American Jewish wishful thinking about Jewish statehood.

For post-World War II developments in American Jewish life, see Zvi Ganin, *Truman, American Jewry, and Israel, 1945–1948* (New York: Holmes & Meier, 1979), for the birth of Jewish statehood; and for a refreshingly critical view of "oneness" between American Jews and Israel, Seymour Martin Lipset and Earl Rabb, *Jews and the New American Scene* (Cambridge: Harvard University Press, 1995). For Jews in Hollywood, inventing American Jewish life as they rolled their cameras, there is the scintillating study by Neal Gabler, *An Empire of Their Own* (New York: Anchor Books, 1988). Deborah Dash Moore, *To the Golden Cities: Pursuing the American Jewish Dream in Miami and L.A.* (Cambridge: Harvard University Press, 1994), offers a rhapsodic account of sunbelt Judaism; Arnold M. Eisen, *The Chosen People in America* (Bloomington: Indiana University Press, 1983), is a fine study of the labored efforts of rabbis to accommodate Jewish chosenness to American conditions. For a book cascading with marvelous insights about the impact of assimilation on American Jewish culture, and an expansively tolerant notion of what is "Jewish" about the residue, see Stephen J. Whitfield, *In Search of American Jewish Culture* (Hanover, N.H.: University Press of New England, 1999).

For American variations on the theme of Zionist perfidy, power, and pressure, see Thomas A. Kolsky, *Jews Against Zionism* (Philadelphia: Temple University Press, 1990); and, for recent examples, Roberta Strauss Feuerlicht, *The Fate of the Jews* (London: Quartet Books, 1983); Edward Tivnan, *The Lobby: Jewish Political Power and American Foreign Policy* (New York: Simon and Schuster, 1987); Paul Breines, *Tough Jews* (New York: Basic Books, 1990); Seymour M. Hersh, *The Samson Option* (New York: Random House, 1991); Milton Viorst, *Sands of Sorrow* (New York: Harper and Row, 1987); and Bernard Avishai, *The Tragedy of Zionism* (New York: Farrar, Straus & Giroux, 1985).

For Zionist and Israeli political leadership, the following were helpful: Shabtai Teveth, *Ben-Gurion: The Burning Ground, 1886–1948* (Boston: Houghton Mifflin, 1987) and *Ben-Gurion and the Palestinian Arabs* (New York: Oxford University Press, 1985); Amos Perlmutter, *The Life and Times of Menachem Begin* (New York: Doubleday, 1987); Eric Silver, *Begin: The Haunted Prophet* (New York: Random House, 1984). For American liberal rage at Begin for demolishing their illusions about Israel, good examples are Arthur Hertzberg, "Begin and the Jews," *New York Review of Books*, February 18, 1982; and Thomas L. Friedman, *From Beirut to Jerusalem* (New York: Farrar, Straus & Giroux, 1989). A thoughtful exploration of the internal Zionist debate over the use of force, with suggestive implications for intramural Zionist conflict after the founding of the state, appears in Anita Shapira, *Land and Power: The Zionist Resort to Force, 1881–1948* (New York: Oxford University Press, 1992).

For critical, if not overtly hostile, scrutiny of Israel in the early years of statehood, marking the emergence of post-Zionist revisionist historiography, there is Tom Segev's *1949: The First Israelis* (New York: Free Press, 1986) and *The Seventh Million* (New York: Hill & Wang, 1993); Benny Morris, *The Birth of the Palestinian Refugee Problem, 1947–1949* (Cambridge: Cambridge University Press, 1987). For an appropriately scathing rejoinder to the new historians, see Efraim Karsh, *Fabricating Israeli History: The New Historians* (London: Frank Cass, 1997).

To comprehend Rabbi Abraham Isaac Kook's attempts to integrate Judaism and Zionism, see Tzvi Feldman, ed., *Rav A. Y. Kook: Selected Letters* (Ma'aleh Adumim: Ma'alyot Publications, 1986). The impact of the Six Day War on Israeli soldiers is evocatively conveyed in *The Seventh Day: Soldiers Talk about the Six-Day War* (Baltimore: Penguin

Books, 1971). The meaning of 1967 and the nature of its transformation of Israeli culture, along with much else, is lucidly analyzed in Harold Fisch, *The Zionist Revolution* (New York: St. Martin's, 1978), a brilliant exploration of the paradoxes of Zionism as it grappled with its own Jewish problem. Amos Oz's eloquent critique of Jewish settlers, and his vigorous defense of the Zionist intermarriage with the West, appears in his *In the Land of Israel* (New York: Harcourt Brace Jovanovich, 1983). His debate with settlement leaders Yisrael Harel and Pinchas Wallerstein in Ofra offers a fascinating glimpse of the chasm between secular Israel and religious Zionism. Further excursions into the land of Oz appear in his *Israel, Palestine and Peace* (New York: Harcourt Brace, 1994).

Jewish settlers have been a favorite target of American and Israeli liberal Jews: Robert I. Friedman, *Zealots for Zion* (New York: Random House, 1992); Ian S. Lustick, *For the Land and the Lord* (New York: Council on Foreign Relations, 1988); and especially Ehud Sprinzak, *The Ascendance of Israel's Radical Right* (New York: Oxford University Press, 1991), who manages to convert the return of Jews to their ancient biblical homeland into an expression of acute paranoia, which has "contaminated" Israel and "stained its democratic record." Sprinzak updates his story of political extremism through the Rabin assassination in *Brother against Brother* (New York: Free Press, 1999). See also Menachem Friedman, "The State of Israel as a Theological Dilemma," in Baruch Kimmerling, ed., *The Israeli State and Society* (Albany: State University of New York Press, 1989); Aviezer Ravitzky, *Messianism, Zionism, and Jewish Religious Radicalism* (Chicago: University of Chicago Press, 1996); and Laurence J. Silberstein, *Jewish Fundamentalism in Comparative Perspective* (New York: New York University Press, 1993). For the accounts of insiders, participants in the Jewish underground whose members were arrested in 1984, see Haggai Segal, *Dear Brothers* (New York: Beit-Shamai Publications, 1988); Era Rapaport, *Letters From Tel Mond Prison* (New York: Free Press, 1996).

An eloquent, impassioned argument for the ingathering of Diaspora Jews in Israel can be found in Hillel Halkin, *Letters to an American Jewish Friend* (Philadelphia: Jewish Publication Society, 1977) (to which *Are We One?* might serve as a belated, and sorrowful, reply). A more recent effort is David Vital, *The Future of the Jews* (Cambridge: Harvard University Press, 1990). For a cynical Israeli view of American Jewry, see Matti Golan, *With Friends Like You* (New York: Free Press, 1992).

Israeli critics of Israel for the Zionist "betrayal" of liberal values include Yehoshafat Harkabi, *The Bar Kokhba Syndrome* (New York: Rossel Books, 1983), a thinly veiled attack on Menachem Begin and the settlement movement; Akiva Orr, *Israel: Politics, Myths and Identity Crises* (London: Pluto Press, 1994), a self-described "anthropocentric critique" of anything Jewish in the Jewish state; Boas Evron, *Jewish State or Israeli Nation?* (Bloomington: Indiana University Press, 1995), arguing for a "democratic" (i.e., non-Jewish) state; Ze'ev Sternhell, *The Founding Myths of Israel* (Princeton: Princeton University Press, 1998), a tirade against the religious right in the guise of a plea for a "truly liberal" Israel; and Yaron Ezrahi, *Rubber Bullets: Power and Conscience in Modern Israel* (New York: Farrar, Straus & Giroux, 1997). Ezrahi, needless to say, finds too much power and too little conscience in Israel, whose post-Zionist task is to retreat from the burdens of Jewish history and inhale a liberal dose of American freedom and individualism. For an extreme post-Zionist vision, from an Israeli who was empowered as foreign minister and prime minister to implement it, see Shimon Peres, *The New Middle East* (New York:

Holt, 1993), an exemplary illustration of the Jewish barrenness of post-Zionist thought.

Just as my manuscript was nearing completion, Yoram Hazony, *The Jewish State: The Struggle for Israel's Soul* (New York: Basic Books, 2000), made its welcome appearance. The title of his introduction, "The Jewish State Doesn't Live Here Anymore," says it all about post-Zionist Israel, which his book is the first to examine from a critical perspective. Hazony's survey of the post-Zionist damage to Israeli culture, politics, literature, education, and law is devastating, even if his attempt to lay all the blame on Martin Buber and his disciples at the Hebrew University is less than convincing. Hazony tries hard to return Herzl and Labor Zionism to the pinnacle of Zionist achievement, but they were, in my judgment at least, part of the Zionist problem, not a solution to it. For exploration of the Americanization of Israel, see the essays in the special issue of *Israel Studies* 5 (Spring 2000).

I was informed by several insightful books, which cannot be easily categorized: Yael Zerubavel, *Recovered Roots: Collective Memory and the Making of Israeli National Tradition* (Chicago: University of Chicago Press, 1995), explores Zionism as "countermemory" to Jewish memory, which goes a long way toward explaining why Zionism once was so creative but ultimately lapsed into Jewish barrenness; Charles S. Liebman and Steven M. Cohen, *Two Worlds of Judaism* (New Haven: Yale University Press, 1990), reject the seductive synthesis of unity between American Jews and Israelis that so captivated American Jews for so long; Lawrence H. Schiffman, *Who Was a Jew?* (Hoboken, N.J.: Ktav, 1985), traces the historical origins of a deeply divisive issue in contemporary Israel; Yosef Hayim Yerushalmi, *Zakhor* (Seattle: University of Washington Press, 1982), offers fascinating insights into the role of memory in Jewish history and culture. R. E. Clements, ed., *The World of Ancient Israel* (Cambridge: Cambridge University Press, 1989), applies sociological and anthropological perspectives to the study of ancient Jewish history; Barry Rubin, *Assimilation and Its Discontents* (New York: Times Books, 1995), resists the temptation, so common in the literature, to applaud assimilation and its dire consequences for Jews.

Two American scholars have written so trenchantly about Israel, Zionism, and the American Jewish Diaspora that it would take a separate bibliography to list all their contributions to what is otherwise an absurdly one-sided debate. Their critique of the pervasive liberal assault against the scandal of Jewish particularity, and their resistance to the malignancy of post-Zionism, have emboldened my own efforts. See Edward Alexander, *The Jewish Idea and Its Enemies* (New Brunswick: Transaction Books, 1988) and *The Jewish Wars: Reflections by One of the Belligerents* (Carbondale: Southern Illinois University Press, 1996); and Ruth R. Wisse, *If I Am Not for Myself: The Liberal Betrayal of the Jews* (New York: Free Press, 1992).

Index

About the Author

Jerold S. Auerbach is the author of *Labor and Liberty* (1966); *Unequal Justice* (1976; a *New York Times* Noteworthy Book); *Justice Without Law?* (1983); *Rabbis and Lawyers* (1990); and *Jacob's Voices* (1996). His essays on Jewish subjects have appeared in *Commentary*, the *Jerusalem Post*, *Jewish Spectator*, *Midstream*, and in scholarly journals and Jewish periodicals. He has been a Guggenheim Fellow, Fulbright Lecturer at Tel Aviv University, Visiting Scholar at the Harvard Law School, and the holder of two College Teachers Fellowships from the National Endowment for the Humanities. He is a professor of history at Wellesley College, where he has taught courses in modern American history, American Jewish history, and the history of Israel.